The Case for the Multinational Corporation

J. Fred Weston
Louis T. Wells, Jr.
Robert G. Hawkins
Thomas Horst
Raymond Vernon
Richard N. Cooper
edited by
Carl H. Madden

Published in cooperation with
the National Chamber Foundation

The Praeger Special Studies program—utilizing the most modern and efficient book production techniques and a selective worldwide distribution network—makes available to the academic, government, and business communities significant, timely research in U.S. and international economic, social, and political development.

The Case for the Multinational Corporation

PRAEGER SPECIAL STUDIES IN INTERNATIONAL BUSINESS, FINANCE, AND TRADE

Praeger Publishers   New York   Washington   London

Library of Congress Cataloging in Publication Data
Main entry under title:

The case for the multinational corporation.

(Praeger special studies in international
business, finance, and trade)
"Proceedings of a two-day conference held in
Washington, D. C. on November 25-26, 1975."
1. International business enterprises—
Congresses. I. Madden, Carl Halford. II. National
Chamber Foundation.
HD2755.5.C38   338.8'8   76-12863
ISBN 0-275-23980-2

PRAEGER PUBLISHERS
111 Fourth Avenue, New York, N.Y. 10003, U.S.A.

Published in the United States of America in 1977
by Praeger Publishers, Inc.

Printed in the United States of America

Because they are successful and powerful, multinational corporations are the cause of much controversy. But even critics admit that internationalization of production must continue. By internationalizing operations, only the multinationals, of all business organizations, have effectively reacted to the prime world economic reality: the unequal distribution of resources, human and physical. By concentrating on factors of production and not upon political boundaries, they have been able to organize, produce and market on a worldwide scale, efficiently mobolizing resources as no comparable economic unit operating from a national perspective can.

FOREWORD
Lee L. Morgan

I would like to set the reader's mind at rest by stating at the
outset that the six papers that comprise the heart of this study do
not constitute either blessings of the multinational business fraternity
or scathing attacks upon it. In the 1970s there has been a virtual
explosion in the publication of material on the multinational corporation. Some of the work has been very good, some has been very bad,
and some of it is just plain nonsense. My associates at Caterpillar,
as well as friends in business associations and other companies, have
been struggling with the problem of how to best get the dialogue on
multinational corporations on the platform of objective discussion
and analysis.

A number of approaches have been tried, including the making
of public speeches on the role of our enterprises in today's world.
Just a few weeks ago, for example, I received copies of no less than
three addresses given on this subject in one day. Please don't misunderstand. These speeches are an excellent device for communicating
activities and points of view; but, in my opinion, they are not enough.

Unfortunately, no matter what corporations themselves say on
this subject, it tends to assume the air of one-sided business propa-
ganda. For these reasons, it was felt that the time was at hand for a
national conference on multinational corporations, conducted in a
serious, objective setting. The National Chamber Foundation was
asked to take on this task because it is an educational and research
tool that can draw from, and is open to, a large spectrum of our
society.

Thus, a two-day conference, held in Washington, D. C., on
November 25-26, 1975, was planned as an educational and research
effort on multinational corporations, with the intent of informing the
public through scholarly analysis and informed discussion of the
issues. Since an educational effort is a two-way street, the conference
program included generous periods for questioning and discussion in

Lee L. Morgan is President and Chief Operating Officer,
Caterpillar Tractor Company. Mr. Morgan's Foreword is a slightly
revised version of his Opening Statement delivered at the National
Chamber Foundation's National Conference on Multinational Corporations for Corporate Leaders, held November 25-26, 1975, in Washington, D. C.

order to stimulate informed and astute analyses of the issues raised. Each of the scholarly papers presented at the conference and included in this volume are followed, therefore, by comments made on that paper at the conference by a corporate leader, and then by the discussion that took place. It was the hope of the National Chamber Foundation that the conference would lend credible and objective insight to some of the problem areas involving multinational corporations so that business can get on with the bigger challenges—for the sooner we replace the misconceptions about multinational business with understanding based on unbiased and factual analysis, the better for all concerned.

The logical question at this point is, How did the managers of multinational corporations get into a situation where they are called upon to define and defend their role as businessmen in a changing world?

It is obvious why they went into business, and it is equally clear that the world is always changing. Therefore, it is often difficult to understand why there is suddenly so much concern, often emotional and moralistic, over multinational business operations.

This study will examine these questions in detail, but let me try to set the tone at the beginning by stating that I believe the world is changing in a different manner than in previous decades, and that the motives and results of our business operations are being more frequently questioned in national and international settings, and in the halls of academe.

As we look at the issue of multinational business, we should not lose sight of its relation to a fundamental formula for economic and social development. The formula holds that the needs and aspirations of all the peoples of the world must be related to the economic system or systems that can best satisfy those needs and aspirations.

It is necessary, therefore, to first identify the needs and aspirations that prevail throughout the world. Only by establishing some agreement on this is it possible to proceed to any meaningful assessment of the relative merits of available means of satisfying those needs—from the international investment activities associated with multinational business to the nonmarket systems associated with Socialist states.

The cataclysmic conclusion of World War II and the postwar redevelopment effort have dramatically changed the course of world affairs. While these activities divided the world into basically conflicting political and economic ideologies, they also produced a world which has come to believe that economic prosperity is an attainable goal for all. While the rich have certainly become richer, the have-nots no longer feel that they can never join the ranks of the haves.

One of the dominant forces contributing to the postwar revolution in human achievement and expectations has been the growth of multinational business. We should therefore recognize that present-day concern over our business activities is predictable, if for no other reason than that the impact of the production, supply, and distribution of goods on an international scale has never been as great as it is today.

Multinational corporations perform over 25 percent of the world's production of goods and services. U.S.-based multinationals are involved in about 60 percent of this total. Even though the bulk of this activity takes place in the developed world, it is of such widespread impact that the developing nations rightly identify multinational business as the key to their own prospects for economic betterment. The problem has arisen where they decided that perhaps another sort of key would serve as well.

As it is, our world is changing in ways few of us would have predicted just a quarter century ago. For example, how many of us in 1950 could imagine that the people of the United States would be so dramatically affected as we are today by what is happening in the deserts of the Arabian peninsula, by the empty stomachs of the people in the Sahel region of Africa, and by the changed ownership of the copper-rich mountains of Peru.

The sheer growth of our world population has placed such demands on our earth's resource system that economic and political interdependence have become facts of life. The multinational corporation has played a decisive role in creating interdependence. It is the main channel through which products, goods, and services flow throughout the world. It also is the structural base on which the world economy operates. As such it has become the target of all those who, for one reason or another, are still searching for the best way to satisfy world aspirations and needs.

Because of these profound changes in our world, and the fact that multinational business is an important force, we have a responsibility to ourselves and to those we serve through our labors, to reflect in a serious, thoughtful manner on our role in a complex and political international environment. We must spare no effort in assembling the facts necessary to demonstrate how world aspirations and needs are in fact achieved through the vehicle of multinational business. And, most importantly, we also must spare no effort in communicating the facts of our operations—and explaining these facts—to those who question the role of multinational business.

Above all, it must be recognized that the best posture for business is to focus not only on the immediate issue—for instance on the domestic employment and taxation aspects of international investment activities—but also on the overriding problems of our times; namely, how are we to feed, clothe, house, educate, and utilize a population that will exceed 6 billion by the year 2000?

It is encouraging to see that many political leaders are also beginning to focus on this imperative concern. The Seventh Special Session of the UN General Assembly, which started with overtones of militant confrontation, responded favorably to calls for cooperative approaches to the problems of food, energy, use of the seas and the environment, and so on.

The general theme of this study is the search for an appropriate role for the multinational corporations in a growing, interdependent world. The following statement from a report of an international agricultural research institute underlines the necessity for us to get this phase of the debate laid to rest:

> The 1970s are a decade of grace in which man must
> bring population growth and food production into balance,
> or watch the world deteriorate into a miserable place
> for human existence. The recent cooperative integrated
> efforts of many individuals, governments, industries and
> international agencies have stirred hope, where there
> was none a short time ago, that this balance may be
> achieved.

CONTENTS

LIST OF TABLES AND FIGURE

NOTE ON NATIONAL CHAMBER FOUNDATION

The National Chamber Foundation was established in 1967 as a non-profit operating foundation for educational and scientific purposes.

The foundation was established to promote understanding of economics, finance, education and training, science and technology, economic planning and development, international relations, and other subjects related to general economic growth and development.

In pursuit of these objectives the National Chamber Foundation conducts research, special studies, seminars, training programs, and economic education activities.

The Case for the Multinational Corporation

In the United States today, the multinational corporation, along with the rest of big business, is under attack. Some have called the multinational "the single most creative international institution of the twentieth century." It is being pilloried by the media, intellectuals, consumer groups, the unions, Congress, and various intellectual organizations as never before.

The great question these attacks raise is this: Will enough political leaders here and abroad, in both developed and Third World countries, see the mutual benefits to be gained in cooperating to settle their differences with the multinationals? Will we avoid serious damage to our increasingly global economy? The answer is far from clear.

In 1970, the multinationals—about half of them American—were growing vigorously in most non-Communist countries around the globe. Their sales and production had moved up so fast since World War II that they were now producing about a sixth of the entire world's output of goods and services—more than $500 billion annually. Direct foreign investment had replaced trade as the major international economic activity.

Today, U.S. multinationals are growing markedly slower. A Department of Commerce study showed that U.S. business investment spending, for plant and equipment abroad—$7.3 billion in 1975—is still rising but not much. The survey, covering 350 U.S. companies and their 5,000 majority-owned foreign affiliates, showed only a

Carl H. Madden is Chief Economist, Chamber of Commerce of the United States.

4 percent increase in 1975 for plant and equipment outlays, a huge
drop from the 25 percent increases of the year before. This drop was
due largely to global recessionary conditions for the period covered
by the survey.

Even so, U.S. multinationals are big. U.S. investment abroad,
most of it by big multinational businesses, reached a total of $118.6
billion at the end of 1974, nearly five times the foreign direct investment ($21.7 billion) in the United States. It brought the nation an
equally impressive $25.2 billion income in 1974, a gain of 48 percent
over 1973, almost entirely from oil price and production rises. In
fact, by 1970 U.S. corporate investment abroad was 25 percent of
total U.S. plant and equipment spending; sales abroad were 13 percent
of total manufacturing sales; and some estimates for 1974 put at
around 30 percent the share of U.S. corporate profits derived from
overseas.

At the end of 1974, of total U.S. direct investment abroad, U.S.
manufacturing affiliates made up 43 percent ($50.9 billion); petroleum,
25 percent ($30.2 billion); and other industries—where the positions
in the finance and insurance, trade, and mining and smelting industries
were the largest—32 percent ($37.5 billion). Developed countries
accounted for 70 percent of total U.S. direct investment abroad,
developing countries accounted for 24 percent, and 6 percent was
"international and unallocated."

Underlying the slowdown in U.S. multinational growth are
changing political and economic developments. In the 1950s, U.S.
corporations rushed abroad to get around high tariffs such as the
European common external tariff, and other barriers to U.S. exports.
By the 1960s, the overvalued dollar had made it cheap to buy assets
abroad. U.S. corporations expanded in an atmosphere of relatively
stable prices, receptive host political climates, rising imports into
the United States, cheap production labor abroad, and rapid world
growth. They even expanded through the Eurodollar market after
restrictions on foreign capital movements had been imposed by the
U.S. government.

Dollar devaluations since 1971 have made U.S. exports more
competitive in world markets. Labor costs are more equalized
through faster rises in wages abroad and new and more realistic
floating exchange rates. And, as U.S. exports grow, Japanese and
European multinationals feel the effects on their sales away from
home. Both U.S. and non-U.S. multinationals are shifting production
to Third World countries that were once mainly the source of raw
materials, as the world climbs the exponential curve of growth, and
raw materials countries gain in bargaining power with industrial
countries.

Oddly enough, nobody quite knows how many multinational companies there are. Indeed, the Group of Eminent Persons, assembled to study multinational businesses, wish the world would call such organizations by another name. They prefer "transnational enterprises"—transnational because not all of the companies are located in enough countries to be multinational, and enterprises because they may be government owned, partnerships, or cooperatives. The fact is, some 3,000 U.S. companies have direct investments abroad but maybe only around a tenth as many have operations in six or more foreign lands.

Also, there are other definitional problems. Is a company multinational when 25 percent of its sales are abroad, or when instead 15 to 20 percent of its manufacturing capacity is located abroad? Authorities differ on this. Even the term "direct investment" is not all that definitive, with most experts arguing that at least 25 percent equity ownership of a foreign enterprise is needed for an investment to be considered direct.

It is not by accident that multinationals have been seen as "arguably the most creative international institution of the twentieth century." In a world of virulent nationalism, the multinational has offered a most effective way to use world human and natural resources. It has offered an adaptable way for people of different cultures, ideologies, and values to work together. It has offered an effective way of transferring a package of capital goods, management, marketing know-how, and technology from one country to another. It has excelled in modern management and in producing and marketing innovative goods and services.

These global corporations harness energies of self-interest, rational choice, and a desire to excel toward producing goods and services people want and can use. As the world becomes the global village of modern communications and transportation, the broad sweep of events pushes the world's people either toward greater cooperation, or else toward stagnation or war. The broad movement toward cooperation is everywhere evident in the birth and growth of such organizations as the European Economic Community (EEC), the Organization for Economic Cooperation and Development (OECD), and the Andean Common Market (ANCOM); even, indeed, in the shaky and uneasy detente of the United States and USSR and the surprising United States opening to China.

And at the bottom of the movement is the growing insight and power of science to unify understanding and shape technology. The modern world has seen world per capita income grow despite the population explosion. In the year of the birth of Jesus, an estimated world population of 250 million had a per capita income in current dollar equivalent of perhaps $200 a year. By 1776 and the signing of the U.S. Declaration of Independence, maybe 750 million people lived on earth, also having only $200 per year in current dollar equivalent per person. Today, even with almost four billion people, incomes (GNP) per person have risen to perhaps $900 per year.

What explains the explosion in economic activity, art, culture, and education of the past 200 years? Surely it has been the creative power of Western civilization. It has been mainly the world impact of European and American freedom of thought and opinion, the English free enterprise system, the resulting waves of innovation, the spread of science and technology, and the pursuit of liberal policies of foreign trade and investment.

What of the future? It seems within reason that, as UN projections suggest, world population growth rates—now somewhere around 2 percent a year—are about to slow down. Economic growth rates also are likely to decline, from an average of 5 percent a year (1950 to the early 1970s) possibly to levels closer in the future to 2-3 percent.

Even so, the prospects for growth in people's incomes are good. Some analysts, such as Herman Kahn of the Hudson Institute, project a world population leveling off near the end of the twenty-first century in the range of 10 to 28 billion people, having average incomes per person between $10,000 and $20,000 per year. In other words, a century of slower but still positive economic growth could create conditions of adequacy spread widely throughout the world.

The world food problem of today is mainly that of the South Asians of India, Bangladesh, Pakistan, and neighboring countries; of sub-Saharan Africa; and of scattered regions of South and Central America. These areas have suffered food shortages for centuries. To be sure, the poorest 1 billion people endure incomes perhaps no more than one-twentieth of those of the richest developed countries. Yet, a much larger portion of the human race and a vastly larger number of people live today under conditions of adequacy than ever before in recorded history. The promise is that in the century beginning now it should be possible to achieve adequacy for effectively all the people on earth.

In short, the prospects for further gains in living standards for the world's people are real, despite valid concerns about population growth, limits to economic growth, and dwindling resources. The multinational corporation, operating in a climate of growing world interdependence, freedom of thought, and rising levels of education, is a brilliant way for people to organize voluntarily for growth, innovation, and technology transfer. It is manifestly to the advantage of all the world's people—as suggested by persistent efforts of the USSR to exchange technology with the West and buy its wheat—to see the multinational grow. And it is quite mistaken to suggest, as

Jean-Jacques Servan-Schreiber did a few years ago in his book The
American Challenge, that the multinational is synonymous with
"American." European, Japanese, and Canadian, as well as U.S.
international corporations, are globalizing production in the world
today and are growing faster in some cases than U.S. international
firms. And there is nothing in principle to stop developing countries
from organizing their own multinationals except lack of capital and
inability of leaders or wealthy landowners to organize know-how.

Projections of growth from today's levels of output for multinationals—now at a value of more than $500 billion a year—suggest
that within a single generation more than half the free world's production may be internationalized. The growth in new jobs, the new
wealth, new ownership, and higher living standards are the way that
economic, technological, and educational gaps can be closed. If, as
some suggest, such global output comes from as few as 300 corporations, surely they will operate under closer scrutiny of governments
and more widespread ownership by people throughout the world.

Already, benefits of multinationals, linked to their responsible
behavior, are plainly evident. Such evidence clearly suggests that
they promote peace and understanding by enhancing the mobility of
people, the flow of capital, the transfer of technology, and the infusion
of modern management, from developed to developing countries, both
industrial and Third World.

The central thrust of criticism against multinationals is that
they undermine and frustrate national power. In 1971, Raymond
Vernon of Harvard, in a book called Sovereignty at Bay: The Multinational Spread of U.S. Enterprises, put forth the central theme that
"sovereign states are feeling naked." He argued that size, strength,
and technological superiority of vast worldwide enterprises made
nation-states needing their jobs, money, and know-how no match for
them in bargaining.

The most popular attack has been that of political scientist
Richard J. Barnet and economist Ronald E. Müller, in a readable
but inflammatory best seller, Global Reach: The Power of the Multinational Corporations, serialized in The New Yorker magazine.
Though it has been condemned by scholarly reviews, the book has
appealed to readers inclined toward scapegoat theory and already
hostile to big business. Revelations of illegal political contributions
at home and of bribery abroad by major U.S. multinationals—conduct
no leader in business would or should condone—have added to people's
suspicions.

The arguments of Barnet and Müller boil down to the view that
multinationals, having too much power, use it to keep host countries
from "optimum development." They argue that the "oligopoly" structure of multinationals causes them to resist bringing in the "best"

technology, overprice their own imports and undercharge for exports, use scarce local capital instead of more plentiful home country capital, and so to "exploit" host countries. They claim that multinationals are independent of host governments and so create political instability by dodging tax and security laws. They hold that multinationals are insulated from market prices by sales from parent to subsidiary or vice versa. Finally, they argue that multinationals "export" jobs from the home country, weakening the U.S. economic structure, making the United States dangerously dependent on the world, and indeed, threatening to turn the United States into a Latin American "banana" republic.

The bargaining power of developing countries is rising, as when Mexico required its U.S. subsidiary auto makers to aim toward selling eventually as many cars abroad as in the local market. Debates over equity ownership are being settled more favorably for developing countries. Even industrial host countries are asking for a bigger share of profits, jobs, technology, and management in the multinationals.

The oligopoly issue is an old one in the United States. It holds that in industries with few competitors, near monopolies can act together to share a monopoly and so boost prices, limit output, and exploit consumers. The theory rests on heroic assumptions that tastes, technology, and product remain constant. These assumptions are of course false in today's world. The evidence shows no significant history among major concentrated industries of either higher prices or profits than among nonconcentrated competitors. And when, for example, autos are looked at from a world perspective, it is obvious that concentration itself drops off to inconsequential levels. So the entire basis of the monopoly thesis slides away in the face of growing world competition, that is, the very growth of multinationals.

As for exporting jobs, the AFL–CIO estimates that from 1966 to 1969, 500,000 jobs in such industries as apparel, radios, and bicycles were lost to American workers and gained by workers in Taiwan, Singapore, or Korea, where labor is far cheaper. The charge is only a partial truth. With the dollar overvalued, the choice for U.S. manufacturers was to lose sales. Lost U.S. sales would have meant lost U.S. jobs. Best academic estimates show that on balance U.S. corporate operations abroad have added at least 700,000 U.S. jobs and repatriated earnings of $7 billion a year—and maybe more. This occurred because production abroad represented expansion of markets. Exports to subsidiaries plus new jobs from foreign earnings generated the added jobs.

Then there is the argument that U.S. multinationals exploit developing countries, a favorite innuendo throughout the Barnet-Müller book. They argue that from 1957 to 1965 U.S.-based firms financed more than four-fifths of Latin American operations with local capital. What they overlook is the patent fact that governments and not corporations set income distribution policies, that urban and industrial nations share income more equally than developing countries, and that wealth (in the sense of the means of production) is most heavily concentrated of all in systems of state capitalism or socialism.

The accusation that multinationals are the major perpetrators of currency crises has been made academic by floating currency exchange rates. These rates make exchange risks symmetrical and no longer reward bets on devaluation of long-overvalued currencies. As for the charge that multinationals evade taxes by rigging prices, the issue in fact is the need for international agreement on a set of rules for pricing transactions among subsidiaries that could be enforced on all. Few U.S. executives would object.

The most serious charge against U.S.-based multinationals, one that may create trouble for all U.S. business, is that of bribery and political corruption. Americans, as polls of opinion show, are far more concerned about such ethical problems than the economic issues affecting multinationals. No company in the United States can condone such practices and responsible executives must rightly forbid them under all circumstances. The underlying reason goes to the political legitimacy of a democratic social system supporting equal rights and unequal rewards. In such a system, bribery denies virtue to accomplishment and instead rewards the vice of status, influence, or contacts.

The result of current developments may well be a period of increased regulation of big business. Lee L. Morgan, President of Caterpillar Tractor, the U.S. multinational with 11 plants in nine foreign countries, has said that the 1970s would see "a rising tide of attempts at control and regulation" of the multinationals.

· Multinationals, already powerful as a group, seem likely to grow in power. It is not so much that they challenge sovereignty as that they unite groups of people across borders giving them a worldwide perspective that casts light on the limitations of national goals. It is essential, therefore, to see where multinationals fit into a benign and rational world order. Since the current world political struggle no longer can be restricted to military-political terms but vitally includes economic and welfare issues, the task is especially important.

What the critics of multinationals say comes out of an intellectual background. It may be nationalism that fears foreign investment, wants to curb the multinational's profits, regulate its behavior, and capture its benefits without its evils. It may be populism, or its modern counterpart naturalism, that fears size itself, standardization,

loss of diversity, increase of complexity, destruction of indigenous
culture. Finally, it may be Marxism, the desperate belief that
capitalist investment by definition has to be exploitative, destabilizing,
and adverse to social development of people. Marxists, by their own
avowed ethic, feel free to use any means of argument or action to
help history move along its predetermined path. And to do this effectively, as the Marxist instruction goes, requires that opinion be
polarized if possible.

Indeed, one new economic order would see the Marxist solution
prevail through an end to private ownership of the huge multinationals,
state take-overs along with liquidation of the current monetary system
by debt moratoria, substitution of world and national state development
banks, suppression of political and ideological dissent, and the rest of
the classic revolutionary tactics now so familiar in this century.

The demands of Third World countries for the most part call
for higher levels of resource transfers—direct and indirect—from
North to South, in trade, aid, foreign investment, and monetary rules.
In trade, the call is for commodity agreements, reduced barriers to
Third World exports, better-financed adjustment assistance to make
less painful imports from the Third World. In aid, the Third World
calls for developed countries to meet UN aid targets (1.0 percent of
GNP), emergency funds, debt renegotiation.

In foreign investment, the call is for more access to world
capital markets, more North-South capital flows, lower charges for
technology flows, more labor-intensive investment in Third World
countries, and the like. Some call for easing restrictions on expropriation—what many developed countries call demands for acceptance
of confiscation.

In technology transfer, more financing of Third World institutions, more adaptation of technology to Third World conditions and
fewer patent restrictions, accompany demands for airlines and steel
mills by some political leaders.

In the monetary system, the Third World wants a greater
voice, more special drawing rights devoted to Third World development, a conscious program to relocate international economic
production, more collective self-reliance among developing countries,
and explicit acknowledgment that colonial injustice and neoimperial-
ism are in great part responsible for present inequities in the distribution of income (a ratio favoring the developed North by twenty
to one in real per capita terms at present).

Perhaps the central aim of U.S. multinationals, looking ahead
to the United States' third century, ought to be to adapt themselves
better, not a simple or peripheral task in the midst of a world political struggle. But even more important, the possibility now looms

of a rapid spread of government intervention—neo-Mercantilism and the politicization of investment decisions.

How can the leadership of the non-Communist world construct a liberal trade and investment policy to meet today's conditions and demands and tomorrow's prospects? True, more than two-thirds of today's direct investment is carried out in developed countries. But from the viewpoint of world order the issue is to establish conditions in the non-Communist world that assure both global equity and freedom of choice.

1

DO MULTINATIONAL CORPORATIONS HAVE MARKET POWER TO OVERPRICE?

J. Fred Weston

The impact of large international corporations on prices has been treated mainly as a by-product of appraisals of other aspects of their activities. A number of views can be extracted from the voluminous and wide-ranging writings on the multinational corporations (MNCs). A central issue is whether MNCs move concentration, oligopoly, and product differentiation into enlarged international dimensions with harmful economic effects. A related consideration is whether transfer pricing is an expression of market power of the MNCs.

An alternative possibility is that MNCs have developed in response to underlying economic forces and, as instruments of competition in international markets, have had on balance salutary effects on efficiency and prices.

This paper will seek to appraise these alternative positions. Since a firm may take multiple approaches to international markets, evidence will be drawn from a number of areas; the field of inquiry is necessarily broad because of the alternative approaches available. These include export and import sales, licensing, joint ventures, foreign operations established de novo, and foreign operations as a result of acquisitions of existing firms. The interactions of these multiple activities are reflected in the available evidence in different ways.

J. Fred Weston is Professor of Business Economics and Finance, Graduate School of Management, University of California at Los Angeles.

ALTERNATIVE THEORIES OF THE ROLES
OF MULTINATIONALS

Richard E. Caves has set forth a theory of foreign direct investment that represents an extension of the structuralist theory for domestic markets. He summarizes his central themes as follows:

> Briefly, the argument of this paper is that foreign direct investment occurs mainly in industries characterized by certain market structures in both the "lending" (or home) and "borrowing" (or host) countries. In the parlance of industrial organization, oligopoly with product differentiation normally prevails where corporations make "horizontal" investments to produce abroad the same lines of goods as they produce in the home market. Oligopoly, not necessarily differentiated, in the home market is typical in industries which undertake "vertical" direct investments to produce abroad a raw material or other input to their production process at home. Direct investment tends to involve market conduct that extends the recognition of mutual market dependence—the essence of oligopoly—beyond national boundaries. [Caves, 1971, p. 1]

But a number of rival theories of direct investment may be found. Robert Z. Aliber presented a theory of direct investment based on exchange risks:

> The central hypothesis is that the key factor in the explanation of the pattern of direct foreign investment is that the world is divided into different currency areas and that there is a bias in the market's estimate of exchange risk. The bias in the evaluation of exchange risk determines whether a country is likely to be a source country or a host country for foreign investment. Moreover, the bias attached to securities denominated in a foreign currency differs from that attached to the income in that currency of a source-country firm. If the world were a unified currency area, exchange risk and a currency premium would not exist; then the analysis of direct foreign investment would be in terms of the economics of location. In this world, tariffs would be a type of transportation cost; the higher the tariffs, the greater the tendency

that demand in each customs area would be satisfied
from production within that area. Tariffs explain
whether a patent is utilized at home or abroad and
not whether a host-country firm or a source-country
firm utilizes the patent.

National differences in capitalization rates are
the major factors that explain the country pattern of
direct foreign investment; otherwise the pattern would
tend to be random. The difference in pattern by industry
reflects differences in the size of the host-country
market and the cost of doing business abroad. Similarly
takeovers can be explained by these differences in
capitalization rates. [Aliber, 1970, p. 34]

Still another view was presented by Stephen Hymer and Robert
Rowthorn in emphasizing increased competitive consequences of both
the European merger movement and internationalization of business:

1. Mergers and rationalizations will lead to
corporate reorganization and the creation of new administrative structures more akin to those of the American
corporation and better suited to multinational expansion.
Or, to put the matter differently, as European firms
increase in size and complexity their administrative
"brain" will increase more than proportionately and
their attention will focus not so much on national or
European markets but on the world as a whole, including the U.S. market itself. In a sense, the vision
of a firm depends on the height of its head office
building.

2. Greater financial strength will enable
European firms to invest more overseas. Investment
in a foreign country often involves a more direct
challenge to established firms than does exporting.
Firms that were previously prepared to tolerate
some competition in the form of exports may not be
willing to tolerate competitive direct investment. To
protect themselves against what they consider to be
a policy of aggressive expansion, they may attempt
to drive the intruder out of the market before he gets
too strong. The outcome of this struggle is likely to
depend upon the relative financial strengths of the
established firms and the firm attempting to increase
its market share by investing, which in turn depend
upon their relative sizes. . . .

3. By consolidating the overseas sales of
European firms, mergers will make them better able
to establish subsidiaries of an efficient size. In any
particular market a big firm is likely to have actual
or potential sales larger than those of a small firm,
either because it is already selling more in the form
of exports or because it can afford to finance a costly
promotion and distribution program for its products.
Equally it can afford to establish a large and efficient
subsidiary which can produce the output necessary to
satisfy this larger market. From the point of view
of both supply and demand the big firm is therefore
better able to produce on an efficient scale. [Hymer
and Rowthorn, 1970, pp. 74-75]

In a later study Hymer and Rowthorn emphasized the rivalrous
nature of foreign investments as follows:

The American response is likely to assign an even
greater role than in the past to increased foreign
investment. For one thing, it is very costly for a
dominant firm to resist incursions into its own market
by serious rivals (since the loss caused by a 1%
reduction in price is greater for the established firm
than for the new entrant). Equally, European attempts
to gain a foothold in the U.S. market are also likely
to be successful, for it will be easier for the U.S.
corporations to counterattack abroad, and to meet
inward foreign investment with outward foreign
investment.
    . . . We can therefore expect a period of
intensified multinationalization (almost amounting
to capital flight) over the coming decade as both U.S.
corporations and non-U.S. corporations try to establish world-wide market positions and protect themselves from the challenges of each other.
    Cross investment is a long-standing feature
of direct foreign investment. In many industries
where U.S. corporations have substantial direct investment in foreign countries, one of the leading firms in
the United States is a foreign firm, e.g., oil, soft
drinks, paper, soaps, and detergents, farm machinery,
business machinery, tires and tubes, sewing machines,
concentrated milk, biscuits, chemicals. [Hymer and
Rowthorn, 1972, p. 81]

Hymer and Rowthorn emphasize the incentives for a rivalrous oligopolist to seek to make incursions into foreign markets. This is far from the theory of "recognition of mutual market dependence" emphasized by Caves. Furthermore, Hymer and Rowthorn's list of industries in which cross foreign direct investment takes place includes products not generally considered differentiated, such as oil, paper, business machinery, and chemicals.

Further counterevidence to a simple theory of direct investment is presented by Thomas C. Lowinger. He runs a regression to explain U.S. industries' export shares of world trade from 1968 to 1970 and changes in the relative export shares of U.S. industries between the years 1960-62 and 1968-70. Generally the most powerful explanatory variable, mostly at the 1 percent level, is scientists and engineers engaged in research and development (R&D) as a percentage of total employment, in 1967-69. The industries with the best export performance record (and investment possibilities) are aircraft, electrical equipment, drugs, scientific instruments, industrial chemicals, and machinery. He concludes:

> U.S. competitive performance in international trade is largely determined by the country's ability to invest a comparatively high proportion of its resources in the development of new products and improved processes. A high rate of generation of new knowledge whether embodied (in capital) or disembodied is typical of a high income country such as the U.S. and may be thought to be the mainstay of its comparative advantage in international trade. [Lowinger, 1975, p. 234]

Another theory of foreign investment is the product-cycle thesis of Raymond Vernon (1966). The product-cycle thesis emphasizes that a large and rapidly growing market is a stimulus to investment. As product markets reach maturity in the United States, growth rates decline so that foreign markets become relatively more attractive. Tests of this thesis have been performed by B. Wilkinson (1968), Louis T. Wells, Jr. (1969), and Martin F. J. Prachowny and J. David Richardson (1974). It has been observed that this theory suggests that certain types of international investment are inherently growth oriented. The implications of the product-cycle thesis have been noted by John H. Dunning:

> This suggests very strongly that certain types of international investment are inherently growth oriented, not only because they are directed to industries supplying products, the demand for

which increases proportionately to the growth in GNP
per head (Wells, 1968), but because of the various
advantages, e.g., access to knowledge and markets,
size, integration, and finance, possessed by the
investing companies over their host competitors.
Even the most cursory glance at the structure of
U.S. firms in Europe reveals that their activities
are heavily concentrated in two sectors, first the
science-based, or research-intensive, industries
supplying both producer and consumer goods, and
second, industries subject to economies of scale and
producing products with a high income elasticity of
demand. Between 1958 and 1964, for example, the four
most research-intensive industries in the United
States spent 2 1/2 times the amount on new plant and
equipment in Europe than 14 other industries (Gruber,
Mehta, and Vernon, 1967). Moreover, these same
"knowledge" industries (e.g., computer, instruments,
electronics, chemicals, etc.), by providing a kind of
infrastructure of knowledge, create substantial spill-
over effects, and act as a catalyst for growth which
may far outweigh the initial demand-stimulating effects.
[Dunning, 1970, pp. 149-50]

These observations also are inconsistent with Caves's simplistic
theory as well as with the paradigm that structure determines foreign
investment and "conduct and performance." In addition, Caves himself presents some very important insights that provide ingredients
for a theory much more rich and robust than the structural theory.
In observing that capital flows are not induced by availability of
equity capital, he observes:

Its investments transmit equity capital, entrepreneurship,
and technological or other productive knowledge in an
industry-specific package: The influence of national endow-
ments of equity capital need not dominate or even significantly influence its actions. [Caves, 1971, p. 3]

Caves also formulates the conditions for foreign investments:

For the possession of some special asset to lead the
firm to invest abroad, two conditions must be satisfied.
First, the asset must partake of the character of a
public good within the firm, such as knowledge fundamental to the production of a profitably saleable

commodity. Any advantage embodied in knowledge,
information or technique that yields a positive return
over direct costs in the market where it is first proven
can potentially do the same in other markets without
need to incur again the sunk costs associated with its
initial discovery. Knowledge would seem to be the
prototypical asset displaying the character of a public
good proprietary to the firm, but it is not the only
one. The essential feature of an asset conducive to
foreign investment is not that its opportunity cost
should be zero, but that it should be low relative to
the return attainable via foreign investment. . . .
Second, the return attainable on a firm's special
asset in a foreign market must depend at least somewhat on local production. [Caves, 1971, pp. 4, 5]

Caves, however, distorts the use of organizational skill that
Servan-Schreiber attributes as the source of The American Challenge.
Caves interprets this as "pure organizational skill," which "would
explain the successful foreign investments by American management
consulting firms, but not by American manufacturing firms." However, what is referred to here is experience in operating mass production industries and developing learning-by-doing in individual
industries, which knowledge is then transferred abroad in horizontal
investments.

A general framework for analyzing the impact of foreign direct
investment has been presented by Harry G. Johnson (1970, pp. 45-47).
He suggests that if foreign investments flow into the more capital-
intensive sectors of the economy (including nonmaterial), the effect
of the inflow of foreign capital may be to raise the return on capital
and reduce the wages of labor. His argument is made in the following
terms, with reference to Figure 1.1:

This point is illustrated in Figure 1, where XX and
YY are the isoquants for the two sectors of the economy
as they are before the foreign investment, and X'X' is
the isoquant for the situation after the introduction of
the foreign technology. If the foreign companies absorb
the whole benefit of their superior efficiency in profits
on the technology, factor prices remain unchanged and
they derive a profit on their technological superiority
as a proportion of cost at the rate MM'/OM'. If they
pass it on to the consumers completely, in the form
of a price reduction proportional to their technical
superiority, the price of X falls by MM' in terms of

FIGURE 1.1

Redistribution of Factor Income from Direct Investment

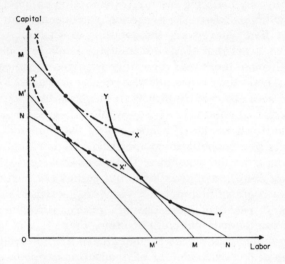

Source: Johnson, 1970, p. 46. Reproduced with the permission of the M.I.T. Press.

capital and factor prices are unchanged; if they keep commodity prices unchanged and let the benefits be absorbed by the community through altered factor prices, the new factor-price ratio is the slope of NN, which implies a relative and absolute increase in the price of the services of capital and an absolute and relative decline in the price of the services of labor. This point may explain the otherwise rather implausible fact that in Britain the employers are favorably inclined toward American investment in the country, while the trade unions are generally hostile toward it.

The attractive feature of the foregoing analysis is that it provides a rationale for the movement of the foreign capital in either material form, knowledge, or training. Within this framework Johnson's observations on the argument for restrictions of foreign direct investment because of the possibility of increased monopoly also are worth noting:

This is a second-best argument, because the intrusion of foreign enterprises may either increase or decrease

competition in the domestic economy, and if more
competition is desired it can be achieved more
reliably by domestic antitrust policy, or still more
reliably, by reducing the tariff protection enjoyed
by industries where the presence of monopoly can
be verified. Moreover, the question of whether
foreign ownership of part of industry leads to social
loss through increased monopoly requires more careful analysis than it has usually received. Social loss
would seem to require either an increase in prices
to consumers above what they would otherwise be,
or additional wastes of resources on the nonprice
aspects of monopolistic competition. Higher profits
derived from the superior efficiency of foreign firms
are not evidence of such loss, but rather the contrary
from a cosmopolitan point of view, reflecting the
saving of resource costs through greater efficiency;
and from the national point of view, there is a gain
to the extent that prices to consumers are lowered,
prices of domestic factors of production are raised,
or the nation shares in the increased profits of the
foreign firms through taxation. [Johnson, 1970,
p. 55]

The same logic is extended to the issue of the take-overs of the
existing domestic firms. If the foreign firm possesses organizational
capabilities and knowledge that will enable them to produce at a lower
price, this increased competition will result in capital losses for
domestic firms. They will receive a higher value for their products
if they are able to sell to a buyer who can use these resources effectively rather than duplicating them.

Other studies have emphasized managerial aspects in the expansion of MNCs. For example, R. Hal Mason, Robert R. Miller, and
Dale R. Weigel write:

Although many United States firms may not have a
technological advantage over local firms, some have
advantages stemming from superior management. It
is widely recognized, for example, that Procter and
Gamble has a competitive advantage over other firms
in the consumer products industries because of its
superior marketing skills. These skills may be exploited, to some extent, by exporting. However,
Procter and Gamble may have to produce in foreign
markets to exploit fully its marketing advantage.

Superior marketing skill includes the ability both to
identify the characteristics of market demand, and to
supply the desired products either in fact, or in the
mind of the consumer through advertising. Local
production is an invaluable marketing aid because it
facilitates adaptation of the product and marketing
strategies to changes in local market conditions.
Moreover, the local plant improves the reliability
of supply—a factor that is of particular importance
when the product has no special technological
advantage.

Other management skills also may have to be
exploited by direct investment. For example, the
advantage possessed by United States food processing
firms such as Heinz and Del Monte is a unique capacity
to organize farmers to produce high-quality products
on a large scale. These skills cannot be adequately
exploited in foreign countries by exporting to them
because canned foods are bulky and heavy and, thus,
are costly to ship. Consequently, foreign investment
is necessary to exploit the organizational skills possessed by these firms. [Mason, Miller, and Weigel
1975, p. 245]

Yair Aharoni (1966) found that foreign investment decisions were
often stimulated as a response to meeting emerging problems. Others
have found that the growth of foreign direct investments has been in
response to sales growth and cash flows in foreign subsidiaries
(Stevens, 1969). The size and prospective growth of foreign markets
also have influenced foreign direct investments (Gordon and Grommers, 1962). Differential tariffs may cause a shift from export to
direct investment (Horst, 1972a).

Thus there are many theories of the MNCs. Each of the theories
can be supported by some appropriate assumptions, and some evidence
can be found both to support and to contradict any individual theory.
Unfortunately, the plethora of theories makes it difficult to develop
a general theory. What we have is a large number of causal variables
operating with widely differing strengths in greatly different com-
binations of circumstances. Different statistical studies, even when
done carefully, will, therefore, yield greatly different results and a
variety of possible interpretations.

Among the alternative theories, the one that has gained widest
acceptance is the extension of the structural theory of oligopoly from
the domestic setting to an international framework. But this ignores
a substantial and increasing body of countertheory and counterevidence.

Even if the structural theory had been established for the domestic economy (and I emphasize that it has not), the different characteristics of the international markets do not permit its automatic extension to the world setting. In the remainder of the paper, therefore, I will concentrate on this and related issues.

OLIGOPOLY THEORY IN AN INTERNATIONAL SETTING

The standard theory of domestic oligopoly can be stated in a sentence. Firms accounting for a high proportion of sales in industries with homogeneous products will recognize mutual interdependence, leading to a form of joint monopoly maximization. If the vectors of decision making in the firm were only price and output, as the standard theory of oligopoly assumes, I too would continue to believe that theory as I did when I was first taught it. Indeed, I wish I could continue to believe the standard oligopoly theory since it would be comfortable to hold to what is the dominant view in the academic world.

The standard theory of oligopoly is simple. It is easy to communicate. It is also satisfying to know that there is a demon causing the world's ills and that by just eradicating the oligopoly demon, most problems will be solved. But the world is not so tidy.

Unfortunately for simple analysis and easy solutions, the decision-making processes in the firm are much more complex than output adjusting. There is a wide range of decision making over the character and quality of products, R&D activities to develop new products and to improve products, and efforts to respond to and stimulate different segments of consumer taste, demands, or responses. In the theory of atomistic markets upon which the structural theory rests, there is no such thing as marketing effort. Nor does the theory of atomistic competition take into consideration firms' organization structures, organization learning, and the time and effort required to achieve efficient management teams with experience and capabilities. Thus in the real world, the managers of firms must take into account a wide range of variables with respect to quality of product, product mix, R&D efforts, marketing strategies, and so on. The many dimensions of decision areas and the wide range over which choices must be made greatly reduce the plausibility of oligopolistic coordination in a multidimensional, dynamic setting.

The risks of falling behind in one of a wide range of areas of R&D, product quality improvement, or marketing effectiveness, stimulate considerable rivalrous activity. As a consequence, the potentials for gains from developing an advantage over rivals exceed the gains from static, joint monopolization. Numerous factors provide stimuli for continued competitive striving and result in the processes of competitive oligopoly.

The foregoing briefly sketches the alternative theory of competition in concentrated industries, but I must concede that it is difficult to win new converts. Laymen prefer to have a demon; scholars are reluctant to discard a dominant doctrine that is simple and has achieved intellectual respectability.

Hence, the central unsettled issues of international oligopoly parallel those of domestic concentration. They are collusion versus competition; market power versus economies of scale and advantages of organizational capabilities and experience; entry barriers versus differential efficiency. Obviously, these issues cannot be settled any more readily in their international dimensions than in their domestic setting.

But studies in the international setting appear to assume that issues of domestic oligopoly have been settled, so a review of some relevant evidence may be useful. The correlation of concentration with profit studies was formulated to establish an association between high concentration and collusion (Bain, 1951). But an increasing number of later studies have called into question the earlier results (Brozen, 1970-73; Demsetz, 1973, 1974, 1975; Ornstein, 1972). Particularly the size stratification of analysis of the concentration-profit relationship by Harold Demsetz (1973) casts doubt on the presumed relationship. The use of two-stage least squares analysis in the framework of an identified econometric system emphasizes the sensitivity of the relationship to industry stratification and equation specification (Intriligator, Weston, and DeAngelo, 1975). But studies of the multinational enterprise treat the concentration-profit relationship as though it were an established fact (for example, Knickerbocker, 1973; Horst, 1974).

A fundamental weakness in the earlier concentration-profit studies was the failure to explain why entry would not be stimulated to ultimately cause above-average profits to decline. In a number of articles Yale Brozen (1970,1973) presents considerable evidence and support of the position that above-average profits noted at any point in time do not in fact persist.

The concentration-profit theory was subsequently buttressed by adding the argument that the existence of entry barriers could explain the persistence of above-average profits (Mann, 1966; Weiss, 1974). The main entry barriers cited are lower costs, economies of scale, product differentiation, patents, and control over scarce raw materials. Patents, of course, reflect the expression of government-endowed monopoly and do not go to the central issues of concentration and profits. Control over raw material supplies is also a form of

overt monopoly and not really germane to the concentration-profit
issue.

The use of the product differentiation explanation is question
begging at best. If product differentiation (along with advertising)
yields differential profits, why doesn't everyone practice the art?
The structuralist explanation is that entry barriers prevent access
to the opportunity for creating one's own entry barriers. But standard
microeconomic theory would predict that competition in the efforts to
erect entry barriers would eliminate the monopoly rents. Furthermore, a number of studies suggest that differentiation efforts through
advertising and other methods, when treated properly from an accounting and economic standpoint, do not, in fact, yield differentially
higher returns over time (Ayanian, 1975; Bloch, 1974).

Another study in the international setting places great weight
on the finding by Scherer that innovative activity as measured by the
employment of engineers and scientists increases up to a four-firm
concentration ratio in the 50 percent to 55 percent range but not
beyond (Horst, 1974, pp. 79-80). A fatal flaw in attaching very great
significance to this finding is that what is being measured is R&D
inputs rather than outputs. The data cited are perfectly consistent
with the conclusion that beyond the 50 percent to 55 percent four-firm
concentration ratio, industries are more efficient in their utilization
of R&D inputs and, hence, can economize on their use.

Thus, there is both a strong theoretical basis and increasing
empirical evidence that does not permit one to assume that the structural theory has been established for domestic markets and that
therefore it can readily be applied to international markets. Furthermore, a consideration of international dimensions of markets casts
doubt on the statistical foundations of the standard structural theory.

Effects of International Markets on Concentration
Ratios: Adjustment of the Conventional
Four-Firm Concentration Ratios

Another basis for skepticism about the view that mutual dependence extends to the international sphere is that measures of concentration in domestic markets are greatly overstated. The presumption
of the existence of a tight oligopoly may not be valid when corrections
to concentration ratios are made. Accordingly, we have adjusted
domestic concentration ratios to account for international dimensions
of markets.*

---

*Nathan Hasson and Marion Klein assisted in this effort. For
a more detailed explanation of the procedures employed, see Nathan

We have made an analysis of the effect of international markets on U.S. four-firm concentration ratios. To apply an initial screening rule, we calculated the sum of the import and export shares in an industry's domestic production plus imports (U.S. Department of Commerce, 1972). For those industries whose imports plus export shares in new supply was 4 percent or more we sought to determine the size of the world market (Trade Relations Council, 1971). In order to match international and U.S. industry classifications as closely as possible, all verbal definitions of U.S. and world industry titles were manually compared for all international industries for which data were available. Sometimes it was necessary to combine two or three international industries or two or three domestic industries to obtain one matching U.S.-international industry. We obtained a final sample of 75 matching industries. From various sources of international production data, estimates of total world production were obtained.* We were then able to develop the data in Table 1.1.

Table 1.1 lists the 75 four-digit industries (approximately) from the U.S. Standard Industrial Classification (SIC): for each industry, column 1 presents the SIC number; column 2 presents the industry

---

Hasson, "Concentration and Performance: A Protection Criterion" (Ph.D. diss., Graduate School of Management, UCLA, 1975).

*These included the following studies by the Organization for Economic Cooperation and Development (OECD): The Engineering Industries in OECD Member Countries: New Basic Statistics, 1963-1970, Vol. 1 (Paris: Organization for Economic Cooperation and Development, 1972); The Engineering Industries in North America, Europe, Japan, 1966-1967 and 1967-1968 (Paris: Organization for Economic Cooperation and Development, Machinery Committee, 1967 and 1969); The Iron and Steel Industry in 1964 and Trends in 1965 (Paris: Organization for Economic Cooperation and Development, Special Committee for Iron and Steel, 1965); The Iron and Steel Industry in 1968 and Trends in 1969 (Paris: Organization for Economic Cooperation and Development, Special Committee for Iron and Steel, 1969); The Chemical Industry 1964-1965 (Paris: Organization for Economic Cooperation and Development, Chemical Products Special Committee, 1966); The Chemical Industry 1967-1968 (Paris: Organization for Economic Cooperation and Development, Chemical Products Special Committee, 1969); and Industrial Statistics 1900-1962, OECD Statistical Bulletin (Paris: Organization for Economic Cooperation and Development, 1964). See also United Nations, Statistical Yearbook 1971 (New York: Statistical Office of the United Nations, Department of Economic and Social Affairs, 1972).

TABLE 1.1

U.S. Four-Digit Concentration Ratios Adjusted for
International Markets, 1963

Standard Industrial Classification (SIC)	Industry Name	Percent Imports and Exports Combined	Percent U.S. to Total Production	U.S.	Adjusted
2011	Meat packing plants	6	19.7	31	6
2022	Cheese, natural and processed	3a	19.6	44	9
2031	Canned and cured seafoods	23	10.3	38	4
2041	Flour	9	11.4	41c	5
2045					
2061	Sugar				
2062					
2063		23	8.4	61c	5
2111	Cigarettes	4	25.6	80	20
2283	Wool yarn mills	5	13.2	26	3
2611	Pulp mills	57	39.1	48	19
2815	Cyclic intermediates and crudes	14	29.3	53	16
2821	Plastics materials and resins	10	38.5	35	13
2822	Synthetic rubber	19	62.3	57	36
2871	Fertilizers	7	40.0b	34	14
2911	Petroleum refining	8	39.6	34	13
3011	Tires and inner tubes	5	49.0	70	34
3031	Reclaimed rubberf	5	74.4	93	69
3141	Shoes, except rubberf	3a	47.5b	25	12
3312	Blast furnaces and steel mills	7	37.4	48	18
3313	Electrometalurgical products	7	30.5	79	24
3316	Cold finishing of steel shapes	7	44.8	36	16
3331	Primary copper	28	27.8	78	22
3332	Primary lead	14	15.1	95d	14
3333	Primary zinc	12	26.5	57	15
3334	Primary aluminum	15	49.5	95d	47
3421	Cutlery	9	44.0	66	29
3443	Steam engines and turbines, and				
3511	boiler shops	12	35.9	44c	16
3481	Miscellaneous fabricated wire products	4	69.2	13	9
3519	Internal combustion engines, not elsewhere classified	16	50.9	49	25
3522	Farm machinery	19	48.6	43	21
3531	Construction machinery	33	62.8	42	26
3532	Mining and oil field machinery				
3533		27	57.7	29c	17
3534	Elevators and moving stairways	2a	44.6	62	28
3535	Conveyors and conveying equipment	10	54.9	28	15
3536	Hoists, cranes, and monorails	8	17.7	36	6
3537	Industrial trucks and tractors	10	64.2	54	35
3541	Machine tools: metal cutting	20	36.9	20	7
3542	Machine tools: metal forming	23	48.4	22	11
3551	Food products machinery	22	46.0	22	10
3552	Textile machinery	29	31.8	35	11
3553	Woodworking machinery	15	32.7	35	11
3554	Paper industries machinery	25	41.4	41	17
3555	Printing trades machinery	23	51.3	44	23

Standard Industrial Classification (SIC)	Industry Name	Percent Imports and Exports Combined	Percent U.S. to Total Production	U.S.	Adjusted
3561	Pumps and compressors	14	57.4	26	15
3562	Ball and roller bearings	9	51.8	57	30
3567	Industrial furnaces and ovens	10	41.7	28	12
3572	Typewriters	20	69.3	76	53
3573	Electronic computing equipment	18	88.5	n.a.[e]	—
3574	Calculating and accounting machines	18	56.4	n.a.[e]	—
3581	Automatic merchandising machines	6	84.0	55	46
3582	Commercial laundry equipment	20	62.0	47	29
3585	Refrigeration machinery	9	64.4	25	16
3611 / 3622	Electrical measuring instruments and industrial controls	10	51.5	44[c]	23
3613	Switchgear and switchboard apparatus	6	54.7	51	28
3623	Welding apparatus	12	78.7	41	32
3632	Household refrigerators and freezers	5	46.2	74	34
3635	Household vacuum cleaners	4	53.2	81[d]	43
3636	Sewing machines	63	19.1	81	15
3641 / 3642	Electric lamps and lighting fixtures	5	59.6	42[c]	25
3651	Radio and TV receiving sets	11	41.7	41	17
3652	Phonograph records	7	41.9	69	29
3671 / 3672 / 3673	Electron tubes and valves	8	63.0	76[c]	48
3674	Semiconductors	12	78.3	46	36
3679	Electronic components, not elsewhere classified	7	74.0	13	10
3692	Primary batteries, dry and wet	7	54.2	89	48
3693	X-ray apparatus and tubes	29	41.5	67	28
3694	Engine electric equipment	9	57.7	69	40
3711 / 3714	Motor vehicles, parts and accessories	9	45.6	77	35
3721	Aircraft	14	85.5	59	50
3722	Aircraft engines and engine parts	11	74.7	57	43
3729	Aircraft propellers, parts, and equipment, not elsewhere classified	15	93.4	38	35
3731 / 3732	Ship, boat building, and repairing	3a	37.1	43[c]	16
3741	Locomotives and parts	11	64.6	97	63
3742	Railroad and street cars	11	67.5	53	36
3751	Motorcylces, bicycles, and parts	34	29.3	56	16
3831	Optical instruments and lenses	18	58.2	41	24
3841 / 3842 / 3843	Medical instruments and supplies	11	83.3	47[c]	39
3861	Photographic equipment and supplies	13	52.4	63	33
3871 / 3872	Watches, watchcases, and clocks	16	16.6	47[c]	8

(continued)

25

(Table 1.1 continued)

aThis industry does not qualify as an international industry in 1963 but does qualify in 1967.

bProduction data available for 1962 only; therefore data are used in 1963 table only, and are an estimate of the percent of U.S. to world production in 1963.

cWeighted average of concentration ratios for bracketed SIC industries.

dConcentration ratio estimated (information which means it is withheld from census data to avoid disclosing figures for individual companies).

eThis industry was not separately identified by the census before 1967, so 1963 data are not available.

fIncludes data for North America and Europe only: international industry market as defined excludes Asia.

n.a.: Data not available.

Sources: U.S. Bureau of the Census, U.S. Commodity Exports and Imports as Related to Output, 1969 and 1968 (Washington, D.C.: U.S. Government Printing Office, 1972); Bureau of the Census, Census of Manufacturers Concentration Ratios in Manufacturing, 1967, Part 1, Chapter 9, Table 5 (Washington, D.C.: U.S. Government Printing Office, 1971).

name; column 3 presents the percent imports and exports to an
industry's new supply; in column 4 we calculated the percent U.S.
to total world production; and column 5 sets forth the U.S. four-firm
concentration ratio. Column 4 is then multiplied times column 5 to
obtain the four-firm concentration ratio adjusted for international
markets.

The impact of the adjustments in Table 1.1 are summarized in
Table 1.2. The average concentration ratio for the 75 industries on
an unadjusted basis is approximately 51 percent. When adjustments
are made for international markets, the adjusted four-firm concentration ratios become 24 percent, representing a decline of over
50 percent.

We also analyzed the distribution of the 75 industries by concentration quartile on both the unadjusted and adjusted basis. On an
unadjusted basis 40 percent of the industries had four-firm concentration ratios of over 50 percent. On an adjusted basis only 4 percent
of the industries exhibited concentration ratios exceeding 50 percent.
The remaining 96 percent of the industries had concentration ratios
of less than 50 percent, with 60 having adjusted concentration ratios
of 25 percent or lower.

These adjustments, however, are subject to an overstatement.
Some of the production outside the United States is, of course, carried
on by U.S. firms. Hence, the four firms in the U.S. four-firm concentration ratio would also account for a portion of production outside
the United States.

A rough estimate of the upward adjustment in the adjusted four-
firm concentration ratios may be made with the help of the Fortune
directory of the 300 largest corporations outside the United States.
In 1974, for the first time, Fortune listed separately the foreign
subsidiaries of U.S. companies. The ratio of sales of the foreign
subsidiaries of U.S. companies to the total sales of the largest 300
foreign firms was 7 percent. I have moved this percentage up to 10
percent as a generous estimate of the average proportion of foreign
production accounted for by the foreign subsidiaries of U.S. corporations. When this is done, the effects on the adjusted concentration
ratios are shown in Table 1.3.

There is now one industry in the over 75 percent concentration
ratio. There are six in the concentration ratio from 51-75 percent for
a total of seven with concentration ratios over 50 percent. This would
represent less than 10 percent of the 75 industries. Hence, even
after a correction for the production of the foreign subsidiaries of
U.S. companies is made, the distribution of the adjusted concentration
ratios is not changed appreciably.

TABLE 1.2

Effect of International Markets on U.S.
Four-Firm Concentration Ratios

Average Concentration Ratio for 75 Industries (distribution by concentration quartile)	Unadjusted, 50.9 percent		Adjusted 24.1 percent	
	Number	Percent	Number	Percent
Over 75 percent	13	17.3	0	.0
51–75	20	26.7	3	4.0
26–50	35	46.7	27	36.0
Less than 26	7	9.3	45	60.0
Total	75	100.0	75	100.0

Source: Table 1.1.

TABLE 1.3

Frequency Distribution of 75 Industries after Adjustments
for World Markets and Adjustments for
U.S. Foreign Subsidiaries

Concentration Ratio	Number	Percent
Over 75 percent	1	1.3
51–75	6	8.0
26–50	29	38.7
Less than 26	39	52.0
	75	100.0

Source: Table 1.1.

More careful refinements will be made in the individual industry concentration ratios in the future. However, the evidence presented demonstrates that the U.S. four-firm concentration ratios greatly overstate the actual concentration ratios that take international markets into account. Thus, even if one takes a structural approach to an analysis of markets, the major industries have much lower concentration ratios than those generally attributed to them. Over 90 percent of the industries have four-firm concentration ratios less than 50 percent of the relevant world market. More than 50 percent of the industries have adjusted concentration ratios below 25 percent. The model of tight oligopoly does not appear to be applicable.

It might be argued that in some economies, particularly in some of the developing countries, individual international firms account for a high percentage of markets. But since they operate in international markets, the constraints of direct competition and potential entry are still there.

BEHAVIORAL CONSEQUENCES OF MULTINATIONALS IN INTERNATIONAL MARKETS

Relevant concentration ratios for international markets have been shown to be predominantly below 50 percent and more than one-half of 75 international markets are shown to exhibit concentration ratios below 25 percent. Thus, even if the paradigm that structure determines conduct were valid, it would not be applicable to the industries of international markets in which the MNCs are found. In addition, much evidence can be found in support of the proposition that MNCs stimulate rivalrous behavior in one another's market.

Competitive Impacts in Individual Markets

In his study, National Interest and the Multinational Enterprise (1969), Jack N. Behrman provides numerous examples of the competitive impact of the MNCs resulting from invasion and counterinvasion of one another's markets. He observes that the entry of several U.S. companies into Britain broke up monopoly positions in watches, tires, soaps and detergents, radiators and boilers, clocks, office appliances, refrigeration machinery, and excavating equipment. He observes further that new production by foreign affiliates in France caused the prices of unrelated products to decline:

By substituting these products for imports, pressures on payments were relieved, thus supporting more liberal

trade policy; trade liberalization in turn increased
competition and reduced prices. Examples of these
effects were found in the chemical, pharmaceutical,
machinery, and electronic sectors. In 1962, direct
competition from the entrance of Firestone and
Goodyear into the tire market caused Michelin, Dunlop,
and Kleber-Colombos to reduce prices of tires. The
simple threat of foreign investment tends to keep prices
down; an unjustified price rise by Kodak-France would,
for example, induce greater penetration by Agfa-
Gavaert into the French market. [Behrman, 1969,
p. 21]

Behrman also refers to what is viewed as overly aggressive
competition:

Industries in the host country have complained about the
aggressiveness of the affiliate; and both industry and host
governments have become concerned over the way in
which the foreigner has entered (e.g., by acquisitions).
French industrialists, for example, have complained that American affiliates in France are responsible for price wars and unrest in the labor force,
are ignorant of the social responsibility of business,
use unfair promotional practices, and disrupt established commercial patterns. [Behrman, 1969, p. 43]

He then gives examples of further disturbing influences of the foreign
companies:

The threat of disturbance is increased by the creation
of overcapacity within an industry sector, and the
consequent competitive pressure. For example, the
French company Moulinex, producing household appliances, lost a "safe" competitive position to the French
affiliates of Singer, Hoover, and Scoville; the last also
raided the staff of Moulinex. The entrance of Ralston-
Purina into chicken processing in France, where
overcapacity was already considered a threat by the
competing companies in Brittany, was the basis of
complaints to the French government by local competitors, even after formal governmental approval had
been given to the American venture. Belgian industrialists have qualified their support of their government's policy of encouragement to foreign investment

by the assertion that foreign companies should not
enter where they would "duplicate the production of
goods already available in Belgium." They have
argued also that foreign-owned affiliates should "be
encouraged to purchase their raw materials from
Belgian suppliers" so as not to create overcapacity
in the supplying industries. The penetration of
American aluminum producers into Europe involved
so many foreign companies—Alcoa, Reynolds, Kaiser,
Edison—that Pechiney and Montecatini feared an overcapacity battle among the American-owned affiliates
for the market, which would harm the Europeans as
well. Pechiney attempted to strengthen its position
through a joint venture with a German firm, which
decided instead to join with an American company,
thus increasing the penetration by the foreigner.
[Behrman, 1969, pp. 44-45]

Numerous other examples could be cited. They all add up to
further competitive dimensions from the invasion and counterinvasion
of MNCs. The basic influence seems to be that the world has become
very small with the tremendous advances in transportation and communication. The veritable revolution in managerial technology that
enables firms to control far-flung operations more effectively also
has stimulated international operations. But the basic and underlying
forces appear to be the considerable potentials for achieving economies of scale in research, in general management, and in marketing.
These economies may also be achieved in production, particularly
where economies of scale are significant in certain segments of
supplying activity. For example, it is my understanding that the
potential economies of scale in the production of automotive trans-
missions are not fully realized even at existing levels of sales of
companies like General Motors and Ford (See also McGee, 1973).

It appears that in some industries, such as chemicals, there
has been a history of careful diplomacy in international expansion.
The chemical industry may be a special case in that the dominant
firms historically were European companies who had followed such
practices in their own markets. A further influence may be that the
impact of a fundamental breakthrough may cause the destruction of
some competing companies (Kahn, 1961, p. 249).

The chemical industry, however, also provides examples of
the nature of entry and potential entry. For example, Alfred E.
Kahn has observed the following:

It has undoubtedly been the promise of high profits
in chemicals that has spurred the widespread and

impetuous entry into the industry in recent years—
by the shipping, whiskey, farm machinery, and
rayon companies, by droves of oil and natural gas
transmission companies, by food processors like
Swift, Armour, and General Mills, paint manufacturers like Sherwin-Williams and Glidden,
producers of rubber tires, and, as Fortune put it,
"such wildly unclassifiable companies" as General
Electric, Minnesota Mining and Manufacturing, Borden,
and the Philadelphia and Reading coal company. It
was the same promise that attracted Eastman Kodak
into cellulose acetate rayon and plastics, du Pont
into film, Allied Chemical into nylon, Olin-Mathieson
into cellophane, Koppers into styrene, Commercial
Solvents into synthetic ammonia. And in this industry
to enter is to innovate. [Kahn, 1961, p. 261]

Overall Effects on Prices

Turning from aspects of behavior in individual industries,
some inferential evidence can be presented on the impact of large
MNCs on price change. The MNCs tend to be in the industries of
highest concentration. Thus, by a comparative analysis of concentration ratios in relation to price change, some inferential evidence
is provided on the impact of multinationals on price changes in the
United States. The data are presented in Table 1.4. They show that
for the 1967-75 period (except immediately after the end of price
controls), the greater the concentration, the smaller the percent of
price changes. Taking 1967 as the initial date (the start of the inflation period), through August 1975 the percent price change is
much lower in the over 50 percent four-firm concentration ratio
industries than in the under 50 percent. Particularly in the category
of greatest concentration (over 75 percent) has the price change been
of the smallest degree of magnitude.

The reason for the better price record of the industries of
highest concentration is found in the reasons they are concentrated.
The most concentrated industries are the most capital intensive.
With larger capital investments, the rate of productivity growth in
the most concentrated industries is higher than for other industries.
Because their rate of productivity growth is higher, the most concentrated industries pay the highest wages, increase wages at a
higher rate, but experience the lowest rate of unit wage cost increases. Competition then holds price increases to their lower rate
of unit cost increases.

TABLE 1.4

Price Changes by Quartile,
1967–August 1975

Concentration Ratio (percent)	Number of Observations in Each Group	Price Change (percent)
Less than 25	17	71.5
25–50	29	71.2
50–75	29	70.6
Greater than 75	12	48.7
All*	87	68.0

*Excludes three sugar industries.
Source: Monthly Labor Review, October 1975.

Probably the most dramatic demonstration of some basic principles emphasized by those who see concentration in the United States as mainly due to economies of scale in plant operations and in managerial technology is the example of Japan. Hymer and Rowthorn point out the following:

> By virtually prohibiting foreign investment, the Japanese government reserved its rapidly growing market for its own firms and frustrated the attempts by U.S. corporations to redress the imbalance caused by the Japanese challenge. This has created considerable tension and may soon have to be modified since Japanese corporations encounter increased resistance to their penetration via exports. [Hymer and Rowthorn, 1970, p. 73]

The Japanese government did the following. A wall was thrown up that prevented foreign corporations from entering. The government provided financial assistance, encouragement, and guarantees to its own corporations. It enabled corporations to be established with plant sizes larger than the plant size of individual firms in other countries of the world. With this encouragement to develop large size the Japanese firms were able to achieve economies of scale. With these economies of scale the Japanese companies were then able to enter the international markets by offering vigorous price competition to existing firms.

Critical to the success of this strategy, then, was the support and protection provided by the Japanese government that enabled these Japanese firms to achieve the large size necessary to realize economies of scale before entering the competitive environment of the international markets. Thus they began in their protected domestic environments and then moved to the competitive foreign environment.

Although a considerable volume of materials can be adduced to illustrate how MNCs increase rivalrous activities, it is acknowledged that the evidence is neither systematic nor conclusive. However, it provides a substantial basis for the competitive MNC hypothesis.

The foreign market forces and influences to which the MNCs are responding also are consistent with competitive oligopoly in the domestic sphere. The writings continuously refer to important factors that may provide a firm with advantages in selling to foreign markets. These include the accumulation of experience and knowledge in a particular line of business; a high rate of research and development activity; economies of scale required by the nature of the industry; managerial economies of scale as well as physical plant economies of scale. These concepts also can be developed by evidence from a number of studies of individual industries, beyond the space limitations of the present paper. A behavioral aspect of MNCs that is a frequent target of criticism is the area of transfer pricing, considered next.

TRANSFER PRICING

The transfer-pricing policies of MNCs have been a subject of much dispute. No critic is without his supply of horror stories consisting of incidents of tax avoidance or of unequal prices charged in different countries. First some background will be developed to provide a basis for evaluating the standard criticisms made.

In transfer pricing many variables will necessarily be taken into account. One study has analyzed national differences in the relative importance placed on factors in transfer-price determination (Arpan, 1972, p. 9). A summary of the findings is set forth in Table 1.5. For U.S. companies, income taxes, inflation, exchange controls, and customs duties appear to have been accorded the greatest importance. Surprisingly, prospective changes in currency exchange rates were found to be of relatively low importance.

The same study analyzed the criteria or objectives in transfer price formulation; these are summarized in Table 1.6. In formulating transfer prices, some firms emphasize market- or demand-based systems and others, cost-based systems. A wide variety of methods can be subsumed under either criterion. But like transfer pricing in

TABLE 1.5

National Differences in Relative Importance Given to Variables in Transfer-Price Determination

Variable	U.S.	Canada	France	Germany	Italy	Scandinavia	England
Income tax	1	1	1	3	1	3	3
Customs duties	2	2	2	3	3	3	3
Inflation	1	2	2	2	2	3	2
Changes in currency exchange rates	3	3	2	2	3	3	2
Exchange controls	2	3	5	5	5	5	5
Improving financial appearance of subsidiary	3	3	3	4	4	4	1
Expropriation	3	3	5	5	5	5	5
Export subsidies and tax credits	4	2	2	4	2	4	2
Level of competition	3	2	2	3	2	3	3

Note: Weighting scale used: 1 = high importance, 2 = medium importance, 3 = low importance, 4 = not mentioned, 5 = mentioned only with respect to non-U.S. operations.

Sources: U.S. data derived from interviews with members of international accounting firms; non-U.S., correspondence and interviews with subsidiary executives and members of international accounting firms.

TABLE 1.6

Objectives in Transfer-Price Determination

Objective	Non-U.S.*	Canada	France	Germany	Italy	Scandinavia	England
				Parent Nationality			
Provide a fair profit to the producing unit	2	2	2	2	2	2	2
Permit top management to compare and evaluate the performance of various corporate units	2	2	2	2	2	2	2
Be acceptable to national customs officials for the purpose of duty valuation	1	1	2	1	2	1	1
Be acceptable to national tax authorities and antitrust officials	1	1	2	1	2	1	1
Enable the purchasing unit to meet profit targets despite the pressure of competitive prices	1	1	1	2	1	2	1
Result in a reduction of executive time spent on pricing decisions and mediation of intercorporate pricing disputes	1	3	1	1	1	2	1
Provide control over the pricing practices of foreign subsidiaries to insure that profit goals are met	1	1	1	1	1	2	1
Provide management with incentives in both the product divisions and marketing divisions	2	2	2	2	2	2	2
Insure that there is a regular and sufficient flow of goods and product information	2	1	2	2	2	2	2
Given a basis for reflecting actual profits (and costs), to maintain the control facets of operating against a budget, and preserving the psychological factor of forcing a manager to meet or exceed profit goals with a wider latitude of action than that which is afforded when operating solely against a set budget	2	2	2	2	2	2	2

*No relative weightings are identifiable for U.S. multinational firms.

Note: Weighting scale used: 1 = important, 2 = not as important.

Sources: Correspondence and interviews with subsidiary executives and members of international accounting firms.

domestic operations, international transfer pricing is not supported by a good implementable theory. Also, a defect of the survey method in this area is that it is likely to elicit a wide variety of respectable explanations. Hence, I turn to a number of analytic considerations.

First, any transfer-pricing system must fit effectively into a good management planning and control system. This should include decentralization of some dimensions of decisions and provide effective managerial incentives and controls. (For amplification of the elements required in an effective planning and control system see Weston, 1971, pp. 35-42). A second principle for transfer pricing is that it should seek to maximize from the point of view of the firm as a whole. Suboptimization from the standpoint of the individual divisional entity must be avoided while incentives to the division are retained and a basis for effective evaluation of division performance is achieved.

The third generalization is that the prices charged in an individual market will reflect the demand and supply conditions in that particular market. Market conditions in fact will determine the ultimate price that will prevail in a given market regardless of how many stages in intracompany transfer pricing have taken place. However, there is also the possibility that control of raw material sources will lead to pricing squeezes at later stages of production or marketing.

The fourth generalization is that in its intracompany pricing practices firms seek to minimize taxes subject to U.S. and foreign governmental regulations. In this regard, the governmental bodies concerned have emphasized the requirement of establishing that an intracompany price has been arrived at on the basis of what would have been achieved in an arm's length relationship between the intracompany units. Business International Corp. sets forth 16 guideposts to a reasonable price and checklist of 34 factors in triangular pricing (1974, pp. 142-43). Business International, however, emphasizes that the Internal Revenue Service requires that "reasonableness" of the intracompany transfer prices be documented effectively. Discussions with business executives indicate that the Internal Revenue Service is vigilant with regard to tax minimization in international transfer pricing. Indeed, the Internal Revenue Service is so vigorous in its efforts in this area that many businessmen complain that it is overly rigid in its requirements.

Business firms also may seek to minimize the impact of tariffs in their intracompany transfer-pricing decision. However, this too is subject to surveillance by governmental authorities. Furthermore, when tariff differentials become substantial, they also are likely to affect the decision of whether to export or manufacture abroad. Likewise other methods of tax minimization are employed, such as decisions with respect to the location of production and sales operations.

It is indeed true that considerable efforts are directed toward tax minimization. For example, Business International, in its publication Decision Making and International Operations, has a number of checklists with regard to taxes. They include "25 Steps to Minimize Taxes on Foreign Company Sales and Services Income," "10 Ways to Use Base Companies," "20 Examples of Non-foreign Base Income," and "Eight Ways to Reinvest Base Company Earnings." It is interesting to note that in its preface to these checklists on taxes, Business International makes the following statement:

> The U.S. Revenue Act of 1962 sharply altered the
> tax roles under which U.S. firms operate inter-
> nationally. Checklists 108-111 provide valuable
> information on how to mitigate the effects of the new
> rules, and thus remain competitive with foreign firms
> that are not similarly hamstrung by their governments.
> But most firms are using the minimum distribution
> escape hatch to avoid the complexities of the 1962
> Act. [Business International, 1974, p. 135]

Tax policy changes by the U.S. Congress in 1962 and subsequently have given rise to the lament that foreign countries treat their MNCs much more liberally with respect to income taxes than the treatment accorded U.S. firms by their government. One might expect to hear such self-serving statements from U.S. business firms, but it is interestingly encountered in a number of places. For example, in a volume on Investing in the Caribbean, the following observation is made:

> Investors other than citizens or residents of the mainland
> United States or Puerto Rico would, today, have much
> greater flexibility for tax purposes with respect to
> planning the form, direct or indirect, of their invest-
> ments in CARINCO. In general, most foreign countries
> do not tax income until its actual receipt by the taxable
> entity. Thus, such investors could accumulate any and
> all income derived from CARINCO free from virtually
> any tax, provided it were not repatriated to, or realized
> by, the local entity. For example, their investment in
> CARINCO could be owned by an intermediate, wholly-
> owned, holding company organized under the laws of the
> Bahamas or Panama. Any dividend distributions to such
> company, or sale or exchange of its investments, would
> be free of tax. The resulting income could be accumu-
> lated for reinvestment, or distributed, according to the

wishes of the stockholders. [Caribbean Economic Development Corporation, 1970]

The more favorable treatment accorded to foreign corporations by their individual governments raises the question as to why foreign governments use tax policies to stimulate export sales and foreign investment by their corporations. The reasons generally indicated are that the expansion of operations by foreign activities leads to greater economies of scale. It is argued that by encouraging export sales and foreign investment, foreign governments have helped foreign firms expand to achieve lower costs of operation, which makes them less vulnerable to imports from other countries and at the same time makes them stronger competitors in other countries.

Economies of scale that foreign tax policies have stimulated have taken a number of forms. In the steel industry in Japan, for example, the economies of scale have taken the form of building steel plants of 5 to 10 million tons of capacity, substantially larger than the size of most steel plants in the United States. For other industries and countries this has involved multiplant operations within the country as well as multiplant operations extending to other parts of the world. This is evidence consistent with economies of scale related to managerial organization and organization processes. One factor is organization learning and experience that is stimulated by foreign operations. Furthermore, there are economies of scale in that a substantial volume of foreign operations can be conducted without adding proportionately to managerial staff and managerial executive personnel. Apparently, an important influence is that the organization's learning and capabilities developed in domestic operations can be utilized abroad, deriving large returns. In addition, products or services developed domestically can be moved to foreign markets, achieving increments of sales without a proportional increase in outlays.

It is frequently argued that a given firm may charge widely different prices in different countries due to transfer pricing differences. I have investigated a number of alleged cases of wide price discrepancies, and several infirmities in price comparisons were observed. First, different products had been treated as though they were identical so that the price quotations were not comparable. Second, the data had been gathered at different time periods so that the price quotations again were not comparable. Third, the comparisons sometimes related list prices to actual transaction prices or prices at different levels of the distribution process. Of course, firms may well charge different prices in different countries. Demand factors may be substantially different among different countries. Rapidly shifting exchange rates would also affect the prices charged.

Other criticisms have been leveled in connection with the reaction of firms in a given industry both to government regulations regarding remitting of royalties or profits, and to currency controls. The criticism has been made that, in reaction to such government restrictions, prices appear to have been arbitrarily raised. However, it seems clear that such government restrictions in a country would affect the supply conditions under which products would be sold or manufactured in that country. The unfavorable impact on supply conditions would be expected to cause a rise in prices.

The scope of this presentation does not permit treatment of individual episodes. But general principles will aid in the evaluation of specific cases. With regard to transfer pricing, nothing in the intrafirm accounting procedures can have any real effects on the prices realized in individual foreign markets. The necessary qualification, of course, is government rules with regard to (1) the determination of tax liabilities in a country, (2) controls on profits in individual industries such as pharmaceuticals, and (3) repatriation of royalties and profits. These government rules will affect the supply conditions under which products are sold. In addition, rules with respect to allowable profits will raise measurement issues. Lopping off profits that are considered high, without consideration of losses on unsuccessful product efforts, changes the risk-return relationships and hence the appropriate level of profit, as well. The issues are complex and require analysis of individual circumstances in some detail.

The central issue of transfer pricing appears to be tax minimization. Two important dimensions are involved. One is to avoid distortion of the world pattern of investment and trade. The other is the issue of whether tax subsidies to MNCs by governments are sound.

The correct principles are readily formulated. Tax policy should contribute to maximizing welfare on a global basis. Tax havens and tax subsidies by the host countries are likely to be more distorting than tax subsidies by the home country. Tax subsidies by the home country will enable the international firm to select the areas of its operations on the basis of market opportunities. Implementation aspects are much more complex.

The basic question is whether tax subsidies by the home country command economic justification. Two of the major historical reasons for tax subsidies have been diminished to some degree. One earlier rationale for the need to provide encouragement to international operations was their greater risks. But with improved communication and transportation technologies, a better basis for predicting political processes and developments, the development of both governmental and private insurance programs, and improved technologies for balancing and managing risks, tax subsidies to improve the risk-return trade-off of international operations are probably less compelling. However, risks due to shifts in governmental policies remain substantial.

Another economic basis for government encouragement of international operations for their domestic firms was the potentials for economies of scale, for multiple sourcing, for diversification of product markets. But foreign operations are significantly correlated with size of firms and the level of concentration in the domestic market. Also, rivalrous response to foreign investment by an initiating firm is swift and strong (Knickerbocker, 1973, pp. 53-99). Further, the average return on foreign investments is correlated with the foreign entry rate (Knickerbocker, 1973, pp. 157-63) and the level of market concentration in the home country (Horst, 1974, pp. 83-87).

The advantage of smaller firms in entering foreign markets is that a small penetration is sufficient to increase their total profits substantially.* The organizational requirements for foreign direct investment are such that large firms in concentrated industries account for the highest proportion of foreign investments. It can be argued therefore that the firms which embark on international operations already have differential advantages for undertaking such activities. If so, they do not require the further encouragement of tax subsidies.

In my judgment, no easy conclusions follow. If economies of international operations are substantial, global welfare maximization may justify incentives. It may be countered that the market incentives are sufficient for large firms and that government incentives should be limited to smaller firms. But it is difficult to administer such discriminatory treatment. Furthermore, if incentives are justified by global welfare reasons, it is not clear that incentives should be used to divert the activity away from firms best qualified to perform the activity.

The issues raised go to the central question of the nature and effects of international oligopoly. The groundwork has now been laid for an appraisal of these issues in the final section of this paper. The present section on transfer pricing and related taxation issues, concludes with two observations. First, we need much more careful

---

*My discussions with owners of small business firms in a series of conferences sponsored by the Small Business Administration suggested the generalization, "If we can achieve foreign sales of 15 to 25 percent of our domestic sales, the foreign sales will represent 50 percent or more of our profits."

analysis of what constitutes tax subsidies versus normal tax treatment. Second, action should not be taken unilaterally by the United States. Any modification of tax policies must be coordinated into the formulation of a broader set of policies toward MNCs by the United States and implemented only after international agreements are reached that accord comparable treatment to MNCs wherever domiciled.

OTHER CRITICISMS OF THE PRICE IMPACTS OF MULTINATIONALS

The MNCs have been criticized in connection with the price impact of their operations on the basis of a number of other criteria. One of these is in the area of import substitution programs. In its effort to conserve foreign exchange and further its economic development programs, a developing country may provide incentives for industrialization, particularly in the form of import substitution programs. Incentives include tariff protection, preferential treatment on imports of capital equipment or other key ingredients, tax subsidies, and subsidized land and building purchases (Mason, Miller, and Weigel, 1975, pp. 396-98).

A number of departures from the operation of free market forces are instituted to stimulate home investment. Since a foreign firm may possess the capital, technology, and managerial experience required to operate in the high-priority industry, it is likely to respond to the incentives rather than a local firm. Since the domestic market is small, a technically feasible plant requires only one firm. Even if more than one firm is established under government encouragement, the conditions for competitive markets have not been met. Typically, a high tariff is required to protect domestic operations from more efficient foreign operations. The prices of locally produced goods are likely to be higher than would obtain without the artificial restrictions.

Clearly, the conditions of competitive market efficiency are not being met by the usual import substitution program. But it is the barriers and incentives formulated by the host governments that create the situation. If foreign firms did not make the investments, the host governments would be required to raise capital to create local firms. The local firms would be operating even less efficiently than the foreign firms. Thus these pathological situations are not caused by MNCs; rather their activities may mitigate to some degree the distortions caused by government programs. Hopefully the developing economies will reach a stage when such operations can continue without artificial stimuli. At this point the foreign firm becomes hostage to various new government policies. Requirements for various forms of local participation may be imposed. Thus the longer-run effects of such programs may operate to the disadvantage of the MNCs.

Another criticism of the MNCs is that their emphasis on efficiency may conflict with other economic objectives of the host government. The nature of the conflicting objectives is indicated by Table 1.7. Eight economic objectives are set forth: efficiency, growth, full employment, income distribution, price stability, quality of life, economic security, and foreign exchange position. (Compare Bergsten, Keohane, Nye, 1975.) And some illustrative conflicts are set forth. For example, the criterion of efficiency may conflict with the objective of full employment if for some products imports are the most efficient method of providing them. Efficiency may conflict with the objective of more equal income distribution if temporary rents are obtained by firms with innovational advantages. The objective of price stability could be disturbed by price increases to stimulate the production of goods in short supply and price declines to discourage the production of goods in excess supply. Economic security may lead to the desire to have local industry in areas such as aerospace, chemicals, and steel. However, such industries might not be established locally by efficiency criteria. Efficiency considerations may lead to an increase of imports. However, this would conflict with the objective of improving the country's foreign exchange position.

The nature of conflicts between alternative economic criteria and objectives is illustrated in the remainder of the matrix set forth in Table 1.7. However, conflicting economic criteria are not fundamentally caused by the operation of MNCs. Rather the conflicting economic criteria are inherent in the processes of international economic development. However, it is recognized that the MNCs are likely to be guided more heavily by considerations of efficiency and growth that may reinforce other criteria such as full employment and price stability, but be in conflict with criteria such as equality of income distribution and quality of life. This is an area in which not only sound individual government policy must be formulated in a long-run context but coordination between governments is required as well. The sound resolution of such issues transcends the operations of individual MNCs.

Further criticism of the MNCs is that increased internationalization of U.S. business and increased concentration in the United States have been reciprocally reinforcing. This view has been stated by Müller as follows:

Two major and empirically well-established characteristics of global corporations are that (1) most of them are conglomerates and that (2) in the many different product groups or industries in which they operate,

TABLE 1.7

Multiple Economic Objectives and Conflicts between Them—Illustrative Major Effects

Objective	Efficiency	Growth	Full Employment	Income Distribution	Price Stability	Quality of Life	Economic Security	Foreign Exchange Position
Efficiency	—	—	Imports	Temporary rents	Price changes to reallocate resources		Desire for local industry	May lead to more imports
Growth	May use exchange rate depreciation, import controls, export subsidies	—	—	Need for increased saving from inequality	Individual sectors may experience price rises		Greater dependence on outside resources	
Full employment	Distort allocation of factors, for example, minimum wage			—	Less efficiency may lead to higher prices			
Income distribution			Inability to cover minimum wage	—				
Price stability	Export controls	Reduction of real growth			—	—	Export controls affect economic security of others	
Quality of life							—	
Economic security	May have other industries with comparative disadvantage				Increased costs of production	Desired industries may be a major source of externalities	—	
Foreign exchange position	Incentives to import substitution industries							—

Source: Developed from discussion in Bergsten, Keohane, Nye, 1975.

44

they compete as oligopolies, not as perfectly
competitive firms. [Müller, 1975b, p. 186]

There is direct disagreement with the assertion that these characteristics are "empirically well established." For example, Caves observed:

Product diversification across national boundaries is
almost unknown, however, and there is some evidence
that the industries and firms most active in conglomerate
mergers in the United States are not among the most
prominent foreign investors. [Caves, 1971, p. 3]

Nor does the evidence support the second part of the Müller
statement. In fact Conglomerate Merger Performance: An Empirical
Analysis of Nine Corporations, published by the Federal Trade Commission in 1972, provides evidence directly counter to the Müller
assertion. The report finds that 82 percent of the acquisitions by the
conglomerates, from 1963 to 1969, represented a "toe-hold acquisition" (market share of less than 5 percent.) Indeed, 54 percent of
the acquisitions represented five-digit product classes in which the
market share in the year prior to acquisition was less than 1 percent.
Further, the postacquisition market position of conglomerates was
predominantly decreased. This pattern was not greatly influenced
by the level of concentration of the market in which the acquisition
was made. After the massive merger activity of the 1960s, the market share of the conglomerate firms of 1969 was less than 5 percent
and was 82.4 percent of that of the five-digit product classes in which
they operated. The pattern is similar for market positions of less
than 1 percent. Thus, there is no factual basis for the generalizations made by Müller.

Other argumenst, by Barnet and Müller (1974), of alleged
increases in concentration fail to take into account the literature
exposing technical defects in earlier generalizations that had been
made. (See, for example, Bock, 1970; Weston, Ornstein, 1973,
pp. 7-14). Indeed, most of the arguments on the evils of MNCs have
been made in exaggerated form by Barnet and Müller in their book
(1974) and in subsequent articles by Müller (1975a, 1975b). But
while their presentations make reference to a number of other works,
little systematic evidence is provided. The nature of their discussions
of the MNCs was characterized in a review by Martin Mayer (1975)
as follows: "What they have produced in short, is a hash of all the
dog food the New Left tried to feed us poor folk through the 1960's,
dishonestly repackaged as a study of multinational corporations."
In general, the exaggerations and oversimplifications employed by

Barnet and Müller do a disservice in misdirecting attention from the
central policy issues involved and from the fundamental institutional
developments required.

Another criticism of MNCs draws on the structural theory
preconceptions with regard to the nature of oligopoly. The barrier
hypothesis provides the basis for a syllogism given much weight in
a study of the relation between profitability and foreign investment:

> If foreign investing is indeed a barrier to entry in the
> U.S. market, then it should be reflected in higher
> profits for firms with foreign investments than for
> those without. [Horst, 1974, p. 119]

The finding of a positive relationship between profitability and
foreign investments is then used to argue that barriers to entry in
domestic markets have been increased. But what are the entry barriers involved? First, economies of plant scale or economies of
scale in research may be enhanced. Second, economies from spe-
cialized plants that produce materials and parts for other plants can
be increased. Outside firms could provide such specialization, but
it appears that there are economies of information flow when such
specialization is performed internally. Third, accumulated experience in international markets enables a firm to achieve cumulative
differential efficiency. And fourth, international operations increase
the size of capital requirements.

These and other increases in barriers to entry can readily be
formulated and listed. But a number of questions remain. Entry
barriers to whom? For new small firms the size and capital requirements for entry in the concentrated industries with their characteristic large plant size and research or marketing activities are already
far beyond their threshold abilities. But for a large firm in a similar
industry the entry barriers are not increased. And for a foreign firm
in similar product lines the entry barriers are not increased.

The most formidable of entry barriers is the competitively
greater efficiency of the firms already existing in the industry. But
this also represents economic efficiency and, therefore, social gains.
Entry and potential entry from foreign firms is already substantial
and will increase, if the relative efficiency of U.S. MNCs does not
continue to increase.

Because of the uncritical extension of simplistic oligopoly theory
into international dimensions, recommendations have sometimes been
made for restrictions on U.S. MNCs. These would include discriminatory tax treatment of U.S. MNCs in comparison with tax treatment
accorded to MNCs by other developed nations. Another proposal is
the requirement, under certain circumstances, of a spin-off of foreign

subsidiaries of U.S. firms who would then export to the United States in competition with their now "foreign" parents.

In part, recommendations for unilateral penalties on U.S. MNCs stem from the general impression that U.S. firms are much greater in size than their foreign competitors. It may be useful, therefore, to present some data on trends in the size of foreign firms relative to U.S. firms. Since 1965, vast changes in the size of foreign firms in relation to U.S. firms have taken place.

I present here a series of tables showing various dimensions of these relationships for the years 1965, 1971, and 1974;* 1965 represents the year prior to the onset of worldwide inflation, and is associated with the escalation of hostilities in Southeast Asia; 1971 represents a watershed year in which the United States made the first of a series of revaluations of the dollar in relation to other currencies; and 1974 was the latest year for which data were available.

In Table 1.8 the relative size of foreign firms to U.S. firms is set forth for the years indicated. Data are presented for the 10, 20, 25, 50, and 100 largest foreign firms in relation to the corresponding number of largest U.S. firms. In 1965 for each of the categories, foreign firms were something under 50 percent in relation to U.S. firms in terms of sales and slightly more than 50 percent in terms of assets. Then 1971 portrays the beginning of a strong upward trend. By 1974 the foreign firms appear to be approaching equal size.

But these relationships can be seen more clearly by analyzing the relationships by groups of firms. Accordingly, in Table 1.9 the relationships are shown for the top 10, firms 11 to 25, 26 to 50, and 51 to 100. What stands out in this table is that it is in the comparative size of the top 10 firms that the U.S. firms have the relative size advantage. However, by 1974 for every group of firms except the top 10, when size is denoted by command over economic resources as measured by total assets, every group of foreign firms exceeds their U.S. counterparts. For example, for the ranks from 26 to 50 the foreign firms have almost 150 percent of the assets of the corresponding group of U.S. firms.

In sales, the foreign firms are approximately equal to the U.S. firms from the eleventh in rank on. Therefore, 1974 represents a threshold year in which foreign firms other than the top 10 have now essentially reached parity in size with U.S. firms. This result is related to the comparatively higher growth rates of the foreign firms in relation to the U.S. firms. The supporting data are presented in Table 1.10. During the 1965-71 period for both U.S. and foreign

---

*Brian Horrigan assisted in these calculations.

TABLE 1.8

Relative Size of Foreign Firms to U.S. Firms,
1965, 1971, 1974

| Largest Firm Group | 1965 | | | |
| | Foreign Firms' Sales to U.S. Firms' Sales | | Foreign Firms' Total Assets to U.S. Firms' Total Assets | |
	Ratio ($ billion)	Percentage	Ratio ($ billion)	Percentage
10	29/75	38	34/65	51
20	42/101	41	44/89	49
25	47/112	42	48/99	49
50	68/149	46	74/128	58
100	98/193	51	108/169	64
	1971			
10	54/118	46	68/102	67
20	86/160	54	105/151	69
25	100/177	57	117/167	70
50	151/237	64	177/219	81
100	208/315	66	245/292	84
	1974			
10	134/210	64	107/155	69
20	198/287	69	173/215	81
25	225/313	72	200/239	84
50	330/413	80	301/306	98
100	450/537	84	421/404	104

Source: Fortune, May–August 1966, 1972, and 1975.

firms, growth rates were higher for firms 11 to 25 than for the top 10. However, during 1971–74, the top 10 grew at the fastest rate for both U.S. and foreign firms. This may reflect the prevalence of petroleum companies in the ranks of the largest both for the U.S. and foreign, and the repricing of oil during 1973–74.

The firms in the 11–25 group that are foreign have grown at double or more the rates of U.S. firms. For the entire period 1965–74, U.S. firms among the 100 largest grew at about a 10 percent compound annual rate when measured by total assets and about 12 percent when measured by sales. Foreign firms grew about 15 percent when measured by total assets and about 19 percent when measured by sales. There is greater unevenness in the rate of growth of foreign firms, with the greatest growth rates being especially in the second size group (11–25).

In 1974 for the first time Fortune magazine began listing separately among the 300 largest foreign firms the foreign subsidiaries of U.S. companies. It should be noted that in our analysis we removed the foreign subsidiaries of U.S. companies because we had no base data for developing growth measures. Hymer and Rowthorn (1970, pp. 70–73) have estimated from the data on direct investments that U.S. subsidiaries in Europe had on average been growing faster than the European companies. They refer to the fact that between 1950 and 1965 the value of U.S. direct investment in Western Europe increased from about $2 billion to about $14 billion representing a growth rate of about 15 percent over a 15-year period. From this they conclude that the growth rate of the foreign subsidiaries of U.S. companies

TABLE 1.9

Relative Size of Foreign Firms to U.S. Firms,
by Groups, 1965, 1971, 1974

| Firm Group | 1965 | | | |
| | Foreign Firms' Sales to U.S. Firms' Sales | | Foreign Firms' Total Assets to U.S. Firms' Total Assets | |
	Ratio ($ billion)	Percentage	Ratio ($ billion)	Percentage
1–10	29/75	38	34/65	51
11–25	18/36	49	14/33	43
26–50	22/37	59	26/29	90
51–100	30/44	68	33/41	82
	1971			
1–10	54/118	46	68/102	67
11–25	46/58	78	48/65	74
26–50	51/60	84	60/52	115
51–100	58/78	73	68/73	93
	1974			
1–10	134/210	64	107/155	69
11–25	91/103	89	92/83	111
26–50	105/100	105	101/68	149
51–100	120/124	97	121/97	124

Source: Fortune, May–August 1966, 1972, and 1975.

TABLE 1.10

Average Annual Compound Growth Rates of the
Largest U.S. and Foreign Companies,
by Groups

Firm Group	U.S. Companies, Percent Growth, 1965–71		Foreign Firms, Percent Growth, 1965–71	
	Total Assets	Sales	Total Assets	Sales
1–10	7.61	7.81	12.52	11.08
11–25	11.86	8.24	22.65	16.95
26–50	10.11	8.45	14.68	15.21
51–100	10.19	9.93	12.68	11.44
	1971–74		1971–74	
1–10	15.21	21.16	16.32	35.06
11–25	8.55	20.75	23.93	25.96
26–50	9.04	18.31	19.00	27.43
51–100	9.75	16.63	20.87	27.96
	1965–74		1965–74	
1–10	10.09	12.09	13.77	18.56
11–25	10.74	12.26	23.07	19.88
26–50	9.75	10.64	16.10	19.15
51–100	10.04	12.12	15.35	16.69

Source: Fortune, May–August 1966, 1972, and 1975.

has been greater than that of European companies. But the growth
rates of the European companies have been greater than the growth
rates of the sales or assets of the consolidated U.S. companies even
including their faster growing foreign subsidiaries.

Hymer and Rowthorn (1970) describe the challenging and counter-
challenging nature of a direct investment by U.S. and European firms.
They suggest that in the long run U.S. and European firms will have
about the same relative market share in all markets. When this con-
dition is reached, the multinational firms from each country will all
grow at about the same rate, therefore, regardless of differences in
national growth rates.

The data in Table 1.9 indicate that the U.S. and foreign firms
are now about the same size. By groups after the first 10, the U.S.
and foreign firms are of approximately equal size in sales but the
foreign firms are larger when measured in terms of assets.

It is difficult to establish the reason for the higher sales to total asset ratios for the larger U.S. firms as compared with the foreign firms. Three possibilities occur. One is that the groupings of the foreign firms are in industries with lower sales to total asset ratios. A second possibility is that the foreign firms are not as close to optimal size as are the U.S. firms so that their ratios of total asset investments to sales is higher than for U.S. firms. A third possibility is that there is systematic underreporting of sales by the foreign corporations. A further analysis would be required to determine the relative influence of each of these factors.

CONCLUSIONS

The comparative size and growth relationships indicate that we are rapidly approaching the situation in which the largest MNCs of the United States are of approximately the same size and occupy approximately the same market position as the largest foreign MNCs. Competition among the U.S. multinationals and the foreign multinationals continues to be intense. There is dynamic competition in research and development, in product quality, and increasingly in marketing efforts.

It is a reasonable hypothesis that the nature of modern technology and production operations has established a technological and economic imperative that these operations can be conducted most efficiently and effectively by the large multinationals. Foreign governments of other advanced economies recognize this and are encouraging the development of their own multinationals. There is increasing criticism in the United States of our own multinationals. Periodically proposals are made to attack our multinationals by various forms of divestiture or by tax proposals that will place them at a disadvantage in comparison with foreign multinationals. If this occurs, it will simply mean that the position of the United States in the international economic world will be handicapped and diminished. Among the consequences, the progress in improving the U.S. balance-of-payments position would be stunted and balance-of-payments difficulties would increasingly be experienced in the future.

The effects of multinationals on concentration within an individual country or on an international scale operate in two directions. By bringing more firms directly into competition with one another, the effect may be to reduce concentration in some markets particularly where single domestic firms may account for 80 to 90 percent of the market, as is true in a number of products in several Western European nations and in Japan.

On the other hand, concentration may increase because if some individual firms achieve differential advantages in economies of scale and managerial efficiency, they may increase their position in the world market. Only a smaller number of national firms will be able to survive, and as a consequence, concentration may be increased in some national markets. Over a period of time the development of multinational firms may result in increased concentration even when measured on a worldwide basis.

However, no such ambiguity exists with regard to the effect of multinationals on competition. The tenuous arguments of tacit collusion made with respect to domestic oligopoly have not been supported by the relevant empirical evidence. The likelihood of tacit collusion on an international scale is even more implausible. Utilizing the framework of comparing the costs of collusion with the gains from not colluding, the analysis supports the likelihood of increased competition.

From the standpoint of the microeconomics of individual firm efficiency the multinationals extend the concepts of the most effective utilization of input factors and achievement of the most efficient production function to international dimensions. Their operations reflect a continuous striving for increased efficiency in all of a nation's industries but particularly those subject to potential foreign competition and which themselves have the potential for extending competition to other geographic markets.

Given the nature of the technology of major industries and their requirements for a high level of managerial and technological capabilities, the large multinationals will continue to be the most efficient way that international trade and investment will be carried on. Because of their operations, products are available at lower prices and higher quality. The multinationals will continue to be the instruments by which the social benefits of international trade and investments are achieved. This is not to argue that in all respects this will be the best of all possible worlds. Some difficult problems of effectively relating multinational corporate operations to evolving international economic and financial institutions still need to be solved. But in the new international economic and financial institutions that are developing, the multinational firms will continue to perform an essential role.

COMMENT

P.F. Cornelsen

Dr. Weston's paper deserves careful reading. Dr. Weston takes things out of the self-serving context and he gets down to the question of whether the propositions and assumptions made by the attackers of MNCs will stand the light of day.

I can't help but wonder, as we reach this point in our history, if there are really any multinational companies who in fact prethought all of these processes as regards pricing, or any of the other things that are now at issue. I think probably what we did was simply to use a more or less entrepreneurial process of trying to maximize whatever circumstances we found ourselves in. Now that we are there, we need to find and define the societal goals to which people everywhere are aspiring. We need to relate what people want to the economic structures that might conceivably be best used to give it to them. Perhaps we could focus more on the future and how to use the multinational corporation, within some international framework that will accommodate national needs, people's needs, and the interdependence that does exist in this world and will exist in this world as long as aspirations continue to grow in people's minds.

I would hope that we could use Dr. Weston's type of work as a springboard to look ahead and grapple with the problems involving this useful resource. Meanwhile, he has laid a great number of things to rest, I think, by pointing out that arguing about what has happened may be a fallacy; what may be important is to try to harness this resource to the benefit of the world in the future.

DISCUSSION

Question. Dr. Weston, when you aggregate all the data, they tend, it seems to me, to support your arguments because most of our investment is in Western Europe and in Canada. However, if you take the same data and disaggregate them, I think you then begin to see where the complaints which led to the UN General Assembly's Sixth Special Session, the proposed Charter of Economic Rights and Duties, and so on, have come from. I am not sure the aggregation, in a sense, will make us feel happy here.

_____

P.F. Cornelsen is Executive Vice President, Ralston Purina, St. Louis.

What it tends to do is to conceal the problems as seen by the
Third World. Therefore, though your arguments may be overwhelm-
ingly correct in developed economies, they tend to minimize and make
difficult to understand the problems as seen by the Third World. When
you say there are certain distortions that occur in, say, a small
country where you have one large company, is that not the very type
of distortion which it seems to me we must begin to discuss?

In other words, how, if we want to forget the past and look to
the future, as our commentator has just suggested, do we reorganize
our thinking? How do we get to the questions of development? How
do we get the corporate community to say what should be done to help
the development of a country? Is it true that it is automatic? Is there
automaticity? I think some of these questions could be discussed by
you, and I think the comments in your paper give us a fruitful way to
begin a discussion.

Dr. Weston. You are certainly correct. A broad survey that emphasizes aggregate data does not get at the concerns of individual countries. I have written on that aspect in other places* and have argued
that policies of individual firms should be formulated in relation to the
stage of development of the individual countries. What is sound from
both a business standpoint and from the standpoint of larger responsibilities is to take the point of view as though the firm itself were a
part of the economic and development planning commission of a nation.
It should determine the kind of business activity that would be best
from the total development needs of that country. Guided by this
criterion, the basic demand needs for that kind of business activity
would be most favorable and the long-run staying power of the firm
would be the greatest.

On the other hand, I think that taking such a far-sighted and
enlightened approach is not going to protect the MNCs from continued
criticism. The basic problem is the inequality and relative disadvantages in the developing country, and that isn't going to be overcome
by the actions of individual firms. It is going to require a broader

---

*See "Teorias del Desarrollo Economico y Estrategia de las
Empresas," Boletin de Estudio Economico 18 (September-December
1963): 621-37; "A Framework for Product-Market Planning," in
Management Sciences in Emerging Countries, eds. Norman N. Barish
and M. Verhulst (Oxford: Pergamon Press, 1965), pp. 1-33; "Eco-
nomic Development Patterns," Long Range Planning Report no. 185
(Stanford, Calif.: Stanford Research Institute, 1965); International
Managerial Finance, written with B.W. Sorge (Homewood, Ill.: R.D.
Irwin, 1972), Chapter 12.

type of international planning to get at those fundamental problems. But I still think individual firm planning related to the development requirements of a developing country makes the most sense from the standpoint of the individual firm. However, the MNC should not be so naive as to think that even though it acts wisely and in a far-sighted and enlightened way, this is going to protect it from continued criticism.

Question. I hear what a lot of the developing country critics are saying—students I have had, and so on. They may not question the efficiency of the multinational corporation, U.S. or otherwise. They are, however, greatly concerned about the increasing concentration in the world and the mergers and acquisitions, U.S. or foreign, that lead to concentrated ownership and concentration of decision making and power. This is quite apart from delivery to the market and efficiency, even if everything you're saying here is quite true, that there isn't any market power affecting price.

I wonder if you could comment on that—how you see the trend toward concentration in the next ten, 20 years.

Dr. Weston. Yes, you make an important point that there are more dimensions to concentration than economic dimensions and efficiency considerations. There is concern about the power aspects of large firms, and I grant that. My own philosophy is one that yearns for more equal distribution of power, and other things being equal, I would rather see smaller business units than larger business units.

But I think the development of concentration and oligopoly has come about primarily because of differential efficiency, and I don't see any way to stem these trends. Even if you prohibited mergers, you would still see the demise of a large number of competitors over a period of time through the bankruptcy and reorganization processes, rather than through the merger route. I think if you look at the history of industries, not only in the United States but in foreign countries as well, that the process of mergers and rationalization has been in considerable measure a weeding out of the less efficient.

I have been studying trends in macroconcentration which measure the quantitative basis for these concerns about the centralization of power. A number of earlier studies pointed to, for example, growth in the share of the total assets of the top 100 firms in the United States. You get into figures such as 58 percent held by the top 100, an increase of 20 percentage points during the last 20 years, and this seems like a very alarming trend. On the other hand, if you look at those data, there are a number of tricks played. They take the largest 100 at any point in time, so you are taking the most successful 100. But if you take the largest 100, let's say in 1948, and follow their position in subsequent years, the largest 100 at any

point in time typically have not changed their share of total manufacturing assets or any other base you want to use. This puts a
different light, it seems to me, on the impact of macroconcentration. What I am saying is if the identity of the largest changes, this
indicates that there is mobility in terms of the possible exercise
of power.

Two other general comments. In these trends of macroconcentration, not only is the identity of the largest changing with respect to
any individual country, but the position of different large firms in
different countries is shifting as well.

And finally, the number of independent centers of power that
are striving still remains large enough so that it prevents the exercise
of arbitrary power by any of these entities. Truly what is more to be
feared is the exercise of power by an entity for which there are no
constraints, and that typically means government rather than individual firms. With individual firms there are counterforces operating.

Dr. Madden. Before you go on, Dr. Weston, would you mind com-
menting further on the last part of his question, about trends for the
next 20 years or so? We read, for instance, forecasts of a sort by
people such as Howard Perlmutter indicating a certain fraction of the
world's manufacturing will be in the hands of 300 or so firms.

Also in your paper there is an implication, a possible implication, that the world scope of the market will no longer provide to U.S.
firms a differential advantage of size that has in the past accrued to
U.S. firms, because our own domestic market has been so much
larger than the domestic markets of other countries.

Would you comment then on the trends of the future as you see
it, or whether you think one can see such matters clearly; and second,
the implication in your paper about size of foreign-based versus U.S.
multinational firms?

Dr. Weston. Well, I think you are certainly correct about the differential advantage of U.S. firms of starting in a large size market.
That comparative advantage has been diminishing. The thesis that
Hymer and Rowthorn had was that at some point in time all MNCs
would be growing at about the same rate because they would all have
similar positions in different countries throughout the world. While
I think that the comparative advantage of U.S. companies is diminishing, I think that the greater growth rate that the foreign MNCs have
had, will in fact diminish in the future.

With regard to concentration as such, I would expect it to continue to increase. I would expect that as time goes on, there will continue to be differential efficiency, regardless of the nationality of the
MNCs. I think that the differential efficiencies in the future will be

determined more by the quality of individual organizations built up by individual firms. It will be a matter of effectiveness in the development of managerial technologies, and I think this will have no nationality. But I think because there will be differential efficiencies in managerial technology, there will be continued increases in concentration when you look at the most successful at any point in time. I think that is virtually inevitable. But I think it will proceed at a slow pace rather than at a very rapid pace. There will continue to be a large number of individual centers of striving and competitive efforts. That means that increased macroconcentration will not pose a threat to the sovereignty of individual nations or to potentials for entry of other individual firms.

Question. Dr. Weston, I would like to ask a question on transfer pricing. Your analysis appears to me, having looked only at one small area of pricing, to have been absolutely correct. From a worm's eye view I know the four factors you mentioned certainly are the determinants of price. What I am wondering is, this being the case, what is going to happen when individual countries become more and more involved in transfer pricing and in the details of the systems of multinational companies? Will the present system be changed radically? Finally, do you see any way of defending transfer pricing as it is in the present situation?

Dr. Weston. I can see a conflict of interest between a host nation and the MNC that is engaged in transfer pricing. I would argue that what determines the price in the individual host country is fundamentally the market conditions in that country for that line of business. Transfer pricing can be used to assign costs in such a way as to record profits in a time-space distribution that will minimize taxes and perhaps tariffs as well.

I don't see any fundamental change in the movitations of transfer pricing even if individual host nations seek to interfere with the principles that I have enunciated here. If host countries behave arbitrarily, what results is a proliferation of other techniques for seeking to achieve the firm's objectives. You have a struggle going on. I think that arbitrary actions of individual host nations will therefore alter, to some degree, the risks of doing business in that country and thereby change the supply conditions for all of the firms operating. This is going to have an effect on realized prices in those countries.

Question. Continuing the transfer-pricing question, is it possible that the fact that two governments are involved in every transfer-pricing situation is going to reduce this issue to a government-to-government conflict, with the company in the middle?

Dr. Weston. Well, I think you've seen a good deal of that already and that is one of the costs to the business firm, that it is in the middle. It doesn't have freedom of decision and you do have distortions of what would otherwise be straight business decisions. Often the real power is outside the business firm, so the apparent power of the large MNC entities is not supreme; it is dominated by governmental authorities.

Question. Dr. Weston, you have mentioned, and there has been quite a little said about, the increasing power of the multinationals. But I wonder what your view is of the probable increase in the nature of the problems to be faced in the coming years, whether or not an increase in the power of private economic units, which I assume to be multinational, may not be absolutely necessary in order to deal with ever increasing problems, as opposed to the suppression of power in the economic private area, leaving problems to government?

Dr. Weston. Well, it is a paradox. It is certainly true that as individual governments seek to express more fully the economic aspirations of their individual countries, this increases the need on the part of a firm doing business in those countries for interacting with, and for negotiating with governmental units, and, this involves increased risks. This increases, therefore, the need for a staff, for executive talent to deal with this dimension of doing business on an international scale. This means that increasingly larger business firms will have a relative advantage because only they can support the kind of staff expertise to perform those functions. So, as the political and governmental environment becomes more complex, more uncertain, requiring more interaction, the comparative advantage of the large firm increases and this, then, is a real barrier to entry for smaller and medium-sized firms.

Question. Dr. Weston, piggybacking on that question, are you equating the future possible increase of concentration that you mentioned with an increase of power as seen, say, by most governments and most people? Do you differentiate that? It seems to me it is one thing to be able to react more ably because you have more resource, but does that necessarily mean that if this occurs in the future the MNC will, in fact, be more powerful vis-a-vis the host nation?

Dr. Weston. My feeling is not. When you have a large number of individual decision-making entities as you do, you don't have a monolithic situation. You don't have a small number of MNCs, you have a large number of MNCs. When I say there is a comparative advantage in dealing with governments for a larger firm, it does not imply that the MNC has greater power in relation to the individual country. But rather that this is a necessary reaction by the firm. This is building up a dimension of management competence required for survival, for performance, for operating a more complex and challenging environment.

Dr. Madden. Could I ask this aspect of the same question? Up to now a casual simplified view of the multinational relegates it mainly to manufacturing. But we of course are aware of the diversification of large corporations, and also what might be described as the increased organization of the market for various services. Is there implicit in what you say, the expectation that multinational operations will in the future extend more toward nonmanufacturing-type activities?

Dr. Weston. Well, we have seen some development of that already in connection with activities in the Middle East in which the role of international oil companies is shifting from ownership to selling management services. I think this is consistent with a broader generalization that the real forms of competition increasingly are represented by differential managerial capabilities. How these managerial capabilities are applied, the levels at which they are applied, the utilization of the more generic forms of managerial expertise—the planning and controlling type of managerial expertise—does have a wider range of applicability. The managerial capabilities that will be sold are not restricted to characteristics of individual industries nor restricted to the traditional managerial functions of production or whatever. I think what we are seeing is development of more general forms of managerial expertise that will have a broader range of potential applicability.

Question. Dr. Weston, you have indicated that concentration is accompanied by higher capital investment; that this in turn leads to lower unit costs. Therefore, in concentrated industries you have a diminished rate of price increases. You have indicated this is obviously an economic benefit, also a social benefit. On the other hand, the structural theory you talked about holds that as an oligopoly becomes a monopoly, whenever that is, there are undesirable aspects of this. Presumably prices go up. There are social disadvantages. So I wonder if you would comment a little bit on these differences, between what is a concentrated industry and what is an oligopolistic industry, the point where the benefits of concentration yield to the disadvantages of oligopoly and monopoly.

Dr. Weston. Concentration and oligopoly have been used as meaning the same thing. Of course, the traditional, standard theory of oligopoly or concentrated industries argues that you have essentially joint monopoly profit maximization, and that theme is then taken by some writers to argue that concentrated industries have been a major cause of inflation in the United States. Others have argued that the global corporations have caused individual nations to lose control over the money supply and this has contributed to international inflation. These are assertions; it has not been documented by the evidence. It represents a difference in philosophic approach. The legal tradition has been to associate the degree of concentration inversely with the extent of competition. What I have referred to as the structural theory says that structure determines conduct and performance. Somewhat higher profits were found to be associated with concentration and it was argued that the differentially high profit indicated some form of collusion. As I indicated in the concentration-profit studies, the box score is at least a standoff here. The earlier studies found a weak association, but more recent ones have not. But what I am arguing is that you can go directly to look at industrial performance in an area such as prices. The careful studies of the impact of concentration on prices have established findings with very little disagreement—I think probably Gardner Means and John Blair are the main dissenters. But even Leonard Weiss, who generally is negative toward concentration, has found that there has been an inverse relationship between concentration and the degree of price change. The difference is explained by the differential higher rate of increase in productivity in the most concentrated industries, in turn for the reason that they are the most concentrated; namely, they are the most capital-intensive.

    This is also indirect evidence that competition is operating in concentrated industries because it is competition that has caused the lower rate of unit cost increase to be passed on in the form of a lower rate of price increase. Again it is an anomaly because it is convenient to ascribe to monopoly labor unions and monopolized industry a major cause of inflation in the United States since 1966. But if you take the period preceding 1966—1958 to 1965—the wholesale price index rose less than one-half of 1 percent per year during that period of time. Yet the strength of labor unions and the degree of concentration in industry is not significantly different in the 1958 to 1965 period as compared to the 1966 to 1975 period. The difference is in monetary and fiscal policy that we have seen in the United States and the world in general, post-1966.

Question. As a practitioner of transfer pricing I find myself comfortable with your four characteristics, but I think maybe there are two or three more we haven't discussed that perhaps have an added influence of considerable degree. In the industry in which I am involved, and I suspect a number of others as well, the transfer-price issue becomes sort of clouded by the fact there is nothing to transfer or there is less and less to transfer as host countries require and demand local investment for greater and greater local participation, and this gives rise to several other characteristics which I think are distorting our business relationships considerably. In more and more countries of the world we have government-instituted price controls. They probably have more to do with the ultimate actual price in the marketplace than all of our own in-house considerations of the matter. There have been many countries with which I am familiar that have added great distortions that have little to do with what we accept and assume is the basic objective of it all, and that is profit. Many of these countries are no longer really interested in profit. Profit is not necessarily an accepted principle any more, and the failure to realize its importance causes more and more problems, I think, in how we really live under these conditions.

I think our objectives are under considerable challenge now. I submit that perhaps employment is more important in many countries than profit and that becomes very evident in the attitude of the governments as they deal with the price issue.

A final observation I would like to make—perhaps this is an emerging trend. I think we are now finding, and it may even be true, that the multinational list is peaking out, and we are really dealing with the private corporation, which is finding itself at great disadvantage with the public corporation. We have seen it in steel, oil, autos, and all of the basic industries that more and more we have government participation, government ownership, government operation, and you can go from one end of that spectrum to the other. I suppose you can go to the extreme, which would be the Socialist scheme in which they perhaps consider the labor cost as a fixed cost and variable costs are really material costs and perhaps investment itself.

As far as transfer pricing is concerned, I think the principle that you mentioned that appeals to me the most is that, in the final analysis, you must deal with the situation as it exists in that market, and you must meet the conditions and challenges of that market. If you are a private corporation dealing in competition with a public corporation in some areas where more than half of the business is conducted by the public corporation, you find the greatest distortions with respect to pricing.

I would like to encourage broadening the discussion of this subject to suggest that it is not just a defensive issue of the multinational trying to defend itself against a number of charges, many of which you have suggested are really not very well founded, but a very serious matter of how we are going to develop the resources of our respective companies in the manner which would be best for the countries and for the participants in that development process.

Dr. Weston. I won't try to comment on every aspect you mentioned.
I think you made some valuable and substantive inputs. I made the
general comment that it is a sound principle for the individual firm to
cast itself in the role or the point of view of the planning agency of an
individual country, that its long-run probability of success will be
enhanced if it takes that view. Individual governments also need to
take the same long-run point of view and the distortions they produce
by price controls, maximizing percentage of local production, don't
really contribute to that country's welfare, taking a long-run point of
view. They are really hurting themselves. Again the MNC has the
responsibility to develop expertise, really to help the country take
the long-run view that really is in the developing country's own self-
interest.

REFERENCES

Aharoni, Yair. 1966. The Foreign Investment Decision Process.
    Boston: Harvard University, Graduate School of Business
    Administration.

Aliber, Robert Z. 1972. "Comments on 'The Internationalization of
    Capital.'" Journal of Economic Issues 6: 113-15.

_____. 1970. "A Theory of Direct Foreign Investment." In The
    International Corporation: A Symposium, ed. Charles P.
    Kindleberger, pp. 17-33. Cambridge, Mass.: M.I.T. Press.

Arpan, Jeffrey S. 1972. "International Intracorporate Pricing:
    Non-American Systems and Views." Journal of International
    Business Studies 3: 1-18.

_____. 1972-73. "Multinational Firm Pricing in International
    Markets." Sloan Management Review 14: 1-10.

Ayanian, Robert. 1975. "The Profit Rates and Economic Performance
    of Drug Firms." In Drug Development and Marketing, ed.
    Robert B. Helms, pp. 81-96. Washington, D.C.: American
    Enterprise Institute for Public Policy Research.

Bain, Joe S. 1951. "Relation of Profit Rate to Industry Concentration,
    American Manufacturing, 1936-1970." Quarterly Journal of
    Economics 65: 293-324.

Baldwin, Robert E., and David A. Kay. 1975. "International Trade
and International Relations." In World Politics and International
Economics, pp. 99-131. Washington, D.C.: Brookings Institution.

Barnet, Richard J., and Ronald E. Müller. 1974. Global Reach: The
Power of the Multinational Corporations. New York: Simon and
Schuster.

Behrman, Jack N. 1970. National Interests and the Multinational
Enterprise: Tensions Among the North Atlantic Countries.
Englewood Cliffs, N.J.: Prentice-Hall.

_____. 1969. "Some Patterns in the Rise of the Multinational Enter-
prise," Research Paper 18. Chapel Hill: University of North
Carolina Graduate School of Business Administration, pp. 166-79.

Benoit, Emile. 1972. "Comment on 'The Internationalization of
Capital.'" Journal of Economic Issues 6: 117-23.

Bergsten, C. Fred, Robert O. Keohane, and Joseph S. Nye, Jr.
1975. "International Economics and International Politics:
A Framework for Analysis." In World Politics and International
Economics, pp. 3-36. Washington, D.C.: Brookings Institution.

Bloch, Harry. 1974. "Advertising and Profitability: A Reappraisal."
Journal of Political Economy 82: 267-86.

Boarman, Patrick M., and Hans Schollhammer, eds. 1975. Multinational Corporations and Governments: Business-Government
Relations in an International Context. New York: Praeger.

Bock, Betty. 1970. Statistical Games and the Two Hundred Largest
Industrials: 1954 and 1968. Studies in Business Economics no.
115, New York: The Conference Board.

Brantner, Paul F. 1973. "Taxation and the Multinational Firm."
Management Accounting, October, pp. 11-16.

Brozen, Yale. 1973. "Concentration and Profits: Does Concentration
Matter?" In The Impact of Large Firms on the U.S. Economy,
ed. J.F. Weston and S. Ornstein, pp. 59-70. Lexington, Mass.:
Lexington Books.

_____. 1970. "The Anti-trust Task Force Deconcentration Recommendation." Journal of Law and Economics 13: 279-92.

Business International Corp. 1974. Decision Making in International Operations. New York: Business International.

_____. 1970. Organizing the Worldwide Corporation. New York: Business International.

Caribbean Economic Development Corporation. 1970. "Legal and Financial Factors Affecting the Establishment of a Private Investment Company in the Caribbean." San Juan: Commonwealth of Puerto Rico.

Caves, Richard E. 1971. "International Corporations: The Industrial Economics of Foreign Investment." Economics, February, pp.1-27.

Comanor, William S., and Thomas A. Wilson. 1967. "Advertising, Market Structure, and Performance." Review of Economics and Statistics 49: 423-40.

Demsetz, Harold. 1974. "Two Systems of Belief About Monopoly." In Industrial Concentration: The New Learning, eds. Harvey J. Goldschmid, H. Michael Mann, and J. Fred Weston, pp. 164-84. Boston: Little, Brown and Co.

_____. 1973. "Industry Structure, Market Rivalry, and Public Policy." The Journal of Law and Economics 16: 1-9.

Dosser, Douglas, and S.S. Han. 1968. Taxes in the EEC and Britain: The Problem of Harmonization. London: Chatham House.

Dunning, John H. 1970. "Technology, United States Investment, and European Economic Growth." In The International Corporation: A Symposium, ed. Charles P. Kindleberger, pp. 141-76. Cambridge, Mass.: M.I.T. Press.

_____. 1958. American Investment in British Manufacturing Industry. London: George Allen and Unwin.

Federal Reserve Bank of San Francisco. 1975. "World Inflation." Business Review, Spring.

Fouraker, L.E., and J. Stopford. 1968. "Organization Structure and Multinational Stragegy." Administrative Science Quarterly 13 (June).

Gabriel, Peter. 1967. The International Transfer of Corporate Skills. Boston: Harvard University, Graduate School of Business Administration.

Gilpin, Robert. 1975. "Three Models of the Future." In World Politics and International Economics, pp. 37-60. Washington, D.C.: Brookings Institution.

Gordon, L., and E.L. Grommers. 1962. U.S. Manufacturing Investment in Brazil. Boston: Harvard University, Division of Research, Graduate School of Business Administration.

Gordon, Paul. 1970. "Organizational Strategies—The Case of Foreign Operations by Non-United States Companies." Journal of Comparative Administration 2, no. 1 (May).

Gruber, W., D. Mehta, and R. Vernon. 1967. "The Research and Development Factor in International Trade and International Investment of U.S. Industry." Journal of Political Economy 75 (February): 20-37.

Hasson, Nathan. 1975. "Concentration and Performance: A Protection Criterion." Ph.D. dissertation, University of California, Los Angeles.

Herring, R., and T.D. Willett. 1972. "The Capital Control Program and U.S. Investment Activity Abroad." Southern Economic Journal 38: 58-71.

Horst, Thomas. 1974. At Home Abroad: A Study of the Domestic and Foreign Operations of the American Food-Processing Industry. Cambridge, Mass.: Ballinger Publishing.

_____. 1972a. "Firm and Industry Determinants of the Decision to Invest Abroad: An Empirical Study." The Review of Economics and Statistics 54: 258-66.

_____. 1972b. "The Industrial Composition of U.S. Exports and Subsidiary Sales to the Canadian Market." The American Economic Review 62 (March): 37-45.

Hymer, Stephen. 1972. "The Internationalization of Capital." Journal of Economic Issues 6: 91-111.

_____, and Robert Rowthorn. 1970. "Multinational Corporations and International Oligopoly: The Non-American Challenge." In

The International Corporation: A Symposium, ed. Charles P.
Kindleberger, pp. 57-91. Cambridge, Mass.: M.I.T. Press.

Inter-American Development Bank. 1968. "Multinational Investment,
Public and Private, in the Economic Development and Integration
of Latin America." Proceedings of conference. Mimeographed.

Intriligator, Michael D., J. Fred Weston, and Harry DeAngelo. 1975.
"An Econometric Test of the Structure-Conduct-Performance
Paradigm in Industrial Organization." Ms.

Johnson, Harry G. 1970. "The Efficiency and Welfare Implications
of the International Corporation." In The International Corporation: A Symposium, ed. Charles P. Kindleberger, pp. 35-56.
Cambridge, Mass.: M.I.T. Press.

Kahn, Alfred E. 1961. "The Chemical Industry." In The Structure of
American Industry, ed. Walter Adams, pp. 233-76. New York:
Macmillan Co.

Knickerbocker, Frederick T. 1973. Oligopolistic Reaction and
Multinational Enterprise. Boston: Harvard University, Graduate
School of Business Administration.

Krause, Lawrence B., and Joseph S. Nye. 1975. "Reflections on the
Economics and Politics of International Economic Organizations."
In World Politics and International Economics, pp. 323-42.
Washington, D.C.: Brookings Institution.

Laffer, Arthur B. 1975. "Global Money Growth and Inflation." Wall
Street Journal, September 23, p. 22.

_____. 1972. "International Financial Intermediation: Interpretation
and Empirical Analysis." In International Mobility and Movement
of Capital, ed. Fritz Machlup, Walter S. Salant, and Lorie
Tarshis, pp. 661-75. New York: National Bureau of Economic
Research.

Lowinger, Thomas C. 1975. "The Technology Factor and the Export
Performance of U.S. Manufacturing Industries." Economic
Inquiry 13: 221-36.

Mann, H. Michael. 1966. "Seller Concentration, Barriers to Entry,
and Rates of Return in 30 Industries, 1950-1960." Review of
Economics and Statistics 48: 296-307.

Mason, R. Hal, Robert R. Miller, and Dale R. Weigel. 1975. The Economics of International Business. New York: John Wiley & Sons.

Mayer, Martin. 1975. Review of Global Reach in Commentary, April, pp. 78-80.

McGee, John S. 1973. "Economies of Size in Auto Body Manufacturing." Journal of Law and Economics 16: 239-74.

Miller, Robert R., and Dale R. Weigel. 1972. "The Motivation of Foreign Direct Investment." Journal of International Business Studies 3, no. 2.

Müller, Ronald. 1975a. "Global Corporations and National Stabilization Policy: The Need for Social Planning." Journal of Economic Issues 2: 181-203.

_____. 1975b. "Globalization and the Failure of Economic Policy," Challenge, pp. 57-61.

National Industrial Conference Board. 1970a. Intercompany Transactions in the Multinational Firm. New York: National Industrial Conference Board.

_____. 1970b. Statistical Games and the "200 Largest" Industrials: 1954 and 1968. New York: National Industrial Conference Board.

Neufeld, E.P. 1969. A Global Corporation. Toronto: University of Toronto Press.

Ornstein, Stanley. 1972. "Concentration and Profits." Journal of Business 45: 519-41.

Prachowny, Martin F.J., and J. David Richardson. 1974. "Testing a Life-Cycle Hypothesis of the Balance-of-Payments Effects of Multinational Corporations." Economic Inquiry 13: 81-98.

Richardson, J. David. "Theoretical Considerations in the Analysis of Foreign Direct Investment." Western Economic Journal 9: 87-98.

Robbins, Sidney M., and Robert B. Stobaugh. 1973. Money in the Multinational Enterprise. New York: Basic Books.

Scaperlanda, A. E., and L. J. Mauer. 1969. "The Determinants of
    U.S. Direct Investment in the EEC." American Economic
    Review 59: 558-68.

Servan-Schreiber, Jean-Jacques. 1968. The American Challenge.
    New York: Atheneum.

Severn, Alan K. 1972. "Investment and Financial Behavior of Amer-
    ican Direct Investors in Manufacturing." In International
    Mobility and Movement of Capital, ed. Fritz Machlup, Walter
    S. Salant, and Lorie Tarshis, pp. 367-96. New York: National
    Bureau of Economic Research.

Shrieves, Ronald Edward. 1972. "Innovation and Market Structure:
    Further Evidence." Ph.D. dissertation, University of California,
    Los Angeles.

Stevens, Guy V. G. 1972. "Capital Mobility and the International
    Firm." In International Mobility and Movement of Capital, ed.
    Fritz Machlup, Walter S. Salant, and Lorie Tarshis, pp. 323-
    53. New York: National Bureau of Economic Research.

_____. 1969. "Fixed Investment Expenditures of Foreign Manufac-
    turing Affiliates of U.S. Firms: Theoretical Models and
    Empirical Evidence." Yale Economic Essays 9: 137-98.

Stieglitz, Harold. 1967. Organizational Structures of Multinational
    Companies. New York: National Industrial Conference Board.

Stobaugh, Robert B. 1974. "More Taxes on Multinationals?" Finan-
    cial Executive 42, no. 4: 12-17.

Stopford, John M., and Louis T. Wells. 1972. Managing the Multi-
    national Enterprise. New York: Basic Books.

Trade Relations Council of the United States, General Counsel. 1971.
    Employment, Output, and Foreign Trade of U.S. Manufacturing
    Industries, 1958-68/69. 3d ed., vol. 1. Washington, D.C.:
    U.S. Government Printing Office.

U.S. Department of Commerce, Bureau of the Census. 1972. U.S.
    Commodity Exports and Imports as Related to Output, 1969 and
    1968. Washington, D.C.: U.S. Government Printing Office.

Vaupel, J.W., and J.P. Curhan. 1969. The Making of Multinational
Enterprise. Cambridge, Mass.: Harvard University, Division
of Research, Graduate School of Business Administration.

R. Vernon. 1971. Sovereignty at Bay: The Multinational Spread of
U.S. Enterprises, New York: Basic Books.

_____. 1970a. "Organization as a Scale Factor in the Growth of
Firms." In Industrial Organization & Economic Development,
ed. J.W. Markham and G.F. Papanek, pp. 47-66. Boston:
Houghton Mifflin Co.

_____. 1970b. ed., The Technology Factor in International Trade.
New York: National Bureau of Economic Research.

_____. 1966. "International Investment and International Trade in the
Product Cycle." Quarterly Journal of Economics 80, no. 2.

Weiss, Leonard W. 1974. "The Concentration-Profits Relationship
and Antitrust." In Industrial Concentration: The New Learning,
ed. Harvey J. Goldschmid, H. Michael Mann, and J. Fred
Weston, pp. 184-233. Boston: Little, Brown and Co.

Wells, L.T. 1969. "Test of a Product Cycle Model of International
Trade: U.S. Exports of Consumer Durables," Quarterly Journal
of Economics 83 (February).

_____. ed. 1972. The Product Life Cycle and International Trade.
Boston: Harvard Business School.

Weston, J. Fred. 1973. "The FTC Staff's Economic Report on Conglomerate Merger Performance." The Bell Journal of Economics
and Management Science 4: 685-89.

_____. 1972a. "Pricing Behavior of Large Firms." Western Eco-
nomic Journal 10: 1-18.

_____. 1972b. "ROI Planning and Control: A Dynamic Management
System." Business Horizons 15: 35-42.

_____, and Stanley I. Ornstein. 1973. The Impact of Large Firms on
the U.S. Economy. Lexington, Mass.: Lexington Books.

Wilkinson, B. 1968. Canada's International Trade: An Analysis of
Recent Trends and Patterns. Montreal: Private Planning
Association of Canada.

2

MORE OR LESS POVERTY?
THE ECONOMIC EFFECTS OF THE
MULTINATIONAL CORPORATION
AT HOME AND IN
DEVELOPING COUNTRIES
Louis T. Wells, Jr.

The debate about multinational enterprises and development is a broad one. It concerns the economic, political, and social effects that they generate. And the parties that are thought to gain or lose by this are in the countries which serve as the origin of multinational firms as well as in the developing countries that host their branches and subsidiaries. This paper concentrates on the economic effects of the firms, in both home and developing host countries. (Chapter 5 of this study will deal with the social and political aspects.)

Economic theory offers no easy answer to the debate about the effects of multinational enterprise. Theory suggests that there could be situations in which the activities of a multinational firm harm the economies of the firm's host or home country. And there are, of course, situations in which the activities can have positive results in the capital exporting or the capital importing country. In fact, contrary to the impression that one might easily obtain from some of the critical literature about multinationals, it is very possible that their activities are favorable for both their home and their host countries. On the other hand, some of the literature designed to defend the multinationals can also give an erroneous impression; it is indeed possible that the activities of multinationals are harmful to both home and host economies.

Although theory gives no answer to the important question about whether multinational enterprises are on balance harmful or helpful, it does provide a framework for analysis. The question of actual

---

Louis T. Wells, Jr. is Professor of Business Administration, Harvard Business School.

effects is an empirical one, involving the collection of data on individual projects. In fact, some projects of the multinationals turn out to be good for an economy while other projects are bad. However, theory and empirical research do suggest that there are some broad generalities that can be drawn about the activities of multinational firms. There are certain classes of investments that are reasonably likely to have predictable effects. There are others about which little can be said without a rather thorough knowledge of the particular project in question. For the purposes of this paper, I have divided foreign investments into two types of projects: those that serve the local market and those that export.

HOST COUNTRIES: PROJECTS THAT SERVE THE LOCAL MARKET

How An Investment Can Be Harmful

For the moment, let me turn to the countries that host foreign investment, to explore how foreign investment that serves the local market can be harmful. Indeed, it may at first seem that foreign investment can hardly harm a host country, at least in economic terms. The multinational firm is certain to bring some capital and some managerial skills. There is also a good chance that it will bring some technical know-how to the country. And it might even provide some other resources that are important to its host; foremost among these are ties to foreign markets that will eventually enable the host country to increase its exports.

A part of the concern with foreign investment is the cost of the resources that the investor brings with him. In the view of many critics of foreign investment, the costs are too high. But let us be clear on what is meant. One possibility is that the cost is so high that the project results in an actual loss for the economy. There are indeed circumstances in which this is possible. We will deal with those later. But what is most commonly meant is not that the costs are such that the overall effects of the investment are worse than no foreign investment at all, but rather that the costs are higher than for some ideal investment the critics can imagine.

Another part of the confusion on effects arises from the fact that the multinational enterprise does not bring with it all the productive resources needed for whatever it is doing. In fact, most host countries would be rather displeased if the investor were not to use some local resources. Thus, one finds that multinational enterprises use local labor, local materials, and, in many cases, some local capital.

A question of critical importance in an analysis of the economic effects
of foreign investment is how efficiently the foreign investor utilizes
the local resources, or indeed any resources that would be available
to the country in the absence of the project. If the foreign investor
uses the resources less efficiently than they would be used in his
absence, then the project may be harmful to the country.

Consider a few examples of bad projects. Say a foreign investor
sets up an automobile plant in a country with a small domestic market.
The investor provides some capital and the basic know-how. A local
investor or bank provides additional capital. Labor is mostly local.
And, of course, land, water, and other resources are local. Using
the foreign and local resources plus imported parts, the automobile
plant produces some cars, similar to those that could be imported.
Sometime later, there is severe criticism that the plant, although
only moderately profitable, is bad for the local economy. The critics
may be correct, but let us examine exactly what they mean. With
reasonable profits from the project, the foreign capital and know-how
are probably not excessively costly. However, the local resources—
labor, land, and so on—may be very inefficiently employed. The
standard should be what they would produce if they were employed in
some alternative activity in the country. The local labor and capital
might, for example, be employed in the manufacture of bicycles,
rather than automobiles. The local bicycle market may be large
enough that a plant could exhaust the economies of scale, while the
automobile market is so small that a local auto plant is terribly inefficient. The rational critic would argue that the value of the bicycles
which the local labor and capital could produce if they were employed
for that purpose is greater than the value of the cars they produce,
even in combination with foreign capital and know-how. Thus, the
foreign project employs local resources inefficiently; the country
would have a higher income without the automobile plant but with a
bicycle plant. [1]

There are some special problems in the calculation described
above in crude terms. One of the major problems is how to evaluate
the output of the bicycle and automobile plants. The common solution
is to turn to the cost of obtaining a similar product from the next
cheapest source. Usually this means imports. Thus, although the
locally manufactured automobile may sell at a high price—indeed, it
probably does if the foreign firm is to obtain a reasonable profit
from the inefficient project—its real value is likely to be calculated
as the cost if a similar car were to be imported.

A second problem is the estimate of what the domestic resources
would produce in some alternative use. Economists have elaborate,
but nevertheless only approximate, ways of determining what labor,
capital, and so on would yield in another activity. The estimates of

this opportunity cost (in a business manager's terms) are labeled "shadow prices" by the government analysts.[2]

I suspect that most readers are familiar enough with small-scale automobile plants to accept that they can be rather inefficient utilizers of a country's resources. But it is easy to overlook how many projects of multinational firms in the developing countries are of this type. In one developing country in which I served as an advisor on foreign investment, I examined fairly carefully eleven proposals from foreign investors. The proposals were selected essentially at random. Of the eleven, analysis showed that four had negative value added. This means not only that local resources would be used inefficiently in the project, but that the country could buy the final product with less foreign exchange than it would require to produce it locally. One example was a watch assembly plant. In that case, the dollar cost of the imported watch parts plus the dollars used to remit interest and profits abroad were greater than the dollars required to import the final watches. In such a case, local labor and capital are not just producing little compared to some alternative employment, but they are literally producing less than nothing, if the value of the output is measured by the import cost. The four projects were, of course, the worst of the eleven. But some of the other projects were very questionable from the point of view of how efficient they were.

How Does It Happen?

The perceptive reader will already have begun to ask two questions: How does it happen that such a project is profitable to a private investor, and cannot a similar situation arise for a local investor as well as for a multinational?

The answer to the first question is simple, in most cases. The host country provides protection from import competition—in the form of tariffs or quotas—that makes it attractive for a private investor to build a local plant. If the protection is sufficiently great, a very inefficient plant can be profitable. Thus, an investor is likely to establish a plant that uses resources inefficiently.

Note that high protection can cause difficulties even if economies of scale do not present a barrier to efficient use of resources. In such a case, the foreign investor may build an efficient plant. However, if local competition is not strong and import competition is constrained, he may be able to set prices so high that he earns extremely large profits. These profits, to be remitted to the foreign investor at some time, mean that the costs of the foreign resources are high. They are too high if an investor could have been attracted at a lower cost or if they are such that it would simply be cheaper to buy the product from abroad.

The problem of inefficient plants is not limited to the foreign firm. Indeed, high tariffs may lead a local investor to establish an inefficient plant as well. But note that if the domestic plant is relatively efficient and the high protection leads only to high profits, those profits presumably remain inside the economy. They are not paid as dividends to foreign owners. Thus, countries feel that the problem is likely to be less in the case of local firms than for foreign investors.

Although protection from competition is the most common reason that inefficient projects are attractive to the foreign investor, there is one other cause that is not unusual. That is that some local resource used by the investor is subsidized. For example, interest rates may be set so low by government policy that the investor borrows money at far less than the opportunity cost of the capital to the economy. In such a case, the investor can put the money to work in a project that is inefficient, but nevertheless make an adequate return on his investment. Of course, capital is not the only resource that may be priced too low, if too low means below opportunity cost. Skilled labor, fuel oil, and foreign exchange are other common examples of resources that lead to investments that are harmful to the host country. I examined a smelting project of this type, which used locally subsidized oil products as fuel; once the export price of the oil was charged to the profit, the project was no longer attractive.

Other Accusations

It is not difficult for economists and managers to reach an understanding, at least in broad terms, that some investments are inefficient users of local resources. The ideas that each has about efficiency are reasonably close. However, there are other charges brought against the multinational firm that are more difficult for the manager to understand because they involve effects on the economy far from the firm itself.

One of these is that investment by a foreign firm actually causes a decline in local investment. Thus, foreign investment reduces the amount of capital available in the country by more than the amount of local capital associated directly with the project. Proponents of this line of reasoning argue that the foreign firm appears as so formidable a competitor to a potential local entrepreneur that the local decides to send his money abroad. Thus, the foreign investor's project must be charged with the lost product from the capital he drives out. And, perhaps, with the loss of the productivity of some would-be entrepreneurs.

A foreign investment can have other effects that are not so clearly visible from the manager's point of view. Important among these are the so-called externalities, which may be either pluses or minuses for the project. Most managers quickly recognize the cost of pollution, so notorious in the capital exporting countries. However, in the host countries the project may generate other costs: the need for schools in remote areas, roads, power plants, police protection, or other facilities to serve the plant. The factory, if in a crowded urban area, may encourage further undesired urbanization, with all its attendant costs—economic as well as social.

Of course, a foreign investment brings external benefits as well. The project may combine with others to provide a market for independent maintenance firms, accounting services, and so on. If these are desirable investments themselves, then the foreign investment should receive some credit.

A further, serious criticism leveled at the foreign enterprise is that its project reduces government revenue. In a simple economic model, this does not matter. If the project is good for the economy otherwise, increased income accrues to nationals. If the government so desires, it can take part of that increased income as taxes. In practice, however, matters are not so simple. First, the taxing capabilities of many governments are not such that they can collect the required additional revenue from increased incomes. The lost revenue usually comes through the decline in easy-to-collect import duties on finished goods previously imported or from forgiven duties on imported inputs to the production process. These lost revenues are usually not offset by the taxes paid by the foreign investor, who often has a tax holiday and duty-free privileges for raw materials. Second, many analysts are not indifferent as to income in government hands compared with income in private hands. They argue that the government is more likely to use its income for investment than is the private sector. A shift of income from the public sector would mean less capital formation, hence less income in the future.

One frequently heard criticism will serve to complete those surveyed here. That is that the foreign investment increases the host country's dependence ("dependencia") on other countries.[3] This is primarily a political issue, to be dealt with in another paper. But it is also partly economic. A major concern is that foreign investors rely heavily on foreign components and raw materials. Before the investment, the country could, in times of foreign exchange crises, cut back on imports of final goods without having immediately disastrous effects at home. However, once the foreigner has built a local assembly plant, for example, an effort to cut back on imports when export earnings fall off results in cutbacks in factory production. Thus, there are layoffs of workers with serious economic as well as political and social costs.

Empirical Studies

When one moves beyond the impressionistic evidence and the
case studies such as the eleven I described earlier, the evidence of
the effects of foreign investment on host countries is still rather
sketchy. This is so in spite of the many studies that have been undertaken. To date, probably the most comprehensive is the one directed
by Grant Reuber for the Organization for Economic Cooperation and
Development (OECD).[4] That study examined 80 foreign investment
projects emanating from eight industrialized countries and placed in
30 developing host nations. In addition, the study carefully incorporates the evidence from many other studies of the effects of foreign
direct investment.

The Reuber study is indeed the best we have to date. However,
in spite of a number of favorable conclusions it draws about foreign
investment, the study does not provide a satisfactory answer to whether
the overall effects of foreign investment in developing countries are
positive or negative. The study does argue that the cost of foreign
direct investment is not excessive, running about 12 percent, compared to a cost of 8 percent for developing country borrowing in
Europe.[5] Foreign investors do buy local goods to a significant extent,
although the export-oriented projects buy less than the projects
serving the local market.[6] Others also have found a similar pattern,
in comparisons with local firms.[7] Reuber suggests that foreign firms
pay more than the going wage rate,[8] as I have found in another study
where job categories were carefully controlled.[9] That foreign investment transfers technology can hardly be disputed,[10] although there
are questions about the appropriateness of that technology.[11]

Reuber argues that foreign investment does not displace local
capital to a significant extent, although the evidence is hardly conclusive.[12] He suggests that his and other studies can say little about
the effect of foreign investment on local entrepreneurship.[13]

Even more complex is the issue of the effect of foreign investment on the balance of payments of host countries. Reuber argues for
a set of conclusions based on the study by Gary C. Hufbauer and F. M.
Adler of the effect of foreign investment on the U.S. balance of payments.[14] Those authors are agnostic in their choice of assumptions,
but pursue the implication of three different models. The outcome
depends on whether the U.S. investor could have continued to export
from the United States (free choice) or would have lost his export
market even if he had not invested abroad (defensive). In the defensive
model, the effects of foreign investment on balance of payments are
negative for Latin America, but positive for other developing countries.
Alternatively, the free choice model shows positive effects in all the
host countries. However, even these conclusions push the data slightly

beyond what can be said with certainty (as Reuber points out in a
footnote). The original study was based on U.S. data and does not
take into account the trade and investment effects generated with other
countries. Although there are other bits of evidence on the balance-
of-payments effects of foreign investment,[15] none resolves the
question satisfactorily.

Even more uncertain are the conclusions with regard to the
basic question of efficiency. Reuber does have some suggestive data.
For projects aimed at the domestic market, efficiency appears to be
low. The host country could have imported the products for about a
third less than it cost to produce them locally.[16] To the extent that
the high costs (in private terms) are caused by high costs of local
inputs, the projects themselves need not be inefficient. However, to
the extent that the high costs are due to the uneconomic scale of production, the projects are inefficient. Reuber does not provide any
hard data as to the relative importance of various causes, but the
impressionistic evidence suggests that small scale is an important
factor in causing high costs.

None of the empirical work available provides a satisfactory
answer to the question of the overall effects of foreign investment
on the developing countries, especially since the critical issue of
efficiency has not been adequately studied. The important question
remains as to whether the host country would use its resources for
more efficient projects in the absence of foreign investment. Clearly,
some of the effects that are viewed as bad, such as the increased
dependency on imports, are primarily a function of the type of industrialization pursued in developing countries. But some of the problems
can be traced directly to foreign investment. Examples such as 14
automobile assembly plants in one small country and 28 pharmaceutical
plants in the very limited market of another country would almost
certainly not be found in the absence of foreign investment. Thus, it
appears likely that there are some cases in which resources would
be better used by local investors.

Although the verdict is not in on the overall effects, there are
certainly many projects that are beneficial to host countries. At the
same time, there can be little doubt that many foreign investment
projects are bad. Cutting off all foreign investment would eliminate
the good with the bad. The problem perceived by many countries is
to institute policies that eliminate the bad projects while still attracting
the good ones.

The Time Dimension

It is important to note that host countries' perceptions of
foreign-owned projects tend to change over time. A project which is

viewed favorably at the outset may be severely criticized a few years
later. Initially, the resources a foreign investor brings to a country
may be seen as outweighing the economic, political, and social costs
incurred by hosting the project. 17
        Consider the technology a multinational enterprise brings.
Without it, the country may be unable to produce the product in question. The costs, in terms of dividends, interest, and royalty fees may
seem to be worthwhile. However, after a few years nationals may have
mastered the technology. Moreover, the technology that was available
only from a few potential investors at the outset may now be available
from many different firms. Typically, the costs of obtaining the technology from abroad decline as more competitors enter the market.
With lower cost options now available, the old deal looks unattractive
in retrospect. From an economic point of view, the host country
would prefer not to continue to pay the costs that seemed appropriate
a few years earlier. At this point, some kind of renegotiation may
make sense to the host country. The form of that renegotiation may
vary from requirements that local owners be taken into the project or
the imposition of restrictions on payments of licensing fees, through
price controls designed to lower profits available for remission
abroad, to outright nationalization. Even in Europe, where the market
is large enough that local competition is more likely to appear
promptly, that competition is often given considerable assistance by
the government to enable it to challenge the foreign investor. 18 The
support of national champions serves a role in Europe that is similar
to nationalizations in the developing countries. The developing countries are usually unwilling to wait for local competition to develop to
the point, even with assistance, that it drives down the returns available for payments to foreign owners.

HOST COUNTRIES: PROJECTS THAT SERVE
EXPORT MARKETS

        This analysis thus far has focused on the most common sort of
foreign investment in developing countries, that designed primarily to
serve the local market. However, the 1960s and 1970s have seen the
emergence of important investments in low-wage countries designed
not primarily to serve those markets, but rather to export to the
markets of the industrialized countries. The assembly of Timex
watch components in Portugal and Taiwan, electronics assembly by
Fairchild in Indonesia, and Rollei camera manufacture in Singapore
illustrate that type of investments.
        Even developing countries that have ambivalent attitudes toward
most foreign investment have competed openly for these kinds of

projects. The Andean Group countries, for example, exempt such
investments from the requirement that foreign investors divest themselves of a certain percentage of ownership and from the strict restraints on remissions of foreign exchange. Mexico offers many
incentives for export projects along its northern border, although it
is much tougher on most projects that serve the local market.

Criticisms: Are They Justified?

In spite of the scramble by developing countries to attract such
projects, criticism of the effects of such investments are beginning to
spread. The critics usually label the projects as enclaves that provide
little benefit to the local economy.
There may be grounds for criticism of the effects of such projects
in the political and social arena, but the odds are low that such projects
harm the host country's economy. For the reasons why this is so,
think again about the earlier analysis of import substituting investments.
Consider first the matter of efficiency. In the case of investments for the local market, projects could be profitable to the private
firm, even though they might be very inefficient. The principal reason
for this discrepancy between the private and social points of view lies
in the protection that surrounds the local market. Tariffs or import
quotas keep out competition from more efficient plants elsewhere. In
such a situation the investor can charge prices high enough to cover
the costs of an inefficient plant and still make a profit.
For an export-oriented project, this particular situation cannot
exist. The manufacturer sells abroad, where price competition rules.
Indeed, some price competition is almost certainly the factor that
drove him to seek out a low-wage production site in the first place.
If the plant is inefficient, he cannot simply jack up his prices as he
would for the local market. Thus, he would not knowingly construct
an inefficient plant in the first place. If he made a mistake in his
forecasts and proceeded anyway, the life of the project is likely to be
short. Not surprisingly, the Reuber study found export-oriented
investments to have costs 30 percent below those in the investor's
home country. [19] The empirical evidence strongly suggests that such
projects are usually efficient.
Protection was, of course, not the only factor that could lead to
inefficient projects. When the prices of some inputs were held down
to the point that the firm paid less than its opportunity costs, inefficient projects were again possible. If inputs are subsidized, even an
exporting firm might use them inefficiently. Indeed, that is a real
possibility: local interest rates may be held down, or utility rates may

be subsidized. In such circumstances, it is possible for an export
project to survive even though it is inefficient from the host country's
point of view. Although I have encountered no research in the matter,
I suspect that the subsidies granted to export projects are generally
offset by the amount local wages exceed the opportunity costs of labor.
That conclusion must remain in the realm of speculation until more
data are available.

Inefficiency has not been the only charge leveled against foreign-
owned projects. Consider some of the others mentioned earlier: for
example, that the projects displace local capital by providing too much
competition. This is unlikely to be the case for the export-oriented
projects. If they are controlled by foreign investors, they tend to be
for the manufacture of products that a local investor would find difficult
to market.[20] Thus, in the absence of the foreign investor no local
investor is likely to take up a similar project.

The issue of externalities provides a more serious possible
charge against the exporters. In many cases, they tend to be crowded
around the principal port, because of their dependence on transport
of incoming materials and outgoing products. Also, because of the
need for administering bonded, duty-free zones, they cannot be widely
scattered. Thus, in some countries they add to urban problems.
Efforts to move them to backward regions have generally been unsuccessful.

On the other hand, export projects are unlikely to cause a fall
in government revenue. In the case of investments for the local
market, the reader will remember, the principal loss in government
revenue comes from the customs collections lost when a previously
imported item is produced locally. The export projects do not displace any imports. True, they might not contribute much to government revenue because they are granted tax holidays, but they would
rarely cause an actual loss in revenue.

Even critics from the "dependencia" school would hesitate to
argue that export projects make the country dependent on imports
that are hard to shut off. After all, the imports are paid for by the
ensuing exports. However, they do level another charge. They argue
that the export projects magnify the effects in the developing country
of business cycles in other countries. Overseas plants, they argue,
are the first to be cut back when a recession occurs in the investor's
home country. The multinational firm prefers to keep its home plants
running at full production levels, where union and government pressures are stronger, and reduce output when necessary in the low-wage
plants. The general impressionistic evidence suggests some truth
in the charge, even though there are exceptions where the multinational
enterprise prefers to keep its newer, more efficient overseas plants
in operation and close its outdated home plants first (it has been said

that this is the case for U.S. automobile firms with regard to their Canadian plants).

Projects Could Do More

Many of the criticisms of the export projects do not really argue that the projects are absolutely harmful, that is, that the host country would be better off without them. Rather, many note only the low value added and the small taxes paid by the projects. The critics would like to see more contribution to the local economy. But low value added and low taxes do not mean bad projects. Host countries would like more benefits from the export projects, but obtaining them has proved very difficult, as foreign investors are able to get the government of one potential site to bid against others to obtain a favorable deal. Unlike the investor desiring to serve a local market, the offshore investor has a wide range of potential production sites.

THE HOST COUNTRY: POLICY CONCLUSIONS

By this point, the reader should have gained a set of impressions about the economic effect of foreign investment in developing countries. Although the evidence in inconclusive, I suspect that the overall effect of all import substituting investment is likely to be positive, as it affects the economics of host countries. But I also have pointed out that one cannot be very sure without more knowledge that the effects of a particular project will be beneficial. In fact, many foreign investment projects for the local market are unquestionably harmful.

For export projects, I have pointed out that it also is possible for them to be harmful. However, the odds are very high that a particular export project will have a positive effect on the host country.

With such different odds for the two types of projects, it is not surprising that one generally finds different government policies for the two classes of investments. For import substituting projects, some kind of screening mechanism is common; export projects are usually sought aggressively, with little or no screening. The studies that are undertaken are typically designed to determine how much incentive should be given, rather than whether the project should be accepted.

In fact, many countries subject foreign investments for the local market to rather severe tests. In some cases, the evaluation is an ad hoc one, involving an examination of each proposed project according to criteria similar to those described earlier. Individual projects that are viewed as harmful are simply not admitted to the country. Rather than relying on ad hoc evaluations, other countries attempt to set up a semiautomatic screening mechanism to eliminate projects of a class that they think are particularly likely to be harmful. For example, countries have lists of sectors closed to foreign invest- ment. The lists are likely to be made up of industries in which local investors can take on projects almost as well as foreigners. Indonesia, for example, takes this approach. In these industries, the government fears that if foreigners are allowed to compete the potential domestic entrepreneurs are not likely simply to shift to another industry. Still another screening mechanism, used by a number of African countries, is one that reserves projects of under a certain size for domestic investors. The reasons are similar.

Ad hoc, project-by-project screening is costly for the host government in terms of the scarcity of skilled administrators. It is costly for firms in terms of managerial time, uncertainty, and long delays in the negotiating process. And corruption finds a comfortable home. On the other hand, semiautomatic screening is usually crude. Bad projects pass through. And some desirable projects do not meet the simple screening criteria. In the face of these problems, managers may wonder why host countries do not simply get rid of the policies that create the disparities between social and private benefits. Indeed, many foreign advisors have recommended that high tariffs and import quotas be eliminated in developing countries. In fact, countries with little protection and relatively free internal markets often do little screening of foreign investment. Singapore and Hong Kong are ex- amples. But for most developing countries, immediate action to create more competitive conditions is not politically possible. More- over, internal prices are particularly difficult to align to opportunity costs in countries with a large public enterprise sector; Egypt, for example. Such countries would be likely to view the required changes in domestic policies to accommodate foreign investment truly as the "tail wagging the dog."

U.S. VIEW: PROJECTS THAT SERVE
FOREIGN MARKETS

The analysis of the effect of foreign investment on capital exporting countries is not all that different from the analysis of the effects on host countries. One must pose the basic question as to whether the resources used abroad return benefits to the home country as great as they would yield if they were used at home.

Remember that I argued, in the case of host countries, that the businessman would probably make decisions that reflected the national interest as long as market prices reflect opportunity costs of re- sources. The economic problems posed by foreign investment in

developing countries usually stem from market prices that lead to bad
decisions. I suggested that import protection is probably the most
important distortion that makes bad projects attractive to the foreign
investor. The same kind of misleading prices in the home countries
could lead their investors to make decisions that are not in the national
interest.

Although major price distortions are very common in the developing countries, they hardly play the same role in the United States.
Although not perfect, prices there are such that society is usually
willing to allow them to serve as the principal guide for investment
decisions. Thus, one can argue that foreign investment decisions
can reasonably be left to the businessman. If he finds it more profitable to invest abroad than to invest at home, then the returns to the
United States should be sufficient. Those returns come not in the
form of goods and services produced at home, but in the form of
foreign exchange earnings from abroad. But these earnings can be
used by the United States to purchase foreign goods and services,
presumably exceeding in value what could be produced at home with
the U.S. management and capital now employed overseas.

This simple model must be slightly qualified, even if prices are
perfectly acceptable. One factor that leads to problems is taxation.
The private investor looks at after-tax returns, while the society
looks at returns captured in the economy. These would include taxes
collected by the government. A foreign investment produces for the
United States the private profit plus only the tax paid to the U.S.
government. Tax paid abroad is lost to the U.S. economy. An investment at home that produces the same private profit would yield more
tax to the U.S. government. Thus, it is possible that a higher return
from abroad to the private investor could lead him abroad, even though
the benefits for the U.S. economy might be less than what would
accrue from a slightly lower private return at home.

The significance of this factor is difficult to determine. Although
rough data on tax payments are available, the data on profitability of
foreign investment are very unreliable. The data that provide the
usual estimates derive from Department of Commerce figures. But
those figures do not report profits captured in the sale of exports by
the parent to the foreign subsidiaries, for example. Reuber estimates
the payback period (based on all repatriations) to be 7.3 years for
North American investors (based only on eight projects, though). [21]
If this is typical, then the rate of return on foreign projects is considerably higher than on domestic projects, probably offsetting the
tax effects.

Still, I doubt that one should accept this simple model of the
economic effects of foreign investment on the U.S. economy. It
assumes a frictionless world that hardly describes what we know.

There are additional costs involved. For example, foreign investment may lead to the need to reemploy labor at home that had been supplying export or home markets. If capital is moved out of the United States, more labor must be combined with a unit of capital to keep employment up. Not only might foreign investment lead to the need for such adjustment, but also it may affect the distribution of income within the United States. Although the comparatively greater return to United States capital that probably results from U.S. investment abroad can be offset by government policy to redistribute income, if that is desired, the required actions involve costs. There can be no doubt that the adjustment costs are real, but for major adjustments, such as reemployment of labor, the question must be addressed as to whether these shifts are actually a direct result of foreign investment or would occur anyway.

Moreover, the simple analysis ignores the possibility that the returns abroad to a particular firm would not be higher than at home if the U.S. government would keep U.S. competitors from going abroad. If this were the U.S. policy, perhaps the potential foreign investor would continue to export from the United States, earning perhaps a higher rate of profit.

Note that the resolution of these problems revolves around what would have happened if the U.S. investor had not gone abroad. If a particular firm had not invested overseas, would the adjustment costs have to be paid anyway? If all U.S. investors were restricted in, say, a particular industry, would the United States be able to continue to supply foreign markets by exporting?

Several studies have argued that U.S. foreign investment is primarily defensive in nature.[22] To the extent the investment is a response to the threat that a firm from the host country or some third country will establish facilities that will close off U.S. exports, then at least a part of the adjustment costs will have to be paid whether or not the U.S. firm invests abroad. The plants that supplied the exports would be closed anyway, and that labor would have to find new employment.

The question as to what U.S. investors are responding to in their defensive investments has not been adequately answered. We do not know whether U.S. investors respond primarily to other U.S. firms that might cut off their overseas markets or whether they respond primarily to potential investors from the host or third countries. However unclear the answer is for U.S. investors going to other industrialized countries, for U.S. investments in the developing countries it is very likely that U.S. investment, if cut off, would be replaced by European or Japanese investment. By the time projects are viable in the developing countries, the technology is usually available from other industrialized countries.[23] Thus, restricting U.S. investment to the developing countries would probably not significantly reduce the adjustment costs arising in the United States.

Saying that the adjustment costs must be paid whether or not U.S. firms invest abroad does not make those costs any less real. In fact, they are substantial for those who must bear them, and they fall especially on labor.

The larger problems of offsetting the loss of capital with more labor intensive technologies and reducing the effects of a relative redistribution of income appear to be minor. U.S. investment in developing countries for manufacturing represents only a small percentage of U.S. investment at home. The shifts in technology and income distribution resulting from these capital movements are unlikely to be significant. It is the issue of labor that is most important.

The simple model of the effects of U.S. investment at home also ignores other factors. If a U.S. investor does not take up a foreign opportunity, but the project is developed instead by a firm from another country, the loss to the United States may go beyond the dividends, royalties, and other receipts that are foregone. Hufbauer and Adler, and others have pointed out that U.S. firms tend to source more of their machinery, parts, and materials in the United States than do firms of other nationalities. Thus, the failure of a U.S. firm to invest may mean less exports and less jobs in the United States, as the sourcing is done elsewhere.

THE U.S. VIEW: PROJECTS THAT SERVE
THE U.S. MARKET

So-called offshore projects, or investments in low-wage areas to serve the U.S. market, provide considerable fuel for the critics of foreign investment. For this kind of investment, the facts have been much less publicized.

Evidence is accumulating that offshore plants are established in response to price competition.[24] Like the investors for overseas markets, the offshore manufacturers are sensitive to threat, rather than opportunity. Few manufacturers appear to take their first steps abroad simply to lower costs, as long as they can retain adequate profit margins from U.S. plants. In fact, the competition that leads U.S. firms abroad appears to be primarily the result of imports. In a study of televisions, semiconductors, and computer core memories, the first steps abroad by U.S. manufacturers of televisions and memories were found to be induced by imports.[25] The risk, from the U.S. viewpoint, is that U.S. firms, once they have established facilities abroad, become more eager to move production of other products to low-wage sites as they view the risks and uncertainties as being less, based on their accumulated experience.

To the extent that offshore investment is a defense against import competition, the investment cannot be charged with exporting

U.S. jobs. Those jobs would have been lost in any case as imports displaced U.S. manufacturers. In fact, the investment abroad by U.S. companies may benefit U.S. labor. The U.S.-owned plant is more likely to use U.S. components than is a foreign supplier. To the extent that the offshore supplier incorporates U.S. components more than a rival foreign supplier would, U.S. labor has more jobs.

Note that offshore investment can be beneficial to the host country as well as to the United States. The imports that presented the challenge to U.S. firms usually originated in Japan. [26] In response, U.S. firms typically move to a lower-wage country. Thus, it is Japanese exports that are displaced, not the output of U.S. plants. In addition, the plant probably does not displace exports of a potential entrepreneur in the country hosting the offshore plant. That country's entrepreneurs would probably not have had the technology or market access to challenge the Japanese for a number of years.

CONCLUSION

In spite of the claims of critics and defenders and in spite of the empirical research now available, the fact is that still too little is known to build a strong case for or against foreign investment as a whole. It is very likely that offshore projects are beneficial to the host countries. However, the effects on the host country of foreign investments for the local market are not at all predictable. Some projects are good and some are bad.

Note that the worst of the bad projects probably come about because of the policies of the host countries themselves. It is import protection, subsidized prices, and other government policies that lead private decisions to differ from socially desirable ones. The foreign investor is not at fault. However, that does not make the effects any more bearable to the host countries. Nor are the policies of the host countries likely to change rapidly in this respect.

Even if one could argue that foreign investment is always beneficial to the host economy, critics of foreign investment would not be satisfied. On the other hand, a large part of the criticism of foreign investment is really not based on a claim that such investment is bad for the developing countries. Rather, the criticism is based on the belief that the benefits could be much greater than they are. The costs of technology transfer, for example, could be lower. The task of the critics is to build government policies that will actually lower the costs while not causing a drop in the flow of technology that offsets the gains. The efforts of groups of countries to act as a bloc in negotiating with foreign investors is an effort in this direction.

The second type of criticism has little to do with economic effects. It is concerned with the political and social issues that surround foreign investment. In these criticisms, matters of who controls various decisions and how social values are formed are of paramount importance. The economic effects play only a secondary role.

In the United States, the usual attacks on investment abroad are based somewhat narrowly on the effect of that investment on jobs. The evidence is now reasonably strong that most foreign investment in developing countries is not harmful to U.S. workers as a whole. The investment aimed at foreign markets is, the data suggest, defensive in nature. Most of the investments appear not to displace U.S. exports, and thus U.S. jobs. The investments are made when those exports would soon be lost in any case. Similarly, the data are beginning to suggest that offshore projects are the result of import challenges. If the investments were not made abroad, U.S. facilities would, in most cases, be closed anyway as imports increase.

This does not mean that labor has no case to argue. As trade patterns change, plants are opened and plants are closed. Society and labor as a whole benefit from the shifts, most economists believe. But the worker (or small businessman) most affected is unlikely to feel comforted by the greater good when he sees his job (or business) disappear. In fact, he is asked to bear the major part of the adjustment costs that result in benefits for the country as a whole. Until those adjustment costs are more evenly distributed in U.S. society, the displaced worker will feel justified in using all his power to influence the political process so that he does not have to pay those costs himself. After the failure of the trade adjustment promised in 1962, those efforts have been aimed primarily at stopping the need to adjust by stopping the shifts in imports and exports that lead to the need to change. The task of management, if it is to reduce those pressures, is to support policies, within firms and from the government, that shift those adjustment costs away from the labor that is directly affected.

COMMENT

E.A. Barr

In worrying about the problems of our industry, it is hard for me to generalize—to get back to the generality from the specific

E.A. Barr is Senior Vice-President, Union Carbide.

problems we worry about every day. However, I must applaud the
stance of Dr. Wells, who points out there are many factors involved.
We talk about the economic but there are also political and social.

We're being drowned in talk of multinational corporations,
worrying about all the things that are wrong with multinational corporations and trying to fully understand them. From what I am hearing,
it appears the jury is still out; there are many factors to consider.
Dr. Wells has not touched on the social and political views and they
are quite extreme. Sometimes we become terribly confused when we
get to a country and there are price controls and other government
involvement. Everybody, I suppose, wants their own petrochemical
venture, for example, just as they wanted their own airlines. And I
am not criticizing that. But it presents some new problems for us
which may overshadow everything else we have seen. So, I want to
commend you and say if you find anyone who can tell us what is going
to happen ten years from now, we'd certainly beat a path to their
door, for we are quite puzzled.

Professor Weston, whose studies certainly impress me, mentioned the book Global Reach. This is quite a book. I wish that all of
the people in industry, at least the ones I know, were as smart as they
are alleged to be in that book.

DISCUSSION

Question. Dr. Wells, I am laboring under the disadvantage of not
having read your distinguished paper in advance, but tell me whether
I am right about this observation. I get the impression some of your
argumentation is based on the assumption of fully employed resources
in a developing country. For example, you were talking about alternative uses of resources. I have lived and worked in many developing
countries where local resources were so underemployed that literally
there were no alternatives other than a given project to use those
particular resources at that particular time.

A second observation—a more general one which has to do with
the general state of the debate on multinational corporations—and that
is, you were referring to accusations against the MNCs. It seems to
me that the quality of the debate would be enhanced by talking about
accusations against government policies. In the final analysis, of
course, MNCs, go into countries where they're allowed to go in and
under conditions that the government itself establishes. To talk
realistically about these things, it seems to me one has to look at
a given government's policy to do a given thing at a given time in a
given place and under given circumstances. The generalizations are
really quite meaningless and misleading.

Dr. Wells. I am reminded of the comment I received from a Latin American country on a consulting report I had coauthored. They said that they were very impressed with the report and as soon as they had time to read it they would send me more comments. I think we were judged only by the weight of the report, not the contents!

But seriously, the issue of fully employed resources is obviously a terribly important one and in such a short presentation I skimmed over it very crudely. If one is dealing with oil that could be exported or capital which would certainly be used in another project, you know, the kind of simple presentation I gave makes good sense. When one is talking about labor that would otherwise be jobless, then the private firm is more likely to view a project as unattractive than the government. The analysis cuts both directions and developing countries know this perfectly well, or many of them know it perfectly well. This is the reason that so many developing countries now offer incentives— and even subsidies—for foreign investors or local investors who will use labor that would be otherwise unemployed. It does cut both ways and I think the paper is a bit more careful on that than the oral presentation I gave.

Secondly, the accusation against government policies: I think there can be little doubt that a substantial number of the projects that are bad for the host country are in some way the result of government policy. Now I don't think that relieves the multinational enterprise; it is still in a position that is very dangerous in that it is going to be accused of doing something that is bad for the country. Government policies are terribly difficult to get right, even if you knew what were the correct ones. Secondly, governments are asked to serve so many different objectives that they almost inevitably generate some bad results along with the good results. I think it is true that an awful lot of bad foreign investment projects do result from government policies that make them attractive to the foreign firm when they should not be attractive to the foreign firm; nevertheless they are dangerous for the foreign investor.

Question. I think Dr. Wells has pretty much answered what I had in mind. I have visited a good many developing countries and I have seen many countries where it is considered that no self-respecting independent country would not have its own oil refinery. I have seen such policies in Central America, where probably one refinery would be enough for the whole area; at least it should be enough. Many countries of course are not satisfied with one automobile assembly plant; they must have four or five. And you can't sell your own automobile unless you make it there, can't sell gasoline unless you refine petroleum in that country. In Honduras they've been trying for years to construct a steel plant, tried to get people interested in constructing

a very small steel plant. They have high-grade ore, no coal, will use
coke which is feasible, I guess, but the encouragement has not yet
become strong enough to build that steel plant. My own comment was
that Dr. Wells might give us some more comment along those lines
but I think he may already have done it.

Dr. Wells. I agree with everything you have said although I am still
frightened by how often I see the policies you are objecting to being
supported by foreign firms. I have seen an awful lot of cases of foreign
firms insisting on higher protection, when the government was not
willing to offer higher protection; I have seen them insist on a monopoly position in the market rather than competition in the market. I
am not saying every investor does this. I am only saying I have seen
it enough times for me to be concerned about the foreign investor's
role in some of these policies.

Secondly, the foreign investors are, I think, justly criticized
in some cases for trying to build too many plants in a market. There
has been some very interesting work recently on the propensity of
investors in international business to copy each other and it is a quite
understandable tendency. If one company in an industry goes into a
potential market, other companies in the same industry try to go into
that same market before it is closed. So, one finds the 14 automobile
plants and the 28 pharmaceutical plants, partly as a result of this
pressure from the multinational firms as well.

Question. I find myself in league with the gentleman who raised the
first question inasmuch as I have not studied the paper of Dr. Wells;
nor do I find myself able to translate what you've said into specifics,
problems which our company faces in trying to deal with a renewable
resource in a developing country where there is basically no infrastructure, no training, no skilled work force in the area. Schools,
religious facilities, camps, hospitals and clinics, and the rest of it
are all part of what the company has put into developing countries.
Obviously the burden of your examples, at least as I heard you, is
related to manufacturing rather than the kind of operation that we are
faced with. I was curious to know whether you have had an opportunity
to look at the primary, secondary, tertiary economic effects associated with the kind of operation a timber company might engage in,
and whether you have come to any conclusions with respect to where
those facts come out, both with respect to the community impact or
the impact on that country overall.

Dr. Wells. You are of course correct that the paper dealt almost
entirely with manufacturing and in a narrow economic kind of analysis,
which was all I was trying to do in the paper. Most natural resource

projects come out much closer to the offshore manufacturers, like electronics firms, which are unlikely to be harmful economically to the developing country. Now the political issues become terribly important in terms of the natural resource industries and I would not as an investor in timber or raw materials feel safe just because someone comes along and argues that the project is economically attractive to the developing country. I think one really has to turn to political factors at this point. And I think political analysis in the first round is relatively simple. ⌈That is that no developing country wants a foreign investor in its natural resources if it can undertake the project by itself. That is a political decision, not an economic decision.⌋

The next question is, can it do it by itself, or at what costs? In making that kind of analysis, I raise three kinds of benefits that the foreign investor might bring, and ask how important those are for that particular project. The first is capital, which is relatively rarely a barrier now. Most developing countries can raise some capital abroad if they have to. Secondly, technology, which can be a real barrier in some industries. And thirdly, access to foreign markets. Can the country sell all of the produce without you? In the case of bauxite, most developing countries fear they can't sell the bauxite without a foreign investor. Copper is a very different kind of analysis. This is the kind of framework I would go through: politically oriented, not simply economically oriented. I have just done a book on this question.

Question. I guess I would add that one highly important contribution you didn't mention is the area of training, whether it be basic language, vocational training, trying to teach someone who does not understand how to operate a machine. The whole range of training is of utmost importance and obviously the internal capacity of the country to do that on its own is almost totally lacking in the kinds of contributions we have got involved in, in Southeast Asia.

Dr. Wells. I think the question is how long you are willing to depend on that benefit assuring that you will stay in an attractive position in the country. I am reminded of a story that one of my colleagues made up about U.S. automobile firms going to Mexico. The story is close enough to the truth. U.S. firms went to Mexico, I guess in the late 1920s, probably telling the Mexicans we have some know-how for you, some technology or training, and how about letting us have a wholly owned subsidiary on our terms and we'll teach you something. The Mexicans said sure, that sounds like a good deal. Almost what happened is that the U.S. firms went down, built a shed on the docks, brought in cars without wheels to them, and taught the Mexicans how to put wheels on the cars. The Mexicans learned this very quickly,

and they said, "Thank you, we were pleased to learn. It was a benefit
to us but we have mastered it. If that is all you have to offer, please
Mexicanize yourself." Mexicanization takes different forms in different
countries. You can be expropriated, or told to sell out equity to local
investors. Price controls can be put on you. Ford obviously had a
lot more know-how than that to offer and gradually they sent completely
knocked down cars, teaching the Mexicans how to assemble them. The
Mexicans mastered that and again said, "if that is all you have to offer,
we appreciate it, Mexicanize yourself." Eventually Ford taught the
Mexicans how to make all kinds of parts and components, transferring
a lot of training and technology. Eventually, by the mid-1960s, I think
the Mexicans could have built their own car had they taken over a U.S.
company. It was very tempting to them to do so, and in many industries they did just that. But the automobile companies had something
else to offer; access to export markets that the Mexicans couldn't get
by themselves. They could not sell those clutch housings or whatever
it is they sell to southern California and Texas assembly plants without the presence of the U.S. company. At that point, many companies
had to, in effect, withdraw from Mexico. They had nothing else to
offer. The automobile companies were in a position that they did have
something else to offer. That is a bargaining model and goes beyond
the idea of simply the net economic benefits.

Question. I was going to inquire, Dr. Wells, if there's some way in
which a company could suggest to a developing country that import
substitution is an undesirable method by which to proceed on the basis
of Reuber's statistics. To deter them, as I recall, is really the path
which many of these countries, developing and developed countries,
tried a few years ago. And, to get to the effects on the home countries,
would you suggest that adjustment assistance, which you use in connection with ameliorating effects on labor of imports coming into the
United States, should also be used as a method of ameliorating the
effect of the so-called export of jobs that Senator Hartke would suggest
are the results of foreign investment?

Dr. Wells. The answer to both questions is no. I think it is a dangerous position for multinational firms to be in, if they are really very
seriously trying to advise the developing countries on their overall
policies. I am just afraid it would get you into more trouble than
what you will gain in the form of benefits. I think you would be accused
even more of being imperialists. I would be rather careful about that.
There are cases where import substitution makes good sense. It is a
very complex kind of argument that I think private firms would be
better to stay out of.

Secondly, let me interpret what I meant when I was talking about the cost of adjustment. I suspect and I guess it is as much an article of faith as it is the result of empirical evidence, that the country benefits, the United States benefits from more open trade policies and continued lack of restriction on U.S. firms investing abroad. That second part I think is borne out by a fair amount of empirical data. Net benefits outweigh the costs we incur by having to adjust to those trade patterns.

Now by assistance to labor I didn't mean we try to eliminate adjustment costs. I meant we try to help labor to adjust to those costs. It is not simply labor; it is often small firms. Small business-men often suffer as much as labor. In fact we have a very good case in the Harvard Business School of a small company in Massachusetts with its plea to the U.S. government to protect it. The plea sounds very much like the plea from labor and is understandable. I think the U.S. government should be involved in helping to make those adjust-ments, rather than eliminating the need to adjust. The Trade Ex-pansion Act of 1962, on paper, was to do that, but in practice it never did anything serious.

Comment. A lot more has been done on the 1974 act; companies and labor might not be turned around in the export-of-jobs situation as well as the import of goods.

Dr. Wells. Oh, yes, I thoroughly agree, both. In fact it's very hard to separate the effects of trade, effects of investment, and effects simply of technological change. The Europeans have in some ways been wiser on this in that they have not tried to keep that separation as clean. They have just tried to help in the adjustment problems.

Question. Dr. Wells, you raised two questions. I don't know what you intended with them. One, if a company enters into an agreement on very favorable terms and ten years later things look very bad in the country's point of view, relatively speaking, were you suggesting we should then push for renegotiation of the contract?

Secondly, you raised the question about incentives. When you were talking about the import substitution industries, you seemed to suggest that maybe the countries were giving away too much; they lose the import tax revenue, from tariffs, and at the same time they are giving a tax holiday. Are you suggesting then that both of these should be modified?

Dr. Wells. It's hard to answer, isn't it? I guess on that issue, when your terms are outdated by events elsewhere, the best kind of maxim for guidance is when renegotiation is inevitable, relax and enjoy it.

There comes a point where fighting it is going to do no good. In fact
I think where management has been most effective is when it has
recognized the point where it is inevitable—not initiated it itself,
which I think is asking for too much—but has initiated ideas for the
renegotiation that will fit the needs of the developing country. I have
seen, for example, some renegotiations occur where it was pretty
clear that, only in financial terms, the foreign firm came out after
renegotiation in as good a position as it was in before the renegotiations. It may have yielded some ownership and often it yielded some
elements of control. But because the firm put together a package that
made sense in terms of the country's needs at that point in time, it
came out much better than if it had simply resisted and maybe even
driven the country to expropriation. Some of you cannot do that as a
foreign investor; that is perfectly clear to me. If you yield too much
in one country, that very seriously affects what happens to you in
other countries. I have seen cases of foreign investors resisting
renegotiation and as a result getting expropriated. But that resistance
probably did make sense, because if they did not resist in that one
country they would face so much difficulty in other countries. It's a
complex analysis. You have to ask, How far off is that renegotiation
in other countries anyway? Is it worth delaying? It takes a very
complex analysis and knowledge of the specifics of the situation to
know how management really should respond, but don't be taken by
surprise. Be ready for it when the terms are outdated.

The second one, yes: I think incentives in developing countries
are sometimes far beyond what is needed. I think the worst of these
is the tax holiday which is offered in developing countries partly because the developing country doesn't know what else to offer. It's
tempting just to pass legislation and hope that legislation will do what
really has to be done through very complex administrative procedures.

It is done, secondly, because often developing countries don't
understand the U.S. tax credit system.

Thirdly, tax incentives are given, from time to time, because
company negotiators get so caught up in the negotiating process that
they forget what is important to the company. I have seen negotiators
insist on tax holidays, insist on them throughout a set of negotiations
when it was perfectly clear, in that case, that the tax holiday was of
no benefit to the U.S. company; it was remitting its earnings back to
the United States and what it did not pay to the host country would be
paid to the United States. A negotiator gets so wrapped up in proving
that he is a good negotiator to his boss, often because the last guy in
there got a tax holiday. There are all kinds of reasons for this.

Question. You say we are moving toward less foreign investment
circulating in this country and we are moving away from direct

investment in the developing countries. As we move toward the public type of corporation, or to alternatives in licensing such as Japanese methods and so on, do you feel we can adequately bring in private initiative, private enterprise into the public corporation? In other words, can the developing country itself properly size up entrepreneurship?

Dr. Wells. I am not sure I agree with the assumptions behind the question, first. The one I am not at all certain about is that there will be a dramatic move to other forms of investment in developing countries, away from wholly owned subsidiaries; I am not sure that will really happen. I think there will be some move in that direction surely, but I think that move has been exaggerated. What one sees is a sort of roll-over. What you see is investors coming in that have strong bargaining power. They get essentially what they want; they get a wholly owned subsidiary or large amount of ownership. Eventually as their industry matures, those arrangements are changed. But new industries come along, either because new technologies are generated or because the country has developed to a point that it needs something it didn't need before. Those new investors also tend to come in on terms more like the old terms. Clearly, I don't want to exaggerate that. Look at IBM in Japan and Mexico. Both countries have accepted IBM on a 100 percent owned basis. When the firm is in a good bargaining position it gets what it wants. IBM has always been in a good bargaining position. That will change eventually. On the other hand I think there is some shift, from a growing awareness on the part of managers about the kind of assumption they used to make. That was that to get the financial flows you want, you have to have control, complete control, and to get complete control you have to have complete ownership. Now they also recognize that developing countries are not interested simply in money, financial flows; they're interested in ownership as an objective in itself and control as an objective in itself. What has happened, I think, is that many managers have decided, look, we can break that tight link, we can work out some arrangements so that we don't really have all the ownership but we have control over those decisions that are critical to our strategy. We can keep the financial flows we need. An extreme case of this is coproduction agreements in Eastern Europe, where the firm has no ownership, yet has, in most cases, a satisfactory amount of control. There is a tendency to work out new arrangements that recombine these factors in different ways. So I would say yes, I agree with you, but I don't think the change will be quite as dramatic as some people make it out to be.

Question. First a comment. I very much agree with the emphasis you placed on the exchange rate and foreign exchange. My observation will run along that line. I take the liberty of asking my question in relation to the topic that Dr. Madden assigned to you, which you referred to briefly in your comments but not very fully in your paper. There is an assumption, I think, throughout the discussion of the issue of export of jobs, that foreign exchange manipulation is a disease of developing countries or at least not one that has characterized so much of the United States. The nature of my comment is that I question that view. My view is that the United States rather deliberately maintained an overvalued dollar from the mid-1960s until the second devaluation in March of 1973, and most of the labor misunderstandings or complaints with respect to the investment process would be rather well understood if the analysis of the foreign investment and the foreign production that was represented by the offshore investment could be related to the overvalued dollar during this fairly extended period.

Now for my question. Have you made an analysis or are you aware of any analysis of this particular problem; namely, the degree to which the direct foreign investment or managing from the United States could be attributed to the maintenance of an overvalued dollar during the period in question?

Dr. Wells. I think the question is well posed. I think it is much more relevant to Western Europe than to the developing countries. Let me talk only to the developing countries, which is the subject I was dealing with. That is, when you are faced with a wage rate of between 15 cents and a dollar a day in a country like Indonesia, the incentive to produce there is not really affected by whether the U.S. dollar is overvalued by 10 or by 20 percent. The orders of magnitude are so different between labor costs here and there that I assume that changing the exchange rate would have virtually no effect on investment in such developing countries. In Western Europe it is a very different matter.

True, in the pre-devaluation, pre-floating exchange rate days, the incentive to produce early in Europe, early in a product's life cycle, was greater as the U.S. dollar had a high value. I think this is hardly the case in developing countries. In fact in developing countries it is a combination of low wage rates, if you look at the offshore manufacturing, and import protection that simply prohibits import of goods from the United States, that causes U.S. firms to go there, not really the difference in exchange rates.

NOTES

1. For an analysis of this project-level approach in a macro-framework, see Michael Bruno, "The Optimal Selection of

Export-Promoting and Import-Substituting Projects," <u>Planning the External Sector: Techniques, Problems, and Policies</u>, Report on the First Interregional Seminar on Development Planning, Ankara (New York: United Nations, 1967).

2. The calculations involved in estimating the efficiency of a project from the economy's point of view are described in simple terms in Louis T. Wells, Jr., "Social Cost Benefit Analysis for MNC's," <u>Harvard Business Review</u> 53, no. 2 (March–April 1975).

3. The "dependencia" arguments are particularly well summarized in the first chapter of Charles T. Goodsell, <u>The American Corporations and Peruvian Politics</u> (Cambridge, Mass.: Harvard University Press, 1974).

4. Grant L. Reuber, <u>Private Foreign Investment in Development</u> (Oxford: Clarendon Press, 1973).

5. Ibid., p. 144.

6. Ibid., pp. 151, 155.

7. Donald T. Brash, <u>American Investment in Australian Industry</u> (Cambridge, Mass.: Harvard University Press, 1966); Albert E. Safarian, <u>Foreign Ownership and the Structure of Canadian Industry</u> (Toronto: McGraw-Hill Co. of Canada, 1966).

8. Reuber, op. cit., p. 175.

9. Louis T. Wells, Jr., "Economic Man and Engineering Man: Choice of Technology in a Low-Wage Country," <u>Public Policy</u> 21 (Summer 1973): 323.

10. See Reuber, op. cit., pp. 185–207.

11. See Walter A. Chudson and Louis T. Wells, Jr., <u>The Acquisition of Technology from Multinational Corporations by Developing Countries</u> (New York: United Nations, 1974).

12. Reuber, op. cit., p. 137.

13. Ibid., p. 209.

14. Gary C. Hufbauer and F. M. Adler, <u>Overseas Manufacturing Investment and the Balance of Payments</u> (Washington: U.S. Treasury Department, 1968).

15. See Safarian, op. cit., and Brash, op. cit., as well as Roderick S. Deane, "Foreign Investment in New Zealand Manufacturing" (Ph.D. diss., Victoria University of Wellington, 1967).

16. Reuber, op. cit., p. 179.

17. For treatments of changing perceptions, see Raymond Vernon and Louis T. Wells, Jr., <u>Manager in the International Economy</u>, 3d ed. (Englewood Cliffs, N.J.: Prentice-Hall, 1976), Chapter 6; and David N. Smith and Louis T. Wells, Jr., <u>Negotiating Third World Mineral Agreements: Promises as Prologue</u> (Cambridge, Mass.: Ballinger, 1976), Chapter 1.

18. See Raymond Vernon, ed., <u>Big Business and the State</u> (Cambridge, Mass.: Harvard University Press, 1974).

19. Reuber, op. cit., p. 179.

20. For the role of marketing factors in the exports of developing countries, see Jose R. de la Torre, "Marketing Factors in Manufactured Exports from Developing Countries," in Louis T. Wells, Jr., ed., The Product Life Cycle and International Trade (Boston: Harvard Business School, Division of Research, 1972).

21. Reuber, op. cit., p. 94.

22. See, for example, Robert B. Stobaugh and Associates, "U.S. Multinational Enterprise and the U.S. Economy," in U.S. Department of Commerce, The Multinational Corporation (Washington: U.S. Government Printing Office, 1971); Yair Aharoni, The Foreign Investment Decision Process (Boston: Harvard Business School, Division of Research, 1966).

23. See Robert B. Stobaugh, "The Neotechnology Account of International Trade: The Case of Petrochemicals," and other articles in Wells, The Product Life Cycle and International Trade, op. cit.; and Gary C. Hufbauer, Synthetic Materials and the Theory of International Trade (Cambridge, Mass.: Harvard University Press, 1966).

24. Richard W. Moxon, "Offshore Production in the Less-Developed Countries by American Electronics Company" (Ph.D. diss., Harvard Business School, 1973), Chapter 4.

25. Ibid., pp. 76, 79.

26. Ibid., Chapter 4.

3

ARE MULTINATIONAL CORPORATIONS DEPRIVING THE UNITED STATES OF ITS ECONOMIC DIVERSITY AND INDEPENDENCE?

Robert G. Hawkins

One of the concerns frequently voiced about multinational corporations (MNCs) is that their unfettered pursuit of foreign activities brings about undesirable effects in the home economy.[1] This paper attempts to examine some of the evidence on this point for the U.S. economy in relation to its own multinationals.

As a point of departure, we will synthesize, or perhaps present a caricature of, the multiple processes which, it is argued, bring about these adverse effects. The position of those who have taken this critical line concerning U.S. MNCs is that foreign activities contribute to the transformation of the United States from an advanced and diverse industrial society to a developing, oligarchic one; that is, that MNCs are tending to "Latin Americanize" the United States.[2] Building upon their oligopolistic advantages in technology, marketing, and finance, and reaping the benefits of interlocking relationships with giant commercial banks, MNCs are able to solidify and extend their market positions in the United States and abroad at the expense of smaller firms. This has led to a concentration of economic wealth and political power within a few large MNCs, and more specifically within the top professional managers of these firms. MNCs have been aided in this aggrandizement of wealth and power by tax laws that favor foreign production at the expense of production in the United States; by international transfer-pricing possibilities that permit higher after-tax profits for foreign source income than for income

Robert G. Hawkins is Chairman, International Business, Graduate School of Business Administration, New York University. The author acknowledges the valuable suggestions made by Professor Ingo Walter.

earned in the United States; and by access to finance unavailable to smaller and nonmultinational rivals. These several competitive advantages of multinationality provide a base for the take-over of smaller competitors by the multinational giants.

The social repercussions of this internationalization and competitive advantage follow directly. First, the growing concentration of economic activity within a few, large MNCs that plan on a global scale places their economic decisions beyond the control of the U.S. government and outside the influence of U.S. macroeconomic policy. Second, in attempting to maximize market share globally, production and investment is moved abroad, thereby displacing output and jobs within the United States. Production in export-platform countries displaces U.S. exports to foreign markets, and supplies imports for the U.S. market that previously were produced locally.

Third, the concentration of wealth and power in the MNC and the transfer of production abroad leads to a deterioration in social conditions in the United States. Income distribution becomes less equal; wealth is more concentrated in the hands of a very few; the middle class shrinks as the share of national income for production workers declines; and the level of living declines for all but the MNC managers and their cohorts.

At the same time, MNC bargaining power vis-a-vis organized labor is enhanced. U.S. jobs of the MNC are expendable due to the availability of foreign production possibilities that can serve the U.S. market. And with the swollen after-tax profits from foreign operations, MNCs are able to enhance their political position and influence favorably their regulatory environment. Another factor contributing to favorable regulation is that the major source of the public regulators of business is in the ranks of the well-indoctrinated MNC corporate hierarchy. Thus, the countervailing powers of big labor and big government become ineffective.

The end result is the loss of national economic diversity and independence. The wealth ends up in the hands of a small number of oligarchs who are in cahoots with the government. The peasant class, robbed of traditional jobs, is powerless against the MNC—which can quickly move production abroad. There are periodic shortages—as the private planning of the MNC fails to consider the national welfare, and as government ratifies this private control of the market. The picture is thus one reminiscent of some Latin American republics in the 1950s.

This is not a pleasant picture, even after discounting its overdramatization. This paper examines some of the evidence relating to the various components of the interlocking arguments.

The issue of whether U.S. MNCs are robbing the U.S. economy of its diversity and independence can be broken into two separate questions. First, has the United States in fact become less diverse and less independent in the postwar period—that is, is it becoming Latin-Americanized? Second, if so, has the growth of U.S. multinational firms been a major or minor cause? This paper addresses both questions as they relate to specific issues of dependence and diversity.

The following sections deal with (1) the matter of international dependence and independence of the U.S. economy and the role of U.S. multinationals; (2) the place of the multinationals in the concentration of industry and of wealth and power in the hands of a few; and (3) the question of the number and quality of jobs in the United States, bargaining power vis-a-vis the MNC, and the issue of income distribution. The final section attempts to place the development of the multinational firm in a somewhat broader context.

GROWING DEPENDENCE AND INTERDEPENDENCE

That the U.S. economy has become more dependent on external economic transactions in the postwar period is not a matter of debate. Exports of goods and services represented 5.5 percent of GNP in 1950 and 10 percent in 1974; imports of goods and services jumped from 4.2 percent of the gross national expenditure to 9.9 percent in the same period. International financial transactions have undergone similar growth rates. As restrictions on trade and investment transactions have been eliminated or eased; as international communications, travel, and transport have become cheaper and faster; and as the awareness of commercial and financial opportunities have become internationalized, the share of economic transactions involving exchanges across national boundaries has, not surprisingly, increased. The implications of this growing macroeconomic interdependence among national economies has been analyzed in detail in the economic literature.[3]

For specific industries or product groups, the level of external dependence of the United States is quite striking. The dependence on imports of critical primary commodities, such as petroleum and bauxite, is currently paramount in the public consciousness. But the rapid changes in the shares of imports in the local market for shoes, textiles, wire rod and other steel products, consumer electronics, and even compact automobiles all provide vivid examples of the increase in U.S. dependence on imported products.

And the history of the dependence of U.S. industries upon exports also contains specific examples of very dramatic increases since the 1950s. In agriculture, for example, soybeans—a negligible U.S. crop in the mid-1950s—turned into the second largest cash crop

by the 1960s, and over one-half of the crop (or its derivatives) is
exported. Commercial jet aircraft companies depend heavily on
foreign sales, as does the earth-moving machinery industry. Thus,
the degree of dependence of the United States, while having great
variation across industry, is very pronounced in some industries,
and has become increasingly so. The same can be said for financial
flows, external payments and receipts for services, and income from
foreign investment, all of which imply that gross balance-of-payments
flows have grown relative to the national economy—one clear indication
of growing interdependence.

Nor is there serious debate that the relative importance of
foreign production by U.S. firms, as compared with total output in
the United States, has increased significantly. Sales by U.S. foreign
affiliates, expressed as a ratio to U.S. national product or to MNC
sales in the United States, have risen rather consistently since 1957.
So also has the capital spending of U.S. foreign affiliates as compared
to investment spending in the United States. It is also true that sales
or capital spending by U.S. foreign affiliates as compared to their
host country counterparts have trended upward since the 1950s. [4]

Furthermore, foreign affiliates of U.S. firms tend to account
for a small, but growing share of international trade. Between 1966
and 1972, U.S. manufacturing affiliates raised the share of their total
sales that were exported to the United States from 6 percent to 7
percent; and the share of such sales exported to other countries from
13 percent to 15 percent. [5] While these are significant percentages,
and evidence a mild upward trend, the overwhelming majority (71
percent) of sales of U.S. foreign affiliates is made in the local
host country market. This then can hardly be taken as indicative of
a strong or growing dominance of world trade by U.S. multinational
firms. Trade within U.S. MNCs does account for a substantial and
rising share of U.S. trade. In 1972, for example, U.S. imports from
foreign affiliates represented about 25 percent of total U.S. imports.

Several U.S. MNCs depend heavily on foreign operations (and/
or exports) as a source of sales and profits. For example, over 50
U.S.-based firms derive more than one-third of their worldwide
production and sales from the foreign component, and a majority of
these attribute one-half or more of the system's profits to foreign
production and sales. Aside from the international oil companies
and other primary commodity-based companies, these firms tend to
be concentrated in the rapidly growing, high R&D, manufacturing
industries—both in the United States and abroad. Their international
involvement has typically grown more rapidly, since 1960, than their
operations in the United States, and in this sense, their dependence
on foreign economic conditions is higher.

The 1960s and early 1970s have thus witnessed an increasing openness of national economies while the role of MNCs, with their superior ability to obtain and integrate market information into their multinational planning and operating structure, has increased in greater proportion. MNCs are thus in a superior position to take advantage of trade and investment liberalization and breakthroughs in transportation and communications. In short, U.S. independence from foreign economic events has lessened, and U.S. (and foreign) multinational firms have played a definite role in that process.

There are two important questions deriving from this confluence of trends. Do the national costs of greater interdependence (less independence) exceed the benefits—or vice versa? And are MNCs the major cause in the lessening independence, and a major factor in any adverse cost-benefit comparison?

The benefits of international economic integration derive from the simple notion of Adam Smith that the degree of specialization is limited by the extent of the market. Extension of the effective market, and specialization across nations, tends to provide cheaper and better products, higher productivities of capital and labor, and frequently more intense competition.

For any country, these benefits are not realized without costs. The costs may take several forms. One is that the domestic market is more subject to external disturbances. There may be induced cyclical instability, required structural adjustments in internal markets, or loss of competitiveness in various lines of activity. There will be shifts in income distribution among groups, as products give way to foreign competition and new ones are developed and produced. A country may be subjected to adverse movements in its terms of trade due to the exercise of monopoly power by foreign suppliers of exports (for example, the Organization of Petroleum Exporting Countries) or monopsony power by importers. In short, there is a wide array of costs involved with interdependence, and any good international trade theorist can argue that, under certain circumstances, autarchy or some optimal degree of control is preferable to free or freer international trade and investment.

In practice this requires that the cost be evaluated quantitatively, and compared with the benefits from interdependence. But both are difficult if not impossible to approximate. The benefit-cost relationship may be more favorable than is commonly imagined. For example, an indication of the benefit from one component of U.S. trade can be found in the estimated cost ($100 billion) and near impossibility of U.S. independence in energy. And the list of commodities that the United States does not have or cannot produce locally is a long one, ranging from bananas to chromium. But more pervasive is the lower

cost of manufacturing products abroad and importing them to the
United States. A calculation of the lower final goods prices permitted
by international interdependence would surely yield a very high benefit
estimate. But the neoisolationists commonly minimize (or ignore)
such national benefits of interdependence, and focus exclusively on
and magnify the costs.

MNCs have obviously contributed to the growing interdependence
of the United States with other economies. Yet interdependence in
the postwar period would have progressed even in the absence of
MNCs, and to focus attention on MNCs as the major cause of heightened
interdependence is to miss a major point. The fact that the major oil
companies developed, refined, and marketed the vast majority of the
world's petroleum does not imply that the United States would have
been less dependent on Middle East crude oil in 1973 if there were no
multinational oil companies. Since the location of mineral deposits
and the location of consumption centers (population and industrial
concentrations) dominate the pattern of international trade and investment in the industry, whether the industry is organized into multinational private firms or into national public enterprises is likely to
matter little. In another example, whether a multinational is the
exporter and foreign distributor of large volumes of grain exports
from the United States can hardly influence greatly whether or not
U.S. agriculture is dependent on foreign markets. And perhaps most
interesting is that some of the most rapid surges in foreign dependence
for the United States have been in industries where multinational firms
are least evident—commercial jet aircraft, shoes, textiles, and steel.
Nor can U.S. multinationals (except by default) be accused of raising
U.S. dependence on foreign cars during the import booms of the
1960s. Volkswagen, Toyota, and Datsun not only are not U.S. multinationals, but until the 1970s were hardly multinational at all by most
conventional definitions.

In short, U.S. multinational firms have not been the only, or
even the dominant, force in the growing interdependence of nation-
states. The rapid rise of foreign operations of U.S. firms during
the 1960s and early 1970s occurred in tandem with, and added to,
the other forces of economic integration. The existence of MNCs
affected the form of the integration, but much less the fact of the
integration. This integration carries benefits as well as costs, and
just as MNCs cannot realistically be considered as its single cause,
neither are MNCs responsible only for its costs and none of its benefits.

There is good reason to expect that the rapid expansion of
foreign investment by U.S. MNCs in the 1960s will not be repeated
in the future, but that a slower growth in operations might be expected.
Although the decline in foreign production and investment by U.S.

MNCs in 1975 may be the result mainly of the worldwide recession, other considerations argue for a slower expansion of foreign operations over the longer term. One is the 25 percent depreciation of the dollar since 1971, which involves a major realignment of cost conditions in the United States vis-a-vis potential production sites abroad. This tends to lower the incentives for U.S. firms to expand abroad and raise the incentives for foreign firms to invest in the United States. Another is the increasing restrictiveness of foreign governments with respect to the conditions for entry and expansion of foreign firms, as for example in Canada. These and other factors suggest that some of the more extreme projections of the future importance of external production by U.S. firms made during the euphoria of the 1960s are likely to be far off the mark.

MULTINATIONALS AND THE CONCENTRATION OF WEALTH AND POWER

One of the alleged adverse effects of the role of MNCs in the internationalization of the world economy is that they are able to employ their financial, tax, and technological advantages to increase their size, power, and wealth. They thus contribute to a top-heavy industrial structure, concentrating markets in the hands of a few producers, and wealth and power in the hands of a small percentage of the population consisting of the technological, managerial, and financial elite. As testable hypotheses, then, one would predict that (1) MNCs control a growing share of output, and this is becoming concentrated in fewer and fewer firms; (2) the degree of monopoly in individual industries is growing; and (3) there is a concomitant rise in the relative political power of the large MNCs. These implications are examined below.

Large Firms in Total Output

It is rightfully argued that the share of the 50 or 100 largest manufacturing firms in total U.S. production, sales, or employment has risen secularly over time.[6] Yet, as will be noted below, the strength and pervasiveness of this trend depends on the time period chosen for observation. A part of the apparent concentration of wealth and power is, no doubt, explained by the financial advantages enjoyed by large firms. They tend to be diversified, better credit risks, and have better cash-flow positions to finance advertising, R&D, and other activities to make their earnings more stable and their market positions more secure. Indeed, these are some of the major objectives of firms and their managers.

Yet the mere observation of such long-term trends, including merger statistics, may be less than fully enlightening. The share of large firms is likely to increase, as the industrial process becomes more complex and interconnected, and as large capital projects are required to achieve minimum competitive scale. Such concentration is evident not only among large manufacturing firms, but also in agriculture and no doubt among governments.

Moreover, a closer look at the measures of aggregate concentration provides quite a dramatic change-over in trend in the postwar period. Using the share of the 50 largest firms in total value added in manufacturing and mining, there has been no change in concentration of output in the largest firms since 1963, and only a 1 percent rise from 1954 to 1970. The data are as follows:[7]

	1947	1954	1963	1967	1970
Percent of value added accounted for by 50 largest firms in manufacturing and mining	17	23	25	25	24

The major part of the increase in concentration of U.S. production in the 50 largest firms thus occurred in the early postwar period, the period prior to the rapid expansion abroad of U.S. MNCs—and the share has remained stable since the mid-1950s while foreign operations have thus expanded so dramatically. A similar picture is found when the share of the largest 100 firms is used, except that the upward trend in share continued until 1967, after which there has been a slight decline.

The simplistic notion that the large firms get relatively larger while the smaller firms get smaller or disappear is further complicated by shifting identities among the large firms. The relative positions of the individual large firms in terms of size and power change quite significantly through time. Today's giant (a firm such as IBM) may have been low in the list sometime ago; yesterday's giants (such as the Pennsylvania Railroad or the Singer Company) may be absent today. The firms appearing among the Fortune 500 (or 100) for 1939, 1950, or 1960 are not the same as those on the list for 1974, and the ranks have changed even more markedly.

Perhaps more systematically to the point is that the average assets of the 200 largest companies grew by 197 percent from 1954 to 1968. Yet the assets held by the 200 largest companies in 1968 were 248 percent greater than the total held by the 200 largest, but different, companies in 1954.[8] This implies that a substantial change in the ranks of the 200 largest companies occurred between the two years.

All of this is not meant to suggest that large firms do not have competitive and financial advantages over smaller firms. It does indicate that largeness per se is not sufficient to assure a stable or rising position in the hierarchy of size and power of firms including MNCs. The interconnecting financial and industrial ties of the Rocke-fellers, the Morgans, and the Mellons have not succeeded in sup-pressing the emergence of firms like Xerox, Polaroid, Honeywell, and Texas Instruments.

If a significant financial advantage arises from the multi-nationality of firms, including any which stem from the preferred and interlocking relationships with the large financial institutions, it should be reflected in a superior financial performance of multina-tional firms over national firms. There is some evidence that profit-ability in the United States and for worldwide operations of U.S. MNCs is, on average, positively related with foreign operations. Both B.M. Wolf[9] and Thomas Horst[10] found such positive relationships, which may suggest that the multinational dimension per se favors multinational firms over strictly local firms (in the same industries) with respect to profitability. Using a different set of data, B.I. Cohen[11] found no systematic difference in profitability between MNCs and non-MNCs, but did find less variability through time of both profits and sales of MNCs, a finding consistent with Horst's. Yet overall measures of pretax return on all U.S. foreign investment yields values comparable to returns on book values in the United States.[12] And a study that compared market rates of return (including appreciation in the stock price) for a sample of U.S. companies showing a high percentage of foreign sales with a sample of firms with little foreign involvement found no significant difference either in the rates of return on the equity or in the stability of those earn-ings.[13] Thus, the evidence is somewhat mixed. Concentration of production in a few large firms is not reflected in the data. On the other hand, there is some evidence that MNCs achieve superior per-formances in their U.S. operations, perhaps an advantage from multinationality.

Concentration of Ownership and Control

Another presumed result of the internationalization of U.S. MNCs is for their ownership, and therefore control, to become concentrated in the hands of a few interlocking interests, including the large money center banks and their trust departments.[14] This apparent concentration of ownership and control presumably allows mutual backscratching, whereby the financing for the expansion of the large MNCs is assured, and their ability to concentrate further the wealth of the nation via merger during periods of economic adversity is enhanced.

There is considerable evidence that large firms do have preferred access to bank credit during periods of restrictive monetary policies, while smaller borrowers and new customers find their credit rationed.[15] And there is some additional evidence that multinational firms have a financial advantage over locally oriented firms in securing funds during periods of restrictive credit.[16] These financial advantages, while they might stem from interlocking directorates and financial relationships, might also be explained by the economic behavior of lending institutions operating at arm's length with corporate customers. Their diversification, large size, earnings stability, and value as a customer may well make multinational firms preferred customers during restrictive credit periods. Thus, while a conspiracy theory of the financial advantage is possible, an economic theory is also consistent with the observed behavior. But the more important question is whether concentration of ownership has really become more pronounced as a result of these financial advantages of MNCs, or whether substantial adverse effects have flowed from it. The importance of the concentration of ownership, and its actual trend, is a matter of continuing debate. The trends after the 1930s, which were toward greater dispersion of common stock ownership and a declining concentration of dividend income and market value of stockholdings in the upper income groups, continued in the period from 1958 to 1969.[17] These trends, which persisted throughout the U.S. foreign direct investment boom of the 1960s, are in apparent contradiction with the supposed growing concentration in the equity ownership of MNCs. Nor is there unambiguous reason to assume that a growing dispersion of stock ownership is socially preferable to a concentrated situation in which control and responsibility are vested in owners rather than in detached managers.[18]

It also seems likely that interlocking directorates among major corporations, while remaining an important issue, are much less prevalent currently than in earlier periods. The vigorous enforcement of the regulations of the Securities and Exchange Commission (SEC) on disclosure and conflict of interest, and of the comptrollers of the currency on board membership by bankers, has reduced the likelihood of company executives serving on the boards of directors of firms with which they compete or on competitive third firms. In short, the regulatory awareness of such concentrations of power and influence, while not as great as might be hoped, has certainly not receded during the rise of the multinational aspect of large U.S. firms, and has in fact probably heightened.

To summarize, while the centralization of ownership and control of big business should be an object of concern and overview, there is little evidence that ownership has become more concentrated in the hands of a wealthy few. Indeed, there are some indications that the contrary is occurring. And while MNCs have financial advantages, these evidently have not become reflected in greatly superior financial performance or in an unalterable market position. Finally, there is little indication that the internationalization of U.S. firms has played a major role in the aggrandizement and irresponsible exercise of power in the hands of a few.

Industrial Concentration

One result of a concentration of financial power of MNCs might be the exercise of market power so as to further concentrate production in a few oligopolistic firms in the major industries. Through conglomerate mergers or industry diversification, or through heightened barriers to entry by competitors, this market concentration may intensify or spread across industries. But as indicated above, the evidence does not support any strong movement since the early 1960s toward overall concentration of total output in a few large firms. Yet the superior financial performance may constitute an additional barrier to entry at the industry level.[19]

What does the evidence show concerning concentration within industries? The argument runs that multinationals, through their superior financial, marketing, and technological power, are able to capture growing shares of the market, suppress entry by competitors, and acquire or force out weaker and smaller nonmultinational firms. To examine the record, one may refer to the evidence on concentration within the U.S. market or in the world market. Aside from the substantial difficulties in defining and interpreting market concentration data,[20] those which do exist offer very little systematic evidence that greater concentration has been associated with the rapid growth of multinational firms.

A careful study of the changes in industry concentration, as measured by the four-firm concentration ratio in 166 U.S. industries, found that the average (weighted or unweighted) concentration ratio rose from 1947 to 1970, but only from 40.5 percent to 42.6 percent.[21] Furthermore, 74 of the 166 industries showed a decline in concentration over the period. Most producer goods industries experienced a decline in concentration; most consumer goods industries saw concentration rise. It was found also that the industries with high degrees of concentration in the initial years (1947 and 1958), and industries with large absolute size tended to experience declines in concentration.

The rate of growth of the industry was also negatively related to changes in concentration in the 1947-58 period, and not related at all in the 1958-70 period. Industries with high degrees of product differentiation (mainly consumer goods industries) tended to have increasing concentration.

These results suggest that multinationalization of U.S. firms has not been used as a base for any major monopolization of markets in the United States. Concentration has varied among industries; has on average risen only slightly; and in fact, has remained almost static since 1958. Only in highly advertised, differentiated, consumer goods industries has concentration tended to increase significantly. For these, the multinationality of U.S. firms might be a factor. While the international role of the MNC may serve as a major source of U.S. market power, it has thus far evidently been of insufficient strength or has not been exploited to visibly affect concentration ratios. For example, the auto industry and consumer durables, which saw concentration rise in U.S. production, got little if any boost from foreign production of the surviving firms. And the decisions by some foreign firms to produce in the U.S. market are likely to slow any strong trend toward concentration.

The concentration of world markets in a few firms shows a very definite tendency to decline in the postwar period.[22] This has occurred as competition from Japanese, German, and other firms has penetrated the markets of U.S. firms, and as medium-sized firms have entered mature industries. As a result, the share of large U.S. firms in world markets has declined markedly since 1962. For example, the percentage of worldwide sales accounted for by U.S. firms among the world's 486 largest firms fell from 67.7 percent in 1962 to 67.1 percent in 1967, and to 59.1 percent in 1972.[23] A similar decline in the U.S. share occurred for the worldwide sales of the 25, 50, and 100 largest companies. And in each of 17 industry groupings, except rubber products and textiles and footwear, the three-firm concentration ratio declined from 1962 to 1972. The presumption, then, that large U.S. multinationals are increasing their control over, and concentration in, world or U.S. markets is simply not borne out by the evidence. Indeed, during the rapid multinationalization of U.S. firms, the concentration in industry has tended to decline or remain static, and evidences of greater, not less, competition exist.[24]

Political Power

The measurement of political power is at best elusive. Yet there is little doubt that large corporations in general, and multinational firms in particular, have wielded and continue to wield great political leverage. The efficient public affairs offices, the available financial support for political candidates, and the relatively easy movement of executives into and out of government have all contributed to this power. Since multinational firms tend to be large, their activities in these areas tend to be correspondingly large, and frequently quite sophisticated.

Attempts to influence favorably the regulatory and economic environment within which firms operate is a legitimate activity, and to be expected. The MNC lobby has, furthermore, been successful on a range of issues, including certain tax policies and foreign trade policy. However, in several of the widely reported cases involving large political contributions and payments for influence peddling by U.S. companies (mainly MNCs), the actions were not only not legitimate, but irresponsible and in several cases illegal. Aside from the damage of the corporate image and the general public revulsion from such actions, a genuine concern must exist over the abuse of corporate political influence for specific private benefit. Furthermore, the liberal interpretation by the Federal Election Commission to permit U.S. companies to establish political committees of stockholders and employees for financial contributions is a reflection of the political power of MNCs and serves to reinforce that power. This cannot but be seen as a move in the wrong direction.

But there are some reasons for optimism. The substantial political influence of the MNCs was not sufficiently cohesive or strong to resist election reform legislation that did limit and regulate campaign contributions. Indeed, some MNCs and their executives supported such legislation. Also, contrary to the allegations, MNCs have apparently not successfully transformed their political power into a superior economic position or very comfortable regulatory status compared to other firms, as the preceding discussion indicates. This is not to say that the economic status of MNCs might not have been worse if their political influence had been less, nor is it meant to suggest that concentration and exercise of political influence does not remain a problem. Indeed, it only suggests that the perennial problem persists, and perhaps has not gotten noticeably worse or beyond regulatory control.

There is no reason to expect MNCs and their employees not to influence the regulatory or political environment, or to insist that they don't. Indeed, this is an integral part of the U.S. political process. Organized labor is able to involve itself directly in the political and regulatory process, and represents the largest single political contributor in the country. Perhaps the sounder solution to neutralize inequalities in financial power is to limit more severely both business and labor (and others) in the exercise of their financial power in the elective and legislative process.

U.S. JOBS, INCOME DISTRIBUTION, AND
FOREIGN INVESTMENT

A further thrust of the Latin Americanization-of-the-United States hypothesis is that MNCs transfer production abroad, eliminate traditional jobs in the United States, exacerbate social problems, harm the income distribution, reduce the middle class, and undermine the power of trade unions in collective bargaining. That foreign production by MNCs contributes to structural change in the U.S. economy is not subject to debate. Some types of production are transferred abroad, others are expanded in the United States, and some jobs destroyed and some created. It can even be argued that MNCs, with their rapid international communication and responsiveness to market conditions, have accelerated these structural adjustments. Yet there are two important and related issues: Do these structural adjustments bring about the major detrimental effects outlined above, and could the structural adjustment really be avoided by controlling U.S. MNCs, except at great cost to the economy?

The Number and Skill Mix of Jobs

The "numbers game" over the impact of U.S. foreign production on U.S. employment has had several players and a long life span.[25] The principal source of disagreement is over whether the markets served from the foreign affiliates could have been retained and served by production in the United States. Spokesmen for organized labor argue that much of that production could have been carried out in the United States, thus retaining employment in the traditional U.S. jobs; the MNCs argue that competitive pressures from foreign firms force the transfer of production abroad in order to retain the market.

Given the evidence of growing competition from foreign firms in world markets and the research findings from several studies, it seems safe to conclude that a large majority of the foreign investment by U.S. firms in the 1950s and 1960s was defensive in nature, and thus should not be considered as destructive of U.S. jobs.[26] Furthermore, there is relatively strong evidence of a positive linkage between foreign affiliate production and U.S. exports.[27] Such a linkage suggests that production abroad by U.S. firms enhances the U.S. export competitiveness, and should thus be counted as job creating, even though different jobs are created from those destroyed.

Some insight into the relationship between U.S. exports and foreign production by U.S. firms, and between U.S. exports and competition from other suppliers in foreign markets, can be seen in a study by Hanan Tell. The study shows the results of calculated gains

or losses of U.S. exports vis-a-vis three other suppliers in 12 industrial countries.[28] The calculations were carried out for 16 separate
manufacturing industries, but only the sum is reported in the study.
The gains or losses were calculated from a base which assumed that
market shares of each supplier to the market remained constant from
1966 to 1970.

The data indicate that, when the growth in the 12 markets is
taken into account as well as the market shares of all suppliers, U.S.
exports actually gained relative to foreign affiliate production in that
period. This is consistent with other findings of a positive linkage
between U.S. exports and foreign affiliate production. Second, both
U.S. exports and U.S. foreign affiliates lost sales to imports from
third countries. While not definitive, this at least suggests that
competitive, or defensive, motives were a significant factor in the
expansion of foreign affiliate production in the period.

The implications of these changes in market share in foreign
markets is that the increase in foreign production by American firms
resulted in a small positive net effect on jobs in the U.S. economy.
But the skill and industry distribution of the estimated jobs created
and jobs destroyed were different.[29] Since the industries in which
U.S. export gained at the expense of foreign affiliate sales tended to
be relatively sophisticated, R&D intensive industries, such as most
chemicals, office and computing machines, electrical machinery,
professional instruments, and the like, the mixture of jobs created
tended to be weighted more heavily in the professional, scientific,
and managerial skill classes, and less heavily in the unskilled and
semiskilled operative classes, than is true for the economy as a whole.
Conversely, those industries that lost production vis-a-vis foreign
affiliates tended to be less R&D and skill intensive, such as textile
products, household appliances, other manufacturing, and the like.
These industries employ lower proportions of scientific, managerial,
professional, and clerical workers, and more semiskilled and unskilled operatives, than the average for all industries. Thus, the
estimated changes in U.S. exports vis-a-vis production by U.S.
foreign direct investment (1966 to 1970) appears to have involved a
very small net creation of U.S. jobs, and tended to shift the demand
for workers from the production worker operatives toward the professional and managerial workers. It should be noted that, while this
estimated shift in the distribution of jobs is substantial when the impact
in the industries directly affected is considered, when allowance is
made for the interindustry linkages between the affected industries
and employment in those industries that supply the affected industries
with material inputs (estimated through input-output data), the net
change in the skill structure of jobs is much smaller, although in the
same direction.

One is led to conclude that the growth of U.S. production abroad has been a relatively minor factor in labor market change in the United States. The direction of the change emanating from MNC operations is broadly consistent, however, with the larger changes taking place in the distribution of jobs in the economy as a whole. White-collar employment rose from 40.8 percent of total employment in 1960 to 45.6 percent in 1970. Blue-collar employment declined from 36.5 percent to 33.4 percent, while farm workers fell from 6.2 percent to 2.9 percent. Nonhousehold service workers rose from 8.9 percent to 10.4 percent while household workers fell from 2.7 percent to 1.4 percent.[30] The international operations of U.S. MNCs may have hastened these structural changes, but not dramatically.

Under the presumption that traditional jobs, as used by Richard Barnet and Ronald Müller, are blue-collar jobs, it is obvious that the multinationalization of U.S. business has played a minor role. Aside from the interesting fact that the decline in blue-collar workers was smaller in absolute numbers and as a percentage of the labor force than was the decline in farm workers, the major declines in the blue-collar occupations simply cannot be associated with foreign direct investment. Among the craft and kindred skills, which lost approximately 1 percent of total U.S. jobs, the major occupational losers in absolute terms were auto accessory installers, blacksmiths, compositors and typesetters, power station operators, and log inspectors— hardly occupations that are transferred to an export platform. And for the class of operatives except transport, which also lost approximately 1 percent of U.S. employment, the major absolute losers were dressmakers, clothing pressers, produce graders, and sailors and deckhands. In short, the notion that large layoffs brought about by foreign production by U.S. firms have induced major dislocations in the national labor market, and resulted in wholesale reductions in traditional jobs—even assuming that traditional jobs are somehow superior and desirable—simply cannot be seen in the relevant statistics. Obviously, some disruptions have occurred in local labor markets as MNCs shifted production abroad, or to locations elsewhere in the United States. And these disruptions are costly to the affected workers, which is the principle upon which adjustment assistance in the Trade Reform Act rests. The relative magnitude of the problem is not as great as is often presumed, however.

Union Bargaining Power

One of the genuine concerns of organized labor is that the presumed flexibility of multinationals in relocating production to other (foreign) production units in the event of a strike in a U.S. (or foreign) plant makes the strike ineffective and erodes the power of the union in the collective bargaining process. There have been some well-reported instances of this (or the threat of it) occurring outside the United States. It is not an unexpected strategy for the MNC.

But organized labor is not powerless or unresponsive. Already there have been movements toward international cooperation among unions within specific industries as attempts are made to share information, arrive at common expiration dates for bargaining agreements, carry out sympathy strikes and other solidarity actions, and the like. [31] As world markets become more integrated and the operations of MNCs become more centrally and coherently planned, these activities on the part of unions will likely increase. But there is little evidence that the multinationalization of U.S. business is about to undermine the labor movement in the United States or abroad. It might well be argued that one incentive for internationalization of U.S. MNCs is to neutralize or offset partially the bargaining power of unions in the United States.

Income Distribution and Concentration of Wealth

Another asserted result of the presumed concentration of power and production in a few large multinationals—a presumption shown above to be misplaced—is a decline in the middle class, a tendency for the distribution of income and wealth to become less equal, and a general polarization of the U.S. society into a few wealthy, powerful "managerial owners" and a massive poor, unskilled, underemployed, powerless "industrial peasantry."[32] Tendencies in this direction have accelerated with the growth of the multinational firms, it is believed.

In the first place, it is quite difficult to observe the disappearance of a middle class. If this means blue-collar, traditional workers, then as a percentage of total employment (and income) it has declined. Yet there is no reason to include an autoworker in the middle class, and exclude a computer programmer. Middle class might also mean unionized workers. Union membership has been relatively stagnant since 1968, and has declined somewhat as a percentage of the labor force. Yet, there is no particular reason to associate middle-class status with union membership.

The process by which multinationalization of U.S. firms concentrates income and wealth presumably involves an increase in the share of national income going to profits (and the compensation of manager-owners), and a decline in the share going to workers as wages and fringe benefits. Although there are major difficulties in measurement, the data on percentage share of national income do not suggest major shifts during the period of rapid growth of multinational operations, as shown below:

Period	Share of Wages and Salaries (percent)		Share of After-Tax Corporate Profits (percent)
	Economy	Private Sector	
1958–60	65.0	53.3	6.6
1964–66	63.9	51.4	7.9
1972–74	65.6	51.6	6.8

Source: Calculated from estimates in Hanan Tell, "Offshore Production by American Multinational Corporations—A Substitute for Manufacturing Activities in the U.S." (Ph.D. diss., New York University, 1976).

The total share of wages and salaries in national income therefore was higher in 1972-74 than in 1958-60. The share for the private sector was smaller, reflecting a shift toward public sector employment. After-tax profits rose significantly from the late 1950s to 1965, then fell again to approximately the earlier level in 1972-74.

These simple national income account measures do not adequately reflect the real rate of return on capital.[33] This is so because borrowing costs change through time, depreciation write-offs change as tax treatment changes, and the replacement cost of fixed capital changes with the inflation rate. Adjusting for these factors, W.D. Nordhaus finds that the genuine share of capital income in total corporate product declined rapidly from 1947 to the mid-1950s, surged up in the cyclical expansion of 1955-58, and fell through the period to 1970 (the period of internationalization of U.S. business), to remain relatively constant thereafter. Thus, neither with the raw data on income shares, nor in the more refined analysis of the real return to capital, is there any indication of a major rise in the share of property income.

The Latin Americanization of the United States should produce growing inequality in incomes and wealth, and rising poverty. But the facts indicate otherwise. Although the Lorenz curve for the measurement of income inequality among families in the United States has remained relatively constant during the postwar period, this fact masks several favorable trends. First, the age distribution of the breadwinners in the households has changed over the postwar period so that the percentage in the younger and older age groups, which traditionally are lower earnings years, has increased while the percentage in the high income years (35-55) has declined. When the

Lorenz curve estimate is adjusted for the age distribution and the average earnings in each category, there is a very significant and consistent trend toward greater equality in income distribution in the entire postwar period.[34] Furthermore, the relative deprivation of the lowest 20 percent on the income ladder looks much less awesome when adjusted to reflect the fact that this group contains a very large proportion in the 14-24, and 65 and over, age groups. When the same age distribution adjustment is applied to wealth, it is found that the age structure explains over one-half of the total inequity in wealth holdings in the United States.

Aside from these data, it also can be shown that the absolute number of people living in poverty has declined. And even when poverty is defined on a relative basis to mean those earning 50 percent or less of the median income, the share of families below this line has remained relatively constant, about 19 percent, even as the median has risen.[35]

While it is not possible to determine whether income and wealth distribution, and other social problems would have been lesser problems without MNCs, the trends should at least be examined carefully. The multinationalization of U.S. business has been accused of producing social, income, and wealth inequalities that in fact do not exist.

CONCLUSION

The multinationalization of U.S. business has been one of several forces leading to more openness in the U.S. economy, and therefore to more interdependence. This heightened openness obviously makes the coordination of policies and planning among countries more necessary, and perhaps requires a closer evaluation of the expected benefits and costs of alternative policies.

But there is little serious evidence to suggest that the growth in foreign production of U.S. firms has stolen the diversity and resilience of the U.S. economy. Production and wealth is now no more concentrated in the hands of a few large firms than in the 1950s. Indeed, there are some indications that competition is now stronger. Production jobs have not been destroyed wholesale, and the skill and occupational mix, while being affected by MNC investment, has received much greater structural pressures from other changes. Nor has the middle class disappeared, nor poverty grown more rampant, nor a major change in income distribution occurred during the period of multinationalization.

One must look elsewhere for causes of whatever Latin Americanization has occurred. The shift to a service economy, the economic and social impact of U.S. involvement in Vietnam, and the pressures of a growing population on production of primary materials all come to mind as more fundamental forces affecting the U.S. economy and its structure since the 1950s.

This is not intended to imply that policy changes with respect to MNC operations are not needed. Antitrust problems still remain. Changes in tax treatment of multinationals are needed; the accounting and reporting for foreign operations should be improved and made more transparent; and the scope of political and governmental involvement of multinationals in the United States and in host countries should be more carefully defined and surveyed. These are continuing problems and action is needed but in its own right and not to save the U.S. economy from an imagined push to destitution by uncontrollable multinational firms.

COMMENT

William Keye

I certainly do not feel qualified to critique Dr. Hawkins's excellent paper, although I must say that I agreed with most of his conclusions and found it very interesting and refreshing. I would like to make a couple of comments and perhaps ask a question of Dr. Hawkins, however.

When I first picked this paper up and read the first three pages, I became very concerned, but I was very pleasantly surprised to see his perspective and conclusions on the points that he raises in the first few pages.

As he says, he is an optimist when it comes to multinational operations. I think his paper reflects that.

I might paraphrase perhaps one of his conclusions: The world is getting more interdependent whether we like it or not. Dr. Hawkins also said that earning power overseas of U.S. multinationals is about the same as it is in the United States. I really think what he thinks about that is that it is difficult to earn a buck anyplace these days.

The one question I would like to put to him has to do with the multinational issue related to the export of jobs. As he states, the total number of jobs in U.S. multinational corporations in the United States has somewhat increased, although the mix has changed.

William Keye is Vice-Chairman, Board of Directors, Control Data.

After all, most of us manufacture overseas because we have to manufacture there in order to get that share of the market, which I think is one of the conclusions he also comes to. There are fewer manufacturing jobs here, however, and more professional or technical jobs. The question I have is, Has not the change in technology and the increase in capital investment had more effect on manufacturing jobs in the United States than multinational operations?

Dr. Hawkins. In the aggregate, that is certainly correct. Let me elaborate a bit on what I think is an appropriate perspective for the question of jobs.

There are labor market disruptions proceeding continuously as a result of the obsolescence of products, or because consumer tastes change and old products are replaced by new and better ones. And technology changes and thereby renders some existing skills obsolete. Thus there are workers, and indeed firms, coming on hard times fairly continuously. A question raised indirectly in the paper is whether one of the national policy objectives should be to maintain the existing structure of jobs. Should we be concerned to keep constant through the future, for example, the percentage of total employment in the automobile industry, or in the electricians trade?

My personal view, and probably that of most of you, is that such quota arguments must be rejected. If we are to have a dynamic and growing economy, adjustments in the structure of the economy and the labor force must occur, and to throttle such adjustments does more harm than good. What does worry me are the downward changes in the number of jobs in an occupation or locality. For example, an absolute and permanent decline in the number of autoworker jobs to exceed losses by normal attrition involves a real economic adjustment problem which the whole economy should bear.

There have been significant losses of jobs, absolutely. But Bureau of Labor Statistics data indicate that the occupations in which the major reductions occurred cannot be connected with the rapid expansion of multinational operations. The occupations which have had the greatest absolute decline had very little to do with multinationals. The paper cites some examples, such as log inspector and auto accessory installer. I would argue that the number of auto accessory installers declined because of technological change and because of the import of compact cars, which were not produced by U.S. multinationals. And this was the rule rather than the exception in the occupational data.

My main point is that we should be very concerned when real structural adjustments eliminate jobs in absolute numbers, whether the cause is foreign production by a U.S. firm or because fewer farmers are needed to pick cotton because of automation. But to then

jump to the idea that a quota or percentage of total jobs should be
maintained is not only economically unsound, but unattainable. It
simply ignores the fact that structural change is going to occur and
that structural change in a growing economy need not involve adjustment costs. They arise and should be absorbed by the community
only when there are absolute declines. My reading of the data suggests
that MNCs have been responsible for some, but relatively few, such
adjustments.

DISCUSSION

Question. Perhaps I just picked a phrase out of context. I just
happened to hear a comment that you made during your discussion
that the United States was dependent on imported automobiles. I
really do not think that we really quite find ourselves in that situation,
but I wondered if that is what is meant.

Dr. Hawkins. Sure, that is what I mean. If people buy a lot of imported automobiles, the economy in a sense is dependent.

Question. What do you mean by a lot?

Dr. Hawkins. I do not mean to imply that we could not live without
imported autos or that there is unavailable an imperfect domestic
substitute. Indeed, some of the domestic substitutes are becoming
more perfect. But by dependent I mean that a substantial share, I
believe well over 10 percent in the case of autos, of total purchases
are of imported automobiles. Dependence means that if in fact we
attempted to substitute local production for imported automobiles in
the short run, it would be significantly costly to shift production and/
or consumer preferences. In this sense, I consider us dependent,
even though it is not a life-or-death situation.

Comment. Well, foreign car imports run about 20 percent of total
auto sales today in the United States. I can assure you that our firm
would be more than happy to provide every customer with our product,
and he would be better off and the U.S. economy would be better off,
and he would have a better car. It certainly would not be costly.

Dr. Madden. Let me say as moderator that we appreciate these
objective comments.

Question. Dr. Hawkins, you say in your paper that accounting and reporting for foreign operations should be improved and made more transparent. This is rather a hot issue at the moment in the OECD [Organization for Economic Cooperation and Development] in connection with the effort to negotiate some guidelines. Do you have any comments as to what you have in mind when you say that this reporting should be more transparent?

Dr. Hawkins. Let me give a few thoughts on this. One is that concern over potential transfer pricing practices and international shifting of earnings for various objectives has become sufficiently severe, not only among MNC critics but also among the more dispassionate, middle-ground observers, that some additional reporting requirements appear to me to be inevitable. What is perhaps unfortunate is that multinationals may be faced with a multiplicity of sometimes conflicting reporting requirements. Some of these disclosure requirements may be deemed desirable by some, but not enforceable. Others may not only be deemed desirable but actually enforced or required by national regulations. It seems to me that we are now at the last possible stage to avoid duplication and inconsistency in disclosure requirements, to perhaps bring about a degree of conformity or harmony among the various proposals for reporting and disclosure which seem to be emerging from various organizations.

As a researcher, of course, I would prefer MNC balance sheet and income statement data, which are in the public domain, to disclose the sales, employment, product lines, and other operating data for each foreign subsidiary. In one sense, this is not only desirable for the academic researchers, but may be desirable from the social point of view. Certainly host countries seek it, and require it in many instances on an ad hoc and frequently uncoordinated basis. That is what I mean by transparency.

When transfer prices, payments for technology, and other kinds of financial flows occur between units in a multinational, the more transparent the payment, that is, the more disclosure, the better it is for the society in that it at least offers the opportunity (even if not utilized) to insure that the public interest is served.

I believe also that corporate secrecy to protect competitive positions is often a red herring, and sometimes does more damage than good. For example, I have held the view for some time that the issue of manipulation of transfer pricing for large tax advantages is greatly overplayed. I believe that the after-tax profits of many MNCs as a whole are very little affected by transfer prices or by the manipulation of transfer prices. If tax rates are fairly comparable across countries, as they generally are, and a firm does not use a tax haven to shift profits, the advantage of using transfer pricing to avoid taxes must be negligible. Yet to find out if this is true, companies need to air their tax payments, and provide a basis for recomputing taxes at other transfer prices. If this amount of transparency were permitted, I am convinced that the tax-avoidance, transfer-pricing issue would be relegated to the more minor position it deserves. And it might very well diffuse some of the more extreme proposals for regulation of multinational operations, which get their strength from the impression that you have got something very definite to hide—which, I may add, some of you apparently do.

In short, MNCs may be faced with a trade-off between more public reporting and much closer regulation by host (and home) countries, even though the latter may in fact be called forth by the ignorance of those who demand the regulation. My own preference is for disclosure, not regulation.

Dr. Madden. Would you favor this unilaterally or would you favor it as a cooperative move on the part of multinationals based in various countries?

Dr. Hawkins. I obviously would favor the multilateral approach. The U.S. heritage and U.S. law and regulations make U.S. firms in general more open and comfortable with financial and operating disclosure than firms anywhere else in the world. And in general, U.S. firms scrupulously pay their taxes, a practice not so evident in some European and many developing countries.

Unilateral imposition of additional disclosure requirements of U.S. firms would certainly harm their competitive positions vis-a-vis foreign-based MNCs. So this is a definite area where one would prefer harmonization of disclosure requirements. But as I noted earlier, we must worry about having several separate codes or disclosure systems when one definitive one would do.

Question. On this whole question of reporting, the Financial Accounting Standard Board [FASB], as you well know, has outstanding its proposal on reporting which would accomplish at least what I understand you to be saying is desirable from the standpoint of transfer pricing. It goes considerably further in the sense of trying to get down to profitability in terms of product lines and all the rest of it. Do you perceive definitional problems when you try to put profitability of product lines on an international basis? Is it too expensive for the benefit that would result, or do you think internationally we should go at least that far?

Dr. Hawkins. It has been years since I took cost accounting, but I obviously appreciate the problem of attributing indirect and overhead

costs to several product lines. This is frequently impossible con-
ceptually, and at best arbitrary. Placing the practice in the international context compounds the complexity and arbitrariness. One
frequently faces the problem then of allocating certain development
and overhead expenses incurred in the United States across production
units [and product lines] which may be located in several countries.
This carries with it great potential for government-to-government
conflict. I doubt that the FASB seriously addressed the problem posed
by international operations in such product lines and profit accounting.

At best, product line reporting by country would require some
harmonization between reporting practices being imposed in the United
States on a unilateral basis and those required abroad, again on a
national unilateral basis. Obviously if U.S. firms have to disclose
product line costs and profitability in the United States, it may very
well place them at a competitive disadvantage with foreign firms in
the U.S. market or in external markets, if foreign firms do not face
such reporting requirements. This is a serious problem. Note that
I did not include product line cost and profit reporting in my support
for fuller disclosure of foreign operations earlier.

Comment. The point I wanted to bring out is that there are many who
feel that the failure to make this kind of reporting is just a reluctance
to live in a goldfish bowl when there are very definitely serious problems of how to go about doing this. I think industry and commerce is
wrestling with the problems, and I hate to see them get a continual
black eye for not having addressed the problem when they are in fact
doing that.

Comment. I would like to just substantiate that statement. I think one
of the major problems that we face here is the capability of providing
the information that is being requested or at least being indicated that
we provide. There is a very technical problem in doing it. There is
a factual problem in that the definition of the information that is requested is different depending on who is asking for it and what country
it is coming from. I think there is a third problem we are all cog-
nizant of, which is that there is a very great difference between reporting information which is legitimate, which has legitimate purposes
and legitimate use and that merely serves as grist for further witch
hunts, you might say. I think this is a very deep concern to us.

We want to help, but we certainly do not want to provide information to those who are our adversaries. If there is some way in
which there can be some consolidation or some general ground, development of general ground on which the information can be provided,
a generally accepted set of definitions, this is one thing.

But to just ask for information for the purpose of getting further information is a useless exercise and an extremely costly one from the economic standpoint.

Dr. Hawkins. My only response is that in general I agree. As to providing additional grist for the witch hunters, my recommendation is that MNCs should not hire or retain witches!

I appreciate the point that duplication of reports and generation of useless data is costly and socially wasteful. On the other hand, now is the time to attempt to harmonize and coordinate the various initiatives to collect different types of information for various organizations. The potential saving in corporate effort is sizable. But the prospect of achieving such coordinated information collection is rapidly slipping away.

Comment. May I just qualify what I said here. All I am saying is this: Those who ask for information have also the responsibility of telling why they want it and how it is going to be used. I realize this means coming clean, but if they would do that, it would not be too difficult to provide the information within the capabilities that we have.

Comment. I just wanted to comment on this information issue. I am very suspicious of it. First, some of these allocations that are supposedly very difficult to make, you must make anyway. You have to allocate your income from one country—among countries—for tax purposes. You cannot avoid it. I agree there is a great deal of arbitrariness in how you do it. There is no way around that. It happens to be done in any case because you have to report your profits to each tax authority on some basis. That I think is done.

Secondly, allocating by product line is clearly difficult, and I am not sure it makes much difference to anybody's policy. Researchers love it. I would love to have it myself. I am not sure it would really affect many countries' policies.

I think much of the debate on information is really a smoke screen. I am not sure who put out the smoke screen. I think part of it hides lack of thinking on the part of policy makers as to what information they would really like and what they would do with it if they had it.

But, policy makers in developing countries are now capable of processing information they do have. What they are really asking for, and what they really need are often two different kinds of information. What they need or like is how you set your transfer prices. That has very little to do with profits by product line. They want to know how you allocate fixed costs such as overhead from the home office. They want to know what you told other tax authorities because they are terribly suspicious that when you allocate home office overhead, you allocate the same overhead to ten different countries and charge all ten the same overhead costs that you incurred in the United States.

It is this kind of information that is being sought. Some of it I think is useful for you to give because I doubt that too many of you do allocate the same overhead expense ten times, but that suspicion will not go away until the data are available. On paper the ability to exchange this kind of information among taxing authorities exists.

A lot of double taxation treaties between, say, the United States and developing countries, call for the exchange of tax information. In practice it is a very rare developing country that is able to draw on this kind of privilege that comes out of double taxation treaties, and I think in many cases it is in your interest to release some of this information.

Comment. One more brief comment on the uniformity question, Dr. Hawkins. I agree that from the standpoint of facility, the uniformity makes a lot of sense. We are having difficulty in getting uniformity even domestically. Witness, for example, the Federal Trade Commission and the Bureau of the Census, just to name two, asking for essentially the same kind of information in slightly different form.

Now if the Financial Accounting Standards Board rules go through, and you have to report to the SEC in a different form, you can see the problem of providing all these breakdowns in so many different fashions. There needs to be a realization by those who want the information that this just is not a one-way street.

NOTES

1. The point is argued forcibly in Richard Barnet and Ronald Müller, Global Reach: The Power of the Multinational Corporations (New York: Simon and Schuster, 1974), especially Chapters 9-11. The same point has been made by various officials of the AFL-CIO in the United States. See, for example, Nathaniel Goldfinger, "An American Trade Union View of International Trade and Investment," in American Labor and the Multinational Corporation, ed. Duane Kujawa (New York: Praeger, 1973).

2. The term and the line of reasoning presented here can be found in Barnet and Müller, op. cit., Chapters 9-10.

3. For example, Richard N. Cooper, The Economics of Interdependence (New York: McGraw-Hill, 1968).

4. These trends have been set out in some detail in U.S. Tariff Commission, Implications of Multinational Firms for World Trade and Investment and for U.S. Trade and Labor, Report to the U.S. Senate Committee on Finance, (Washington, D.C.: U.S. Government Printing Office, 1973).

5. Data are from U.S. Department of Commerce, Survey of Current Business 54, no. 8 (August 1974): 27. The percentages for all U.S. foreign affiliates (regardless of industry) were very similar.

6. Barnet and Müller, op. cit., pp. 229-30.

7. These data are in Betty Bock, "Concentration as an Economic Scapegoat," The Conference Board Record 12, no. 6 (June 1975).

8. See Ibid.

9. B.M. Wolf, "Size and Profitability among U.S. Manufacturing Firms: Multinational versus Primarily Domestic Firms," Working Paper no. 7420 (Louvain: University Catholique de Louvain Institut des Sciences Economiques, 1974).

10. Horst's findings are reported in F. Bergsten, Thomas Horst, and T. Moran, American Multinationals and American Interests (Washington, D.C.: Brookings Institution, 1976), Chapter 8.

11. B.I. Cohen, "Foreign Investment by U.S. Corporations as a Way of Reducing Risk," Discussion Paper, no. 151 (New Haven: Yale Economic Growth Center, 1972).

12. See Survey of Current Business 54, no. 8 (August 1974): 15. The measured rates of return were quite similar throughout the 1960s, and until 1973, when the average return (measured in dollars) on foreign direct investment jumped significantly (to 17.4 percent), mainly as a result of the depreciation of the dollar in terms of the European currencies.

13. Martin Lawrence, "The Relative Financial Performance of U.S. Multinational Firms" (Ph.D. diss., New York University, 1971).

14. Barnet and Müller, op. cit., pp. 233ff.

15. See D.G. Harris, "Some Evidence of Differential Lending Practices at Commercial Banks," Journal of Finance 28 (December 1973) and W.L. Silber and M.E. Polakoff, "The Differential Effects of Tight Money: An Econometric Study," Journal of Finance 25, no. 1 (March, 1970).

16. See D. Macaluso and Robert G. Hawkins, "The Avoidance of Restrictive Monetary Policies in Host Countries by Multinational Firms," N.Y.U. Working Paper no. 75-63 (July 1975), forthcoming in the Journal of Money, Credit and Banking.

17. M.E. Blume, J. Crockett, and I. Friend, "Stockownership in the United States: Characteristics and Trends," Survey of Current Business 54, no. 11 (November 1974).

18. A recent examination of the Berle-Means argument concerning ownership and control, and the economic implications, can be found in L. de Alessi, "Private Property and Dispersion of Ownership in Large Corporations," Journal of Finance 28, no. 4 (September 1973).

19. This possibility has been thoroughly explored by Horst. See Bergsten, Horst, and Moran, op. cit.

20. See Bock, op. cit., for a discussion of the weakness in market concentration measures as evidence of the existence or absence of competition.

21. W.F. Mueller and L.G. Hamm, "Trends in Industrial Market Concentration, 1947-1970," Review of Economics and Statistics 56, no. 4 (November 1974).

22. Raymond Vernon, "Competition Policy Toward Multinational Corporations," American Economic Review 64, no. 2 (May 1974).

23. See John H. Dunning and R.B. Pearce, Profitability and Performance of the World's Largest Industrial Companies (London: Financial Times, 1975).

24. See particularly Vernon, op. cit., and the literature cited therein.

25. Among the frequently cited literature are Stanley Ruttenberg, Needed: A Constructive Foreign Trade Policy (Washington, D.C., 1971), U.S. Tariff Commission, op. cit., Chapter 7; and Robert Stobaugh et al., "The Effects of U.S. Foreign Investment in Manufacturing on the U.S. Balance of Payments, U.S. Employment and Changes in Skills of Employment," Occasional Paper no. 4 (Washington, D.C.: Center for Multinational Studies, February 1973).

26. See particularly Stobaugh et al., op. cit.; see also, R.G. Hawkins, "Job Displacement and the Multinational Firm: A Methodological Review," Occasional Paper no. 3 (Washington, D.C.: Center for Multinational Studies, June 1972); and R.G. Hawkins and M. Jedel, "U.S. Jobs and Foreign Direct Investment," in International Labor and the Multinational Corporation, ed. Duane Kujawa (New York: Praeger, 1975).

27. See Thomas Horst, "American Exports and Foreign Direct Investments," Discussion Paper no. 362 (Cambridge, Mass.: Harvard Institute of Economic Research, May 1974); see also, R. Lipsey and M. Weiss, "Analyzing Direct Investment and Trade at the Company Level," Proceedings of the American Statistical Association (Washington, D.C.: American Statistical Association, Business and Economic Statistics Section, 1972).

28. These countries were those of the European Community, the Scandinavian countries, the United Kingdom, Canada, and Japan. The calculations were carried out for each country and for each product group. For a detailed description of the methodology and other

results, see Hanan Tell, "Offshore Production by American Multi-national Corporations—A Substitute for Manufacturing Activities in the U.S." (Ph.D. diss., New York University, 1976).

29. These conclusions rest upon the analysis in Elizabeth Webbink, "The Effect of Foreign Trade and Investment in Manufacturing on the Structure of the U.S. Labor Market" (Ph.D. diss., New York University, 1976).

30. C.B. Discesare, "Changes in the Occupational Structure of U.S. Jobs," Monthly Labor Review 93, no. 3 (March 1975).

31. See Hawkins and Jedel, op. cit., for a more elaborate description of the areas of international cooperation or organized labor.

32. Barnet and Müller, op. cit., pp. 292ff.

33. This point follows the analysis of W.D. Nordhaus, "The Falling Share of Profits," Brookings Papers on Economic Activity (Washington, D.C.: Brookings Institution, 1974).

34. See Morton Paglin, "The Measurement and Trend of Inequality: A Basic Revision," American Economic Review 65, no. 4 (September 1975).

35. On these points, see Alice Rivlin, "Income Distribution—Can Economists Help?," American Economic Review 65, no. 2 (May 1975).

4

ARE MULTINATIONAL CORPORATIONS GETTING PREFERENTIAL TREATMENT IN U.S. TAX POLICY?

Thomas Horst

John Maynard Keynes once made the tongue-in-cheek suggestion that during a depression the government should consider paying one group of workers to dig holes and another group to fill them in. I assumed that no one had taken this suggestion literally until I tried to understand U.S. income taxation. The Internal Revenue Code, as I see it now, is really a set of holes dug by tax lawyers in the government to be filled in by their colleagues in private practice. While Keynes would have appreciated the benefits of this arrangement, he doubtless would have seen the costs as well. The least of these costs is the one we must pay right now—before we can evaluate U.S. taxation of foreign-source income, we must go to some trouble to find out what that policy is.

If charity begins at home, the taxation of foreign investment income starts abroad. Every country has its own distinctive tax laws with its own statutory tax rates, depreciation allowances, capital gains rules, and so on. Fortunately for us, a researcher for the International Tax Staff of the U.S. Treasury has sifted through U.S. corporations' income tax returns, corrected as much as was possible for differences between foreign and U.S. definitions of taxable income, and calculated realized income tax rates for the many countries in which U.S. firms invest.[1] We have reproduced these estimates for 24 countries in column 2 of Table 4.1. We should note that these are average tax rates and may be considerably higher or lower than what was paid by any one subsidiary, and that they cover only manufacturing

---

Thomas Horst is Associate Professor of International Economics, Fletcher School of Law and Diplomacy, Tufts University.

TABLE 4.1

Taxes Paid to Foreign and U.S. Governments per $1,000 Taxable Income in Various Foreign Countries

Country	Realized Foreign Income Tax	Foreign Withholding Tax Rate	Dividend Payout Rate	Foreign Withholding Taxes Paid	Total Taxes Paid to Foreign Government	Tentative U.S. Tax Liability	Tentative Foreign Tax Credit	Tentative U.S. Tax Less Tentative Tax Credit	Total Foreign and U.S. Taxes Paid When Total Tax Credits are Less Than Overall Limitation
Canada	428	.15	.32	27	455	154	164	-10	445
United Kingdom	386	.0	.52	0	386	250	201	49	435
France	480	.05	.39	10	490	187	197	-10	480
Germany	430	.15	.59	50	480	283	304	-21	459
Italy	411	.05	.34	10	421	163	150	13	434
Netherlands	345	.05	.24	8	353	115	91	24	377
Denmark	325	.05	.50	17	342	240	180	60	402
Norway	458	.10	.20	11	469	96	130	-7	462
Spain	395	.15	.19	17	412	91	92	-1	411
Sweden	431	.05	.26	7	438	125	119	6	444
Switzerland	222	.05	.36	14	236	173	94	79	315
Japan	415	.10	.49	29	444	235	232	2	446
Australia	406	.15	.49	44	450	235	243	-8	442
New Zealand	487	.15	.32	25	512	154	181	-27	485
South Africa	358	.15	.62	60	418	298	282	16	434
Mexico[a]	422	.20	.47	54	476	130	169	-39	437
Panama[a]	139	.10	.52	45	184	215	107	108	292
Argentina[a]	217	.295	.89	206	423	334	357	-23	400
Brazil[a]	300	.25	.22	39	339	74	85	-11	328
Colombia[a]	473	.20	.51	54	527	129	181	-52	475
Peru[a]	321	.30	.91	185	506	297	383	-86	420
Venezuela[a]	300	.15	.55	58	358	185	174	11	369
India[a]	570	.257	.65	72	642	312b	443b	-131	511
Philippines[a]	296	.35	1.00	246	542	338	454	-116	426

130

aDeveloping country exempted from grossing up.

bGrossing-up exemption not advantageous and not exercised.

Notes: Taxes shown in column 2 and in columns 5 through 10 are per $1,000 of foreign subsidiary income using U.S. rules for calculating taxable income. Realized foreign income tax is the ratio of income taxes paid to a foreign government per $1,000 of taxable income in 1968 using the U.S. definitions and rules for measuring taxable income. Foreign withholding tax rate is the statutory withholding tax rate applied to dividends paid to U.S. share-holders. Dividend payout rate is the ratio of dividends to earnings after taxes for U.S. manufacturing affiliates in 1972. Foreign withholding taxes paid are calculated by subtracting realized foreign income taxes from $1,000, and multiplying that after-tax income by the product of the foreign withholding tax rate and the dividend payout rate. Total taxes paid to a foreign government are the sum of realized foreign income tax and foreign withholding taxes paid. Tentative U.S. tax liability equals 48 percent, the statutory U.S. income tax rate, of the tentative taxable income from the country. For the developed countries, tentative taxable income equals the $1,000 times the dividend payout rate. For the developing countries, tentative taxable income equals the $1,000 less the realized foreign income tax, the difference then being multiplied by the dividend payout rate. Thus, income from both types of country is entitled to deferral, but only that from developing countries is exempted from the grossing-up obliga-tion. When the realized foreign income tax exceeds $480, as in the case of India, grossing up is an advantage, not a disadvantage, and presumably the exemption would be waived. Tentative foreign tax credit for income from devel-oped countries equals realized foreign income tax times dividend payout rate, the product then being added to foreign withholding taxes paid. Tentative U.S. tax less tentative tax credit equals the tentative U.S. tax liability minus the tentative foreign tax credit. Total foreign and U.S. taxes paid when total tax credits are less than the overall limita-tion equal total taxes paid to a foreign government plus tentative U.S. tax less tentative tax credit.

Sources: Data on realized foreign income tax are from M.E. Kyreuz, "Foreign Tax Rates and Tax Bases," National Tax Journal 28, no. 1 (March 1975): 61–80; foreign withholding tax rates, from Price Waterhouse, Corporate Taxes in 80 Countries: Information Guide (New York: Price Waterhouse, 1973); dividend payout rates, from Survey of Current Business (U.S. Department of Commerce), August 1974, Part 2, Table 10B, pp. 20–21.

subsidiaries and not petroleum, mining, banking, or any other nonmanufacturing affiliates. Because the tax issues surrounding these
nonmanufacturing industries are so different from those in manufacturing, I will focus my remarks on the manufacturing investors.

If U.S. investors were content to reinvest all their earnings,
they would pay no additional taxes, foreign or domestic. But if the
subsidiaries pay out some of those earnings as dividends, the investors
will pay an additional dividend withholding tax to the foreign government and, perhaps, U.S. income taxes as well. Given the withholding
tax rates shown in column 3 of the table and the average dividend
payout rates shown in column 4, we have computed in column 5 the
withholding taxes U.S. investors pay as a fraction of pretax income.
We can add this withholding tax to the realized income tax in column
2 and compute the total taxes, income plus withholding, paid to foreign
governments.

We should perhaps also look at these total taxes paid to foreign
governments as they are shown in column 6. The conventional wisdom
seems to be that U.S. investors pay substantially lower taxes abroad
than they do when in the United States. This is certainly true in several
low-tax countries, such as Taiwan, Hong Kong, South Korea, and
Ireland, which we have omitted from the table because of inadequate
dividend data. But as a general rule, the conventional wisdom that
taxes are much lower abroad than they are at home is quite wrong.
In 11 out of the 15 developed countries shown in the table, foreign
governments collected 40 percent or more of the affiliate's taxable
income. Since these large developed countries are the recipients of
the vast majority of U.S. manufacturing investments, we must look
to them and not to the developing countries in drawing any broad conclusions about U.S. investments overseas.

Having described foreign taxation of U.S. investments abroad,
we can focus on the taxes paid in the United States—or, more accu-
rately, the taxes not paid in the United States. The United States
requires corporations to include foreign-source income in calculating
their U.S. income taxes, but gives a tax credit for the income and
withholding taxes paid to foreign governments. Because the foreign
tax credit almost always turns out to be as large as the income taxes
due the U.S. Treasury on foreign-source income, we end up collecting
little or nothing on the income earned by the manufacturing subsidiaries of U.S. companies.

Let us see how this works. We have shown in column 7 of the
table the income taxes that would be paid to the U.S. Treasury were
it not for the foreign tax credit. These calculations are described in
the notes to the table and are distinctive in two respects. First and
foremost, U.S. income taxes are based only on that portion of foreign
subsidiary income paid out as dividends—U.S. taxes on reinvested

earnings are deferred. The deferral of U.S. taxes until dividends are
paid was an application of the broader principle of not taxing income
until it was actually received by the taxpayer. Furthermore, while the
dividend income from developed countries must be grossed up to include the foreign income taxes deemed paid on those dividends, the
dividend income from developing countries is exempted from grossing
up. Prior to 1962, dividend income from all foreign countries was
exempted from grossing up, and the effect was to create a small and
unintended tax advantage to investing abroad. Congress eliminated
this tax preference in 1962 for developed countries, but retained it
for developing countries as an aid to development. In column 8 we
show the foreign tax credit that the U.S. investor can use to reduce
U.S. income tax payments. For dividend income the tax credit will
equal the withholding taxes plus the portion of foreign income taxes
corresponding to the dividend.

   The United States may limit, however, the total tax credit
claimed by U.S. investors. While foreign tax credits can be used to
offset U.S. taxes on foreign-source income, they cannot be used to
offset U.S. taxes on domestic income. The rationale for this limit
is simple and pragmatic: if there were no limit on the foreign tax
credit, foreign governments could increase their income and withholding taxes and know that the U.S. investors could pass the cost of
higher foreign taxes on to the U.S. Treasury. If this limit were
applied to each country separately, then U.S. investors would have
to pay U.S. taxes whenever an entry in column 8 (of the table) were
positive. But U.S. tax policy is not so strict. We allow corporations
to match their total U.S. tax liability against their total foreign tax
credit. Surplus tax credits from one country can be used to offset
deficits in others—the minuses in column 8 can be matched against the
pluses. The corporation pays additional income taxes on its foreign-
source income only if it has an overall insufficiency of foreign tax
credits.

   What all this boils down to is that the total taxes paid on income
from a particular country depends not only on the tax and dividend
circumstances in that particular country, but also on the U.S. investor's overall tax position. If the investor has sufficient foreign
tax credits overall, no U.S. taxes are paid on any of the foreign
investments, and the total tax burden is as shown in column 6. On
the other hand, if the U.S. investor has insufficient tax credits overall, then the total burden is as shown in column 10. In cases where
foreign taxes are lighter, such as the United Kingdom, Italy, and
the Netherlands, the additional taxes paid in the United States increase the total tax burden on foreign investment income. In others
where foreign taxes are heavier, such as Canada, France, and
Germany, the opportunity to use excess foreign tax credits reduces

the total tax burden on the foreign investment income. Thus, the
overall method of computing the allowable foreign tax credit serves
to raise the total tax burden on income from low-tax countries and
to lower the tax burden on income from high-tax countries.

Let us summarize what we have found so far and then move on
to the more interesting questions of what is right and what is wrong
with existing U.S. tax policy. Perhaps our most surprising conclusion
is that the tax inducement to invest abroad is usually small, not large.
Through a combination of income and withholding taxes, most foreign
governments of the larger, more developed countries tax the income
of U.S. subsidiaries at a rate approaching that in the United States.
While the low-tax countries of the Far East and elsewhere are exceptions to this general rule, they are the exceptions and not the rule.
U.S. multinationals on the whole do not reap substantial tax savings
by virtue of investing abroad. And, finally, because the United States
allows a tax credit for these foreign taxes, it collects little or no
income tax on the foreign-source income of its manufacturers.

U.S. Tax Policy: Are Reforms Needed?

Should we be satisfied with U.S. tax policy as it now stands?
If not, what can or should we do about it? What specific reforms
would serve our broad national interests? To answer these questions,
we need to set forth explicit standards by which our current policy
and any proposed reforms can be judged. My own preference and that
of most economists would be for equalizing the tax burden on U.S.
investors whether they were investing at home or abroad. This
standard has much to commend itself. Equity demands that taxpayers
with comparable incomes pay comparable taxes. And as long as we
tax corporations and not just individuals, I can see no reason for
treating multinational corporations any more gently than domestic
corporations. Secondly, the AFL-CIO has a legitimate gripe when
it claims that the U.S. tax system should not foster tax incentives
for U.S. firms to export their jobs. Whether it is true or not that
the tax system is biased against U.S. production, we cannot afford the
political cost of appearing to favor foreign workers over our own.
The illusion of discrimination may be as intolerable as the reality.
Thirdly, when the tax burden on domestic income is heavier than that
on foreign income, U.S. multinationals can lighten their global tax
burden by shifting taxable income from U.S. to foreign jurisdictions.
These shifts may be effected by selling U.S. exports to overseas
affiliates at bargain-basement prices, by not charging foreign affiliates for their share of R&D costs, and by making other such adjustments in intrafirm accounts. Although the Internal Revenue Service

(IRS) has the power to prevent flagrant abuses of the transfer-pricing mechanism, as long as foreign income is taxed at lower rates than U.S. income, U.S. investors have a tax incentive to minimize their U.S. taxable income. And that is regrettable indeed.

Having stated that the objective of U.S. tax policy should be to equalize the tax burden on the foreign and domestic production of U.S. corporations, I should add that our current tax system favors U.S. exports over most foreign affiliate production. This tax bias in favor of exporting appeared in 1971 when the Domestic International Sales Corporation (DISC) legislation was passed. Although DISC is as complex a piece of tax legislation as I have yet encountered, it serves to reduce the U.S. tax on export income from the usual 48 percent to a more advantageous 36 percent. When DISC was passed, it was justified as necessary to offset the tax advantages of the U.S. deferral of taxes on reinvested foreign subsidiary earnings. Judging from the effective tax rates on foreign investment income in columns 5 and 9 in Table 4.1, a tax reduction from 48 percent to 36 percent tilts the balance from foreign investing to exporting in all but a handful of cases. Of course, no U.S. corporation chooses exporting over foreign subsidiary production on the basis of tax considerations alone. The additional tariffs and transport costs borne by exports, the economies of scale in foreign versus domestic production, the intangible advantages of locating close to the final market, are much more important than tax considerations are. But it is worth noting nonetheless that DISC has tilted the tax advantage toward U.S. exporting and away from foreign production for the local market in most countries.

When the U.S. Treasury proposed DISC and the Congress agreed to create it rather than to eliminate deferral, they made a most regrettable choice. As a cure for the balance-of-trade deficit, the substantial depreciation of the U.S. dollar in foreign exchange markets, also initiated in 1971, was far more effective than DISC. Because of the legal and administrative costs of establishing a DISC and keeping it in compliance with law, DISC has benefited the large exporters, who could afford the costs, and not the small ones, who could not. Between half and two-thirds of the tax savings afforded by DISC have gone to corporations with more than $250 million in total assets.

If DISC unwittingly favors large exporters over small ones, that is the least of its inequities. DISC reduces taxes for U.S. exports and does absolutely nothing for manufacturers beleaguered by import competition. Why are the machinery manufacturers any more deserving of tax relief than shoe producers? Why are the high-skill jobs that typify the export industries any worthier of tax protection than the low-skill jobs in the import-competing industries? If DISC did nothing more than offset the deferral of foreign investment income,

DISC and deferral taken together favor foreign over U.S. consumers. While I am sure that this bias against U.S. consumers was not intended by the supporters of DISC or of deferral, it is the inevitable by-product of the two measures.

The remedy for these substantial inequities is simple. Eliminate DISC and deferral; make all subsidiary earnings subject to U.S. taxes, not just those paid out as dividends. Deferral has been a part of our corporate income tax since that tax was instituted in 1908. Deferral was permitted not because anyone looked far into the future and decided that this was the best policy, but because a similar deferral also was given to individuals owning shares in corporations. While consistency may be a virtue, a foolish consistency is the hobgoblin of little minds. As a matter of tax policy, deferral of foreign investment income is looking more and more foolish.

Although in theory eliminating deferral represents a major change in U.S. tax policy, in practice the consequences would probably be minimal. The net effect would be to increase the total taxes collected by the foreign and U.S. governments from their present levels to 48 percent. But as we have shown in Table 4.1, the effective rate of taxation on foreign investment income from most developed countries is already between 40 percent and 50 percent. Although it is impossible to estimate the impact with scientific precision, my best guess is that eliminating deferral would encourage U.S. investors to reduce their overseas investments by only 2 percent to 3 percent of their current values. Since overseas investments often grow by 10 percent per year or more, deferral might be eliminated without any detectable impact on aggregate foreign investment levels.

Although the impact on aggregate investment levels would be small, we still have much to gain by eliminating deferral. Perhaps the largest gain would be the least tangible one, that of showing U.S. workers and consumers that the tax deck is not stacked against them. Eliminating deferral would also reduce the attraction of investing in the low-tax countries for export back to the United States. Although the export platforms in the Far East are a small portion of U.S. investments abroad, their presence and growing significance inflames protectionist sentiment here in the United States. If we don't want to go back to the world of the 1930s with its high tariffs, tight quotas, and other trade restrictions, the least we can do is limit the artificial tax incentives to make this type of investment.

While eliminating deferral would take us a long way toward a standard of tax neutrality, two additional changes also must be made. First, taxable income derived from developing countries should be total earnings before foreign income taxes, not after taxes. The tax bill reported out of the House Ways and Means Committee in November 1975 would do just that. This may be a small step, but it is a

welcome one nonetheless. Second, corporations should be required
to compute a separate limit on the foreign tax credit for each country.
As long as excess tax credits from high-tax countries can be used,
directly or indirectly, to reduce income taxes paid to the U.S. Treasury, U.S. investors will have a tax incentive to invest in low-tax
countries rather than the United States.*

Although we have emphasized the impact of U.S. tax policy on
the choice between investing at home and investing abroad, the United
States may reap some additional benefits from the reallocation of
taxable income. Our current tax system encourages U.S. investors
to avoid the higher, U.S. taxes by lowering export prices to overseas
affiliates, by paying more than they have to for imports from their
affiliates, by allowing U.S. operations to bear the full cost of R&D
programs, or by allowing the affiliates to pay less than their fair
share of global interest costs. Although the IRS has the authority
under Sections 482 and 861-64 of the Internal Revenue Code to challenge transfer-pricing practices, the inherent ambiguity of the arm's-
length standard works to the investors' advantage. Tax avoidance can
be reduced, but not completely eliminated. The treasury has proposed
to issue new and more stringent guidelines for allocating R&D expenses and other joint costs. Since in 1973, royalties, management
fees, and all other intrafirm charges amounted to just over 1 percent
of sales by manufacturing affiliates, the treasury would seem to have
good reason to ask for more. The multinational firms have been
resisting the treasury, not only because U.S. taxes tend to be somewhat higher than foreign taxes, but also because they fear that foreign
governments will not allow new deductions from the subsidiaries'
income. While this fear of double taxation is understandable and
real, it is hard to imagine any other way of getting U.S. investors
to make fair and reasonable allocations. An important by-product of

---

*This proposal may seem to be at odds with the part of the
Tax Reduction Act of 1975 which required petroleum companies to
use the overall limitation, not the per-country. The conflict is only
superficial. The Congress was trying to limit the petroleum companies' ability to write off foreign drilling and exploration expenses
against U.S. domestic income, which the producers could do under
the per-country method, but only with difficulty under the overall
method. Since this ability to deduct foreign drilling and exploration
expenses could be limited directly rather than indirectly through the
foreign tax credit, it is possible to compel all firms to use the per-
country method without allowing the unwanted write-offs in the
petroleum industry.

the tax reforms proposed above is that they would eliminate the tax incentives to minimize U.S. taxable income. In trying to change the status quo, it is nice to have both a carrot and a stick.

Before summing up, let me discuss the foreign tax credit. The tax credit eliminates double taxation of foreign investment income by giving the host country first crack at taxing that income. As we showed in Table 4.1 above, first crack usually turns out to be the only crack. While the various tax reforms outlined above would contribute modestly to U.S. tax revenues, as long as the foreign tax credit remains, foreign governments will collect the lion's share of the taxes on foreign investment income. With foreign investment in the United States amounting to less than a fifth of the value of U.S. investments abroad, the United States gets the short end of the long stick and the long end of the short stick. Unfortunately, we have no good or effective way of redressing this imbalance. Eliminating our foreign tax credit unilaterally would not only invite foreign governments to do likewise, but would probably jeopardize the whole network of trade, tax, and financial relations among developed countries. For better or for worse, we seem to be stuck with the foreign tax credit.

In conclusion, then, we found that U.S. tax policy does not discriminate as badly against U.S. production as is often supposed. In fact, if we limit our attention to exporting, the advantages of DISC have outweighed the tax preferences for foreign investment in most developed countries. We do not, however, find DISC to be an equitable solution to the problem of neutralizing the impact of taxes on the location of investment. DISC helps U.S. exporters, but does nothing to assist the U.S. companies or their workers who must contend with growing import competition. The only remedy for these tax inequities is to eliminate DISC and the tax incentives to invest abroad—deferral, the grossing-up exemption for developing countries, and the overall method of calculating foreign tax credit. While these may seem like major reforms of U.S. tax policy, in actual practice their impact on aggregate international investment would be small. But since they would instill both the illusion and the full reality of equity and neutrality in this area of U.S. tax policy, these reforms are well worth the effort.

COMMENT

John T. Estes

Dr. Horst and I have one thing in common. I am also not a tax lawyer. Rather than engage, as this paper does, in slogans, such

John T. Estes is an attorney for Allied Chemical.

as equalizing the tax burden and tax neutrality and the emotionalism that those slogans generate, I think we should ask ourselves some hard questions.

First, will foreign competitors of U.S. enterprises be able to manufacture, free of U.S. taxes, products which the U.S. corporation will no longer be able to manufacture without paying a U.S. tax? Is this desirable?

Second, will the foreign-owned competitor take over the relevant market? Is this desirable?

Third, will U.S. labor in fact be deprived of jobs if U.S.-controlled foreign manufacturing operations are taxed only at the local foreign tax rate?

Fourth, how important is the foreign manufacturing operation to U.S. national security?

Fifth, to what extent is the ability to compete with foreign-owned enterprises impaired because the income is ultimately taxed on distributions to the domestic parent?

The paper, as I see it, raises really, or advocates, three standards of tax policy. First, it suggests we equalize tax burdens— that is, have the same burden at home as we do abroad; second, that we not encourage the export of jobs; and, third, that we do not permit the reduction of U.S. taxable income by transfer-price gimmicks and other types of chicanery.

Looking then at equalizing tax burden proposals, that of course should be a two-way street. It would mean extending to foreign operations of U.S. companies certain U.S. tax benefits now generally denied them. For example, if we are to equalize the tax burden, would the investment tax credit now extended U.S. property be extended to foreign property? If we are to equalize the tax burden, would we change the rule of nonavailability of losses incurred by foreign subsidiaries to reduce current income of the U.S. shareholder? If we are to equalize the tax burden, would we change the rule that only U.S. companies can be included in consolidated income tax returns? Last and probably most important, would the U.S. government grant a cash refund to the taxpayer in those cases where the host country tax rate is higher than the U.S. rate in order to equalize the rate on U.S. and foreign income?

The second principle advanced is that we should not export jobs. Agreed, we should not. To do that, we should not repeal DISC. In fact, DISC is designed to foster and encourage jobs. DISC should be liberalized. DISC clearly does preserve and create U.S. jobs.

The very purpose of DISC was to discourage location of U.S. operations abroad. Unilateral dismantling of DISC would seem to me to jeopardize portions of the GATT [General Agreement on Tariffs and Trade] negotiations now going on. We should get something for this chip from our foreign trading partners, particularly in the Common Market.

Next, the paper advocates elimination of deferral since this would be consistent with the principles of tax neutrality. This would mean tax discrimination, not neutrality. Deferral permits U.S. foreign subsidiaries to compete on an equal footing with foreign competition, for both the foreign market and the U.S. market. Why place U.S. companies at a competitive disadvantage?

Assistant Secretary of the Treasury [Tax Policy] Walker, has said that elimination of deferral would not be welcomed by developing countries who are encouraging U.S. investment. They grant tax reductions to encourage investment. The U.S. Treasury would find repeal of deferral disadvantageous.

We should be cautious of adoption of proposals advanced in this paper, particularly the elimination of deferral, because that would place U.S. multinational corporations in a unique and completely unviable position, because neither the shareholders of U.S. corporations nor foreign-owned international corporations are subjected to similarly accelerated taxation of undistributed earnings.

Another serious problem with these proposals is that they would involve the taxation of reinvested foreign profits that might never be received by U.S. shareholders for a variety of reasons: capital needs abroad, subsequent losses, exchange blockage, expropriation, or any other business-related reason.

Finally, elimination of deferral would ultimately lead to tax retaliation that could leave both the U.S. corporation and the U.S. Treasury worse off than before. These proposals are not in the best interest of the United States. In general, I would say that this paper fails to appreciate the intensively competitive world in which multinational corporations find themselves today.

Dr. Madden. Apparently there is a slight disagreement here. Would you like to comment, Dr. Horst?

Dr. Horst. Yes I would. It seems to me there is always going to be a problem of equity in the tax system as long as foreign governments or the United States are taxing income at different rates, and if we try to put U.S. corporations on an equal tax footing with their foreign competitors, we have to take them off an equal tax footing with firms that supply the U.S. market. So there is basically a question of which kind of equity you want to have. I believe that equity should be vis-a-vis domestic firms not vis-a-vis foreign competitors. My defense is based on why we have an income tax and who should be paying it. I would be happy to contemplate the general lowering of income tax. I am more concerned about the structure of that tax and who pays it. The multinational firms should be on the same tax footing as domestic firms.

I am willing to go the whole way in striving for neutrality. Investment tax credit is something that applies to domestic investment and not to foreign investment. The answer to the question of would I be willing to extend investment tax credit to foreign investment is, yes, I would be willing to do that. I would be willing to consider other requests for extending to foreign investment the same favorable tax treatment given to domestic investment.

Capital export neutrality is an appropriate standard, and we really should go the whole way, and not just concern ourselves with reforms working to the disadvantage of United States business. The one place that I would not go the whole way, for pragmatic reasons, is the limitation on the foreign tax credit. If you do not have any limitation on the foreign tax credit, whether it is calculated on a per-country or an overall basis, you are opening up the U.S. Treasury to a tax raid by foreign treasuries working through the multinational firms. And I prefer to put the limitation on per-country basis rather than on overall basis.

Let me just talk a little more about DISC. I would not deny that DISC creates jobs. I think the extent of the job creation has been somewhat overstated by proponents of DISC. More importantly, there are many other ways of using tax reductions to create jobs. There is investment tax credit. There is accelerated depreciation. There are general cuts in U.S. income taxes.

The question then becomes, Which one of these tax instruments are you going to use? That gets down to questions of basic equity in the tax system. Why shouldn't you try to pick out those tax reductions most effective in creating jobs or at least the most equitable in its benefits, rather than DISC, which singles out one small group of firms, gives them the lion's share of the tax benefits, and leaves all the other firms out in the cold.

That is the basis for my objection to DISC, not that I am against using the tax system to create jobs, but that I am against this particular way of using the tax system to create jobs.

Now let me, lastly, comment on the question of the developing countries' possible opposition to the elimination of deferral. I can appreciate their opposition. Our current policy does give them the opportunity to use their tax system to attract U.S. investors and attract U.S. jobs, and that really goes to the heart of the labor unions' complaint.

Now I do not think that U.S. investment abroad has been a tremendously significant factor in the export of jobs. But this is a very contentious and decisive issue in the United States. It upsets labor unions very much. I think that the least that we can do to

remove foreign investment as a political issue is to eliminate the
artificial tax incentives to invest in developing countries.

I do not think that that is going to stop firms from investing in
those countries. The labor cost differentials are very large. There
is a good competitive reason why U.S. firms might want to produce
in those countries. Surely they would continue to make those investments whether or not they had deferral, whether or not they had the
overall tax credit limitation, whether or not they had no grossing-up
exemption. There are good hard economic reasons for making those
investments. All I am saying is that I do not see why those incentives
should be augmented by tax incentives.

                                    DISCUSSION

Question. I certainly could not improve on Mr. Estes's comments.
But I would like to add a footnote to what he said. That is that it seems
to me that one of the basic problems with the kind of presentation we
heard is that it seems to ignore completely the competitive situation
in which the United States increasingly finds itself in the world.
Some of these proposals, like those that come out of the Treasury
Department of a legislative or administrative nature, demostrate a
great inconsistency in what is supposed to be a U.S. foreign economic
policy of encouraging foreign investment as well as foreign trade.
It is highly important for practical reasons never to lose sight of
where we stand competitively.

According to about seven authoritative sources that I know of,
it seems unmistakable that governments of various other countries,
industrial countries, either tax not at all or tax at greatly reduced
rates the foreign-source income of their own MNCs.

In Switzerland there is no Swiss tax on foreign-source income
and to the same extent or to a lesser degree, one can say the same
think about Japan, Germany, France. So in the increasingly competitive world we live in, taxation as a matter of competition must
increasingly be taken into account.

Dr. Horst. I think there are just factual questions that maybe we
differ on. First of all, how large a competitive impact would these
changes in U.S. tax policy have on U.S. firms and on their ability
to compete in foreign markets?

My judgment from looking at the tax figures in Table 4.1 suggests that the elimination of deferral, and other changes I favor,
are not the draconian steps that I think you are interpreting them to
be. There is also the issue of what it is we want to imitate in the
international system. Foreign governments have looked to the United

States for a number of years as a leader in taxation. They have emulated the Internal Revenue Code and Internal Revenue Service procedures. This has been all to the good.

They have upgraded their procedures for collecting taxes, made tax systems more equitable, and put things out in the open, rather than behind closed doors. We can see this in areas like transfer pricing, where I think that our action on that front has been imitated in other foreign countries like Germany.

It is a sad day when we imitate Switzerland rather than trying to set an example, which I think we have some reason to expect that foreigners might follow.

Question. My position simply is instead of further unilaterally adding handicaps to our competitive position in the world, why not push for the fair shake that we say that we are seeking in international negotiations?

Dr. Horst. Would you be very optimistic for substantial progress through international negotiations? Does it strike you as an area in which the United States could effectively move on a multilateral basis? Because if it were, I think I would agree with you that it is something that we should do on a multilateral basis instead of a unilateral basis.

But I am under the impression that this is an area in which a number of foreign countries would find it difficult to move at this time. Maybe ten years down the road their revenue services and tax laws will be at a stage where one can imagine successful multilateral agreements. I just do not really see we are at that point right now.

Dr. Madden. Could I interject just to follow that question? Looking at the distribution of world income, is it so clear as an assumption that neutrality as between domestic and international investment is an appropriate choice of a criterion for the richest country in the world, presumably, to take with respect to its corporations? I do not wish to argue the case but I wonder if that is a legitimate question to raise.

I also wonder whether that criterion is not open to challenge on the part of other developed countries as well, and therefore, following the other countries in favoring foreign investment is not at all a deterioration in the leadership of the United States, but on the contrary, a catching up to the implicit leadership of countries with longer experience in international relationships. Now, that is a very favorable picture of the point. But I put it in those favorable words in order for you to respond.

Dr. Horst. I am not sure I understand what you think the standard is.

Dr. Madden. Are you saying neutrality between domestic and foreign investment is the appropriate criterion for the United States? I am asking this question: If you consider the income distribution in the world, would not a better criterion for taxation—not only for the United States but also for other developed countries—be to favor foreign investment over domestic investment?

Dr. Horst. Well first of all, I think that the defense of the basic standard on neutrality and equity as I interpret it is very much a part of U.S. approach to taxation, that income taxes are to be in proportion to ability to pay, that in calculating ability to pay we not only look at income from domestic investment, but income from foreign investment. And it is this notion of ability to pay that leads to the standard of neutrality and equity that I have set forth. So at the very least, when we move to other standards, standards that favor investment in foreign countries rather than the United States, we have to move away from this basic cornerstone of U.S. tax policy.

Furthermore, I am rather reluctant to use the tax system as a foreign aid mechanism, which is essentially what you are proposing. When you suggest that we should encourage firms through the tax system to invest abroad to spur development, you are essentially saying we ought to use the tax system as a way of disguising foreign aid. You are trying to use the tax system to redistribute some of the benefits of investment from the United States to foreign countries.

Dr. Madden. Would you prefer foreign aid directly?

Dr. Horst. I would prefer a system where I was fairly sure to whom the aid was going. Under our current tax system, a lot of the aid, if you will, that is implicit in the tax system is going to other developed countries, to Saudi Arabia and other oil countries in the Mideast, and it is not typically going to Bangladesh and the really poor countries of Asia and Africa. So I do not think that the tax system is very efficient as an aid-channeling mechanism.

Question. I would like to follow this along, leading to a question and making a couple of comments. I have been surprised that we are talking of the U.S. national interest and not of tax minimization by multinational corporations; why, Professor Horst, you take neutrality as really being the key criteriion, as Dr. Madden mentioned. I know certain people in the treasury talk about it, and I really believe it is a very conceptual and provincial concept in terms of the hard-nosed interest of the United States as a nation in a highly competitive world. You missed a very strong reason for believing this is the best approach. Is not this the question—is not the question,

What do other nations that compete with the United States do for their exporters, not just businesses and corporations, but their workers in export industries, and what do other competitor nations do for their companies that are engaged in foreign investment? The answer is they have very strong export incentives. That is one of the main reasons we have DISC—regardless of what treasury put into its papers—to compete with the European Common Market and others at this time. On deferral, it has been the tax system of the world. Maybe that is wrong. Maybe we should change deferral. I am puzzled about why, in a pragmatic world, people who are not tax theorists like Stanley Surrey would really feel we ought to approach it on a tax neutrality concept, looking only to the United States with blinders on, instead of seeing what would happen. I think there may be a number of U.S. multinationals who—not out of spite or as a threat or anything else—might elect not just to go to tax havens like Panama or some of those places, but to Switzerland or Holland. The relatively Socialist government of Holland favors its multinationals, and goes much farther than our concept of deferral.

In determining U.S. policy, could you give us a little more backing for tax neutrality versus what is really going to happen if we do get rid of DISC and deferral?

Dr. Horst. The notion of neutrality that I have set forth, and I realize that is not everybody's definition of neutrality, is based on equity, on the impact of the location of investment, on what is fair to U.S. workers, and finally on the consequences for transfer pricing.

A very dangerous road for the United States to start down, and I think it did start down when it instituted DISC in 1971, is to try to emulate the tax-cutting practices of foreign governments. Unfortunately things never stop there, but rather what we do just gives additional incentives to foreign governments to try to outdo DISC, and then when the United States finds that DISC is no longer doing what it was supposed to do, there will be pressures to do better than DISC, to give 100 percent deferral rather than 50 percent deferral. If we could negotiate an effective multilateral convention for the taxation of foreign investment income, that would be just fine with me.

Question. Is this what OECD [Organization for Economic Cooperation and Development] is supposed to be doing?

Dr. Horst. Yes. What I worry about is whether and when that is going to happen. If that does not happen, what should the United States be doing unilaterally, given that all it can do is move unilaterally? One of the reasons why I do not want to repeal the foreign tax credit, is because the repeal would frustrate international cooperation on the negotiation of international treaties and conventions.

I am not trying to pick a fight with the foreign governments. But all I want to do is to find ways that the United States, if it cannot get multilateral movement, can move unilaterally to protect our legitimate interests.

Question. I think you are probably getting, expectedly, a sort of negative reaction from this group based on intuition that disagrees with your conclusion. I do not react negatively to the conclusion, partly because I do not think it will make much difference—what you indicated yourself.

I do have another negative reaction, and that is an argument from an economist that starts with the principle of equity or fairness. Let me try taking a different tack, and I am not sure it comes out with a conclusion that would make this group any happier.

Let us take your premise that it is really the U.S. national economic interest that we ought to start with. That has got nothing to do with fairness. If that is the starting point, I think an economist— (not being an economist, you will have to correct me—I do not know why noneconomists get the job of writing papers about economic effects) would start by asking, would the tax legislation lead investors to make decisions in the national interest concerning which you would measure the foreign investment effects by asking whether the foreign exchange earnings from foreign investment would be large enough to allow the United States to buy from abroad, by importing more goods than it would have produced if that capital had been invested in the United States? That seems like a reasonable way of starting on a purely economic criterion without any concept of equity or fairness.

Now that is going to lead down a complicated path. I am not sure where the answer will come out. I think it may come out less attractive to this group than where you went. It seems like an effective way to start from the economic point of view.

The next step is to expand beyond economics and ask whether it is politically feasible—what the international implications would be, whether there would be retaliations such that the economic benefits we thought we got would be wiped out. I guess that is not really an economist's question; it is a political scientist's question.

Then, I would go to the step, Is it fair? Is it equitable? I suspect we begin to raise questions about whether really we are happy maximizing U.S. economic interests as objectives. That is where fairness comes in. We might try some other objectives, such as maximizing world income, maximizing something else, to see whether we reach different conclusions, and then pose the choice for politicians to decide.

<u>Dr. Horst</u>. Let me make a couple of comments. One of the standards
I passed over, believe it or not, was even less favorable to multinational business, and that was the standard Peggy Musgrave advocates,
called national neutrality. The bottom line there is, you ought to
eliminate foreign tax credit as well as deferral.

That conclusion derives from a very straightforward calculation
of what is right for the United States, and it bases that calculation
not only on the income that the multinationals earn from their investment, but also the taxes collected by the U.S. Treasury. I think that
is the conclusion of what is in it for the United States.

<u>Dr. Madden</u>. U.S. government, you mean?

<u>Dr. Horst</u>. No, I think the definition of U.S. welfare to be maximized
is taxes collected by the government plus income earned by multinationals.

<u>Dr. Madden</u>. I see.

<u>Dr. Horst</u>. And that standard leads to the conclusion that you ought
to repeal the foreign tax credit and not just deferral.

The standard that you suggested at the end, maximizing international gains from investment, leads to the standard that I am proposing, of equalizing the tax burden on investment regardless of the
location of the investment. This standard ignores to whom those
taxes are being paid. Is it the U.S. government, or is it a foreign
government? The more liberal standard that you suggested comes
out at the same place I do.

I think the only way that you come out in favor of either the
current tax system or something that does not tax foreign investment
income at all is a standard that would say that U.S. multinationals
ought to be put on the same tax footing as their foreign competitors.

<u>Question</u>. It seems to me that we should go back to some basic con-
cepts; this might clear up things in the first place. I would like to
point out that what are determined as earnings of U.S. corporations
are the consolidated earnings reported on the balance sheets. That
is an arithmetical accumulation, more or less adjusted, of the earnings of U.S. components of the group. Those are not U.S. earnings.
They are not the earnings of the U.S. parent. The earnings of the
U.S. parent only develop when it has utilization of the earnings of
the components from overseas. Those earnings are not distributed
at the will of the U.S. parent. Many of us wish they could be. But
they are not. The distribution depends to a great extent on the
minority shareholders, on the host country, and on a number of other

considerations. So that those earnings, although they appear in the reported statements, are not available to the U.S. parent.

The second thing is that control by virtue of ownership is considered to be absolute control. You may have the absolute control of your operations overseas up to the point of distribution of earnings, and there it stops. You do not have control of those earnings.

The third point is that earnings as reported on the U.S. earnings statement are a computation according to U.S. accounting standards as determined by the IRS and the SEC, largely, and mainly the SEC.

This results in some distortions. I can tell you from our own experience, we have one overseas operation, a major one, which in its own currency, according to legally required determination of earnings in that country, will be deficit by over a million dollars. Our U.S. reporting will show a U.S. profit of $2 million. Therefore, you tax that, you are taxing nonexistent earnings. I think there are these practical considerations that are rather important.

Dr. Horst. Very briefly, I believe that the Internal Revenue Code has a provision for branch earnings blocked by the host government.

Comment. Pardon me, these are not branch earnings. These are separate subsidiaries.

Dr. Horst. What I am saying is I would presume if deferral were eliminated, and earnings were blocked, the same rule would apply to them as currently applies to blocked branch earnings. It seems to me if dividends were blocked, U.S. taxes would not be due until they were unblocked.

Comment. Out of this debate that is based upon Table 4.1 (like a good many other people around here, I am not a tax lawyer, but I do know), there is no way that you are going to pay German taxes of 43 percent. There is no way you are going to pay Japanese taxes of 41.5 percent. The basic data from which you draw your conclusion are, at least in a few instances I know something about, erroneous.

Dr. Horst. What would you suspect the rates are?

Comment. For German taxes, with 60 percent payout, it would be 56 percent; Japanese taxes would be 46 percent before dividend payout—just to pull a couple of them off the list. There are others I could go into. The basic data are suspect.

Dr. Horst. If you have better data for me, I would be happy to see them. I thought it was important to assemble what data there are.

These data were compiled by the International Tax Staff of the U.S. Treasury, and income tax data are 1968 data, and the rates that you are quoting may be more recent rates; I do not know.

Comment. The German rates were in effect in 1958.

Comment. They have adjusted for different definitions of income. You would not expect to come out with the same rates.

Dr. Horst. These are not statutory rates. These are realized rates. If accounting rules differ, the measure of the realized tax rate would differ.

Comment. Sorry, gentlemen, but the definition of income in Germany is not that much different from the United States.

Question. After you take into account accelerated depreciation?

Comment. Yes. I am sorry, the data are faulty.

Question. I would like to raise a question of equity. Given the fact that the vast majority of U.S. foreign direct investment is for the purpose of serving local markets in host countries and that the vast majority of those investments involve local indigenous personnel producing for those markets; that in very significant degree those facilities are even financed by local financial resources within the host country markets; that production is in competition with local competitors within those markets; that the purpose of the investment is at least in part to get return on investment for U.S. shareholders so that it will at some point in time be repatriated (as in fact better than 50 percent of it is in a typical year)—given that set of conditions, can you not make a case at least as well that the concept of equity should be equity within the host country market between the U.S. firm and the foreign competitor as distinguished from equity for domestic investment and foreign direct investment in the United States?

Dr. Horst. You certainly can make a case for it. And a number of writers have. I personally do not think it is the appropriate standard of equity. I think the standard should be on the basis of the U.S. taxpayers' ability to pay. That is the notion that has been incorporated into the U.S. income tax laws.

Certainly, as you say, a case can be made. I do think, on the other hand, one can go a little bit further to look not only at where labor and financing come from for foreign investment, but also where technology comes from. In many cases the technology comes from the United States, which gives rise to the question of whether or not the U.S. Treasury might have a tax claim on that income. It is not a tax claim that they are currently exercising, but if you open up the question of what really would be a fair international distribution of the tax revenues from foreign investment income, I doubt you would come out with foreign governments collecting something on the order of 90 or 95 percent of tax revenue from foreign investment income, and the United States getting the residual.

NOTE

1. M.E. Kyreuz, "Foreign Tax Rates and Tax Bases," National Tax Journal 28, no. 1 (March 1975): 61-80.

THE POWER OF MULTINATIONAL ENTERPRISES IN DEVELOPING COUNTRIES

Raymond Vernon

"Guard yourself against the Standard Oil
Trust and all who are in league with it."

From a speech by Dimitrie A.
Sturdza, Prime Minister of Romania,
delivered in 1904

Although multinational (or transnational or international)
enterprises come in all shapes and sizes, they generate some fairly
common reactions in the developing countries in which they operate.
One reaction associates the multinational enterprise with power—
power of a sort and on a scale that leaves commentators in the host
country uneasy and concerned. Multinational enterprises, according
to this perception, are in a position to shape the consumer demands
of any such country in which they operate, to determine the industrial
technology that will be used in satisfying these needs, to avoid the
restraints that governments seek to apply on business, to bolster
the political position of the classes that the multinational enterprises
favor, and to magnify the diplomatic influence of their home countries.

To most managers of multinational enterprises, this reaction
generally seems puzzling and wrong-headed. From their point of
view, the job at hand has been to use a pool of resources—money,
patents, trade names, knowledge, and organization—in the execution
of a global strategy. With the firm's resources spread out all over
the world and the firm's threats and opportunities similarly dispersed,

Raymond Vernon is Director of the Center for International
Affairs, Harvard University.

the managers have seen themselves as exposed and vulnerable. As
they see it, the sovereign states can apply arbitrary force with little
or no restraint. With impunity, they can break previous commitments,
raise taxes, cancel patents, nationalize properties, and expropriate
assets.

How to reconcile these two views? Do multinational enterprises
represent an overweening and uncontrolled force to which the governments of developing countries have been obliged to give way? Or is
the impression of managers closer to reality? What I shall suggest in
the analysis that follows is that the debate, when stated in these terms,
runs the risk of encouraging a dialogue of the deaf. The two rival
perceptions both have elements of validity; but both are misleading
unless they are considered in a much larger framework.

THE IMPERFECT FIT

The disconcerting fact is that there is an imperfect fit between
a political world composed of responsible nation-states and an economic world in which multinational enterprises play a leading role.
The imperfect fit between the two systems generates stresses and
strains that lead each to regard the other at times as a source of
unbridled power, potentially dangerous to its interests.

Consider the relationship from the viewpoint of leaders in the
developing countries. Those located in Asia and Africa for the most
part formally acquired their political independence after World War II.
Those in Latin America, although politically independent much earlier,
nonetheless reached a new stage of national self-awareness about the
same time. At the very time when these developments occurred,
however, spectacular improvements in international communication
and in the international transportation of people and goods were
strengthening the links between these new countries and the rest of
the world. Trade and investment were growing faster across international borders than within the national economies of the developing
nations.[1] The circulation of foreign periodicals, books, music,
movies, and television programs was rising faster than those of
national origin.[2]

One thing that has troubled the developing countries in this
process is the risk that the industrialized countries might be reestab-
lishing their old political or military hegemonies through these new
interdependencies. Individuals and enterprises in the higher-income
areas had a palpable starting advantage over those based in the
developing areas. In industry, the professions, culture, and the arts,
the developing countries seemed doomed to a new dependency.

In many ways, the growth of multinational enterprises has epitomized the new threat. These enterprises, headquartered in foreign countries, have come to account for, say, 30 or 40 percent of the total output in developing countries and an even larger proportion of their industrial output. The giant strides in international transportation and communication have strengthened multinational enterprises not only by allowing them to project their products and services to distant places, but also by allowing them to control their distant operations with greater efficiency. In the 1950s or 1960s a parent that sought to maintain some sort of control over remote operations had often run up against the uncertainties of international travel and communication. But then the commercial aircraft, the radio, and the computer rapidly helped to ease that constraint. As a result, as the data were graphically demonstrating, multinational enterprises could spread their reach a good deal further in the 1970s than in the 1950s.[3]

In what sense was the spread of the multinational enterprise to be regarded as a threat? Consider the nature of a multinational enterprise. Such an enterprise is a cluster of corporations, not a single company. The cluster contains units of diverse nationalities, linked together by a parent with a distinct nationality of its own. To the extent that the collective resources of the system are applied to some common strategic purpose, the parent unit generally takes the leading role in defining the purpose and allocating the collective resources. This structure, operating in a world of separate nation-states, offers certain points of conflict with the nation-state system.

One ineluctable fact in a system of nation-states is that the objectives of different states are often mutually incompatible. When one unit of a multinational enterprise is in one of the differing states while another unit is located in the other, trouble can ensue. When the U.S. government lays down regulations that oblige a U.S. parent to withdraw funds from its British subsidiary in London, sterling may suffer while the dollar may be given a boost. When the Mexican government directs the Mexican subsidiary of a U.S.-owned automobile company to produce components for export to affiliates in Detroit and Sao Paulo, Mexican workers may be helped while U.S. and Brazilian workers suffer. When the U.S. government instructs a U.S. firm not to permit its Mexican subsidiary to export to Cuba, U.S. policy may be helped but Mexican policy may be hurt. When the Saudi Arabian government forbids Aramco (a partnership of four U.S. companies) to ship oil to its parents' bunkering stations that serve the Seventh Fleet, the interests of the United States are placed in jeopardy. In brief, as long as the units of a multinational enterprise are located in different countries, there is always the risk—and often the reality—that the interests of one nation will be served at the expense of another.

When the interests of states conflict, there may be some energetic hauling and pulling on the different units of a multinational enterprise. In that kind of situation, the developing countries assume that they generally are on the losing end. Though the evidence on this point is not at all clear, still these countries think of themselves as relatively weak.

Even when the pressures of other countries are not involved, multinational enterprises are thought at times to present a special problem for developing countries. Such enterprises are in the business of deploying their global resources of money, knowledge, and organization in ways that serve their own interests. In the ordinary course, their activities may be quite compatible with those of the states in which they operate; all may conceivably be benefited. But conflicts of interest cannot be ruled out. The enterprise that shifts its resources from one country to the next in response to its strategic needs may, quite incidentally, be contributing to one economy at the expense of the other.

Of course, an enterprise that operates wholly within the borders of a single country—a national enterprise—can be presumed to be just as devoted to the pursuit of its own interests as any multinational enterprise. But in terms of their social accountability and their social legitimacy, national enterprises have only one nation to satisfy. By contrast, the multinational enterprise confronts no public entity charged with weighing its contributions and legitimizing or controlling its operations; each nation will evaluate that part which falls within its jurisdictional reach, without concerning itself with the effects on other nations or on mankind at large. Therein lies the imperfect fit.

It may be, however, that the bitterness with which the multinational enterprise is denounced in some sectors of the developing countries stems from still another factor. Many leaders in those countries, like leaders everywhere else, are struggling with a pervasive sense of doubt and misgiving about their national performance. Where economic growth and industrialization have actually occurred in the developing world, they seem to have generated new problems no less disconcerting than the old: on the economic front, unemployment in the cities and new extremes in income distribution; on the political front, unrest in some areas, authoritarianism in others. As doubts have developed whether progress of any real sort was being achieved, the tendency to question every established institution has grown. The multinational enterprise—powerful, expansive, and foreign—has been an obvious target for the new wave of concern.

Elements of Conflict

The sense that multinational enterprises represent a source of
uncontrolled power generally gets expressed in much narrower and
more concrete terms than I have so far suggested. The list of worries
that representatives of developing nations express from time to time
concentrates on several problem areas.[4] These include the choice of
products and services supplied to the consumer in the developing
country and the choice of technologies used in the country.

The Choice of Products

Anyone who has traveled in developing countries is aware that
Coca Cola, Datsun, Hoffmann-La Roche, Philips, and Martini-Rossi
are almost as familiar in the cities and villages of Asia, Africa, and
Latin America as in their home precincts. But, the leaders of developing countries, like many leaders in the industrialized countries,
are inclined to question whether their national interests are greatly
served by a heavy emphasis on these soft drinks, automobiles, tran-
quilizers, radios, and aperitifs.

On this issue and on others relating to the multinational enterprises, the key policy question at times is not whether foreign-owned
enterprises should exert so much influence on the local economy but
whether any privately owned enterprise, multinational or national,
should exercise that influence. Many leaders in the developing countries would agree—indeed, would insist—that their own national enterprises were no more likely to improve the mix of goods and services
than were multinational enterprises; for them, hopes are pinned on
the performance of state-owned enterprises, not of national privately
owned firms. Although the record of state-owned enterprises in the
development and adaptation of products and services is far from
impressive so far,[5] such enterprises are commonly seen as the
answer to the problem of providing a more socially useful mix.

Nevertheless, concern over the products offered by multinational
enterprises is related in some respects to their foreign origin. Assuming that soft drinks, automobiles, and radios in some form or
other may be a good thing, the question is commonly asked whether
it is good for the developing countries to have their needs satisfied
by the particular products and services that multinational firms
design—to have their soft drinks in the form of Coca Cola, their
automobiles as designed by Datsun, and their radios out of the minds
of Philips' engineers. One problem with the products of multinational
enterprises is that they often command premiums over competing
local goods in the markets of developing countries. Such premiums
are not always based on objective measures of performance, such as

reliability and efficiency; they are thought to be based, in some cases, on the more effective use of trademarks and advertising. [6] Where that is the case, leaders in the developing countries see no social purpose served in paying the premium.

The concerns of developing countries regarding the product mix do not involve only questions of unnecessary cost; they also are linked to the nature of the products themselves and, through that link, to questions of employment and balanced growth. It is commonly assumed that the products promoted to the poor by multinational enterprises tend to use relatively more capital and less labor than the products that the poor would otherwise consume. [7] Homespun cloth is compared, for instance, with factory-spun cloth of cotton or synthetic materials; thatched roofs are compared with roofs of galvanized or aluminum sheet; plastic pails with clay pots. The peasant's preference for these manufactured products, according to the argument, makes no sense in social terms; it does not satisfy his material needs and it puts a strain on the process of economic development.

Judgments over the welfare implications of competing mixes of consumer goods involve some profound questions, which often get answered according to the social and economic background of the beholder. When the Manhattan Indians sold Manhattan island to the white settlers for a quantity of wampum, the white settlers may conceivably have exploited the Indians by applying their superior knowledge. But the peasant's preference for tin roofs over thatch and for aspirin pills over coca root does not seem to fall in the Manhattan island category; it appears to stem from the peasant's perception of what constitutes superior performance. One observes, for instance, that preferences of this sort seem to surface both in Brazil, where the peasant is exposed to the multinational enterprise, and in Tanzania, where he is shielded from it.

On issues such as these, it should be emphasized, the spokesmen for developing countries are characteristically not drawn from the ranks of the poor for whom they speak. They tend to be writers on the more cosmopolitan newspapers, professors and students, poets and novelists, and politicians. In some measure, therefore, the preferences of the spokesmen represent the perennial battle between the classes, the struggle over the choice between Beethoven and the Beatles, proteins and calories, Heineken beer and Coca Cola. The problem, when stated in these terms, is a universal one, relevant to all nations including those that provide a home base for multinational enterprises. It is one that involves the multinational enterprises only in the sense that such enterprises contribute to the satisfaction of mass wants, including some wants that appear at times shoddy and antisocial.

The Choice of Technologies

The subsidiaries of multinational enterprises in developing countries are found clustered in the more capital intensive industries of the country. The subsidiaries of multinational enterprises also tend to establish larger installations than their local competitors, a fact which usually gives them an edge in terms of efficiency; but larger scale also goes hand in hand with greater capital intensity. In spite of labor-using adaptations that subsidiaries in developing countries characteristically institute in goods handling and assembly operations, their installations still appear to be more capital intensive than those of their local competitors. [8]

There is evidence that, under the influence of the engineers, some subsidiaries of multinational enterprises indulge a nonrational preference for capital intensive facilities in developing countries, not justified in terms of local factor costs. [9] But this unfortunate bias seems to be shared by national firms and even state-owned firms, provided they are big enough and affluent enough to indulge it. [10] Moreover, the governments of the developing countries themselves, by insisting on the "latest and the best," have been known at times to override the preferences of multinational enterprises for less capital intensive equipment. So weighing the causes of the bias is not very easy.

The problem of developing and applying the right technology, however, runs deeper. Most of the work on the development of new industrial processes is done in the environment of the industrialized countries, an environment with relatively cheap capital, expensive labor, and well-developed infrastructure. This is all very well for processes that serve the needs of the industrialized countries; but it is less than ideal for the developing world. The subsidiaries of multinational enterprises, pursuing the economic principle of least effort, tend to select their production processes from the existing menu of technologies. Their choice, therefore, tends to be determined by the conditions of the industrial countries. [11]

Finally, there is a problem more subtle than the others, adumbrated in my earlier references to plastic pails and clay pots, thatched roofs and aluminum roofs. The growing edge of modern industrialization, it may be, pushes developing economies in the direction of more capital intensive activities, at a rate that contributes to unemployment even as it adds to total growth. Multinational enterprises, as various studies repeatedly confirm, are represented most strongly at the growing edge of the developing economies. [12] Their clustering in the growing industries may speak well for their contribution to the growth of the developing countries, if growth is measured in terms of aggregate output. But it also identifies them with some disconcerting problems that accompany such growth.

Control at the Borders

At bottom, developing countries allow foreign-owned subsidiaries to settle in their territories because the countries assume that they will derive some advantages from the relationship. The advantages they usually foresee and commonly realize are manifold: increased employment, increased exports, and increased taxes lead the list. Whatever the advantages may be that are associated with the foreign-owned subsidiary, however, there is also a sense that the subsidiary cannot be quite as effectively monitored and controlled as a national enterprise engaged in comparable activities.

The reasons for that expectation have already been suggested. Other governments, especially home governments, are in a position to put pressure on the enterprise, sometimes in ways that may be hurtful to the developing country. On top of that, the subsidiary is seen—rightly seen—as a unit of a larger multinational system with goals and strategies of its own; and some of these at times could prove inimical to a developing country's interests. Because of factors such as these, three consequences are generally thought to ensue: the host country may not receive all the taxes to which it is entitled; the balance of payments of the country may be subject to special threats, short-term and long; finally, most important of all, the commitment of the multinational enterprises to continued operations in the country may be weak.

The materials that explore and evaluate each of these allegations are quite overwhelming, and no brief summary can do them justice. Yet some generalizations are appropriate.

The Payment of Taxes

Managers of multinational enterprises, like the world at large, take no great pleasure in the payment of taxes. Accordingly, the financial strategy of multinational enterprises is commonly shaped with an attentive eye to opportunities for tax avoidance. Some of this tax avoidance is achieved by decisions of the enterprise that redistribute profits between competing tax jurisdictions. The redistributions, in general, take two forms. One means of tax avoidance is to divert profits to a tax haven company, located in a jurisdiction such as Panama or Bermuda. The function of such a company is to interpose itself in transactions between affiliated units located in other tax jurisdictions and to absorb some of their profit. Most multinational enterprises have the facilities for engaging in such practices, having set up the necessary subsidiaries in tax haven areas. But according to a compilation performed by the U.S. Treasury Department, only about one-eighth of the foreign profits of U.S.-based companies find their way into tax haven companies. [13]

The second form of tax avoidance is achieved without necessarily using a tax haven company, by setting the price on products or services that move between operating affiliates at levels that achieve some desired redistribution of profits. The profit shifting that is achieved by appropriate price-setting policies presents an exceedingly tough problem to the tax authorities of any country, however well trained and sophisticated they may be. As a rule, such pricing decisions do not involve fraud or evasion; they usually relate to situations in which a wide range of discretion exists. What, for instance, is the appropriate price for the subsidiary's use of a parent's trade name, for access to a central research laboratory, or for a license to a patent? And how are products to be priced when the full cost differs enormously from the marginal cost and when no independent market is available?

When multinational enterprises have some leeway in the setting of transfer prices, the developing country may be the loser; but the opposite outcome a priori is just as plausible. With corporate tax rates in the United States generally a little higher than in most developing countries, [14] there is a presumption in favor of keeping the funds out of the United States. Some of these funds may be sequestered in safe haven countries, but the data suggest that such amounts are relatively small. For all the rest, questions of access and convenience presumably determine the distribution. On top of that, in the early years of operation of a new subsidiary, it is common practice among multinational enterprises to price their goods and services to the new subsidiary on the low side, in order to allow the local manager to absorb his start-up costs more readily and to avoid an early sense of failure. [15] (When the growth of the subsidiary levels off, on the other hand, there is apparently a tendency for the multinational enterprises to lean in the opposite direction.)

Since transfer pricing is an area of decision making in which the sovereign state appears at the mercy of the multinational enterprises, it has been a subject that has understandably evoked strong reactions in developing countries. The reaction has been particularly strong at times because multinational enterprises have sometimes demonstrated how important their price-setting discretion can be. In the 1960s, for instance, Colombia set ceilings on profit remissions, fixing the ceiling at 14 percent of invested capital. The ceiling formula fell with particular weight on pharmaceutical companies, whose capital consisted mainly of development costs expended in the United States, plus patents and trademarks. On top of that, the Colombian government was imposing price controls on pharmaceuticals, setting prices that were related to production costs. Spurred on by these regulations, multinational enterprises increased the prices of their intermediate products to Colombian subsidiaries and licensees, hoping both to secure higher prices and to withdraw larger profits.[16]

Whatever the facts, multinational enterprises are discovering that the taxing authorities of all jurisdictions, host and home, are concerned at times that the multinational enterprises may be setting the transfer prices of goods or services in ways adverse to the jurisdiction's interests. India, Mexico, Brazil, and many other countries place ceilings on the payment by foreign-owned subsidiaries to their parents for all licenses to patents and for access to unpatented technology.[17] In the Andean Pact countries, foreign-owned subsidiaries are prohibited from paying a foreign parent anything at all for such licenses. Meanwhile, the tax authorities in the U.S. government harbor the opposite concern—that U.S. parents may not be charging enough to their foreign subsidiaries for products and services rendered. Accordingly, the U.S. authorities have been requiring U.S. parents at times to refigure their U.S. taxes by applying higher prices on the sales of goods to their subsidiaries, and have been studying formulas for the allocation to overseas subsidiaries of the U.S. parent's system-related costs, such as research costs.[18]

Although measures such as these threaten to catch the multinational enterprises between the scissor blades of conflicting jurisdictions, the room for maneuver that they still possess continues to appear as a substantial problem from the viewpoint of authorities in many countries in which they operate. The capacity of government bureaucrats to regulate is ordinarily matched by the capacity of business bureaucrats to find some remaining room for maneuver. The race is clearly on.

The Movement of Foreign Exchange

A somewhat different concern that contributes to the sense of diminished control on the part of developing countries relates to the flow of foreign exchange associated with the presence of the foreign-owned subsidiary. There are, in fact, two different worries on this score.

One is a long-term concern: the fear that the foreign-owned subsidiary will "decapitalize" the country. The term itself is not easy to define. Operationally, it means that money outflows associated with dividends, royalties, and debt service exceed the fresh capital being brought into a developing country by foreign-owned subsidiaries. Figures of this sort cannot be obtained precisely. But their relative magnitudes are suggested by U.S. balance-of-payment data. In 1974, for instance, fresh capital moved into the developing countries by U.S. parents from the United States amounted to $4,900 million while reported outflows of the type mentioned earlier amounted to $5,800 million.[19]

Whatever calculations of this sort may produce, however, the fact is that they do not measure the impact of foreign-owned enterprises on the country's balance of payments. Foreigners' investments in developing countries probably make their largest impact on the country's balance of payments through the trade accounts, not through the accounts covered in the figures quoted above. To estimate the net balance-of-payment effects of an investment, one has to estimate the impact of the foreigners' investments on the imports and exports of the country. Objective studies of this sort are difficult to do and are never altogether unambiguous. In the few instances in which they have been done, they have failed to support the decapitalization worry.[20] Indeed, I read the evidence, such as it is, as leaning in just the opposite direction—that is, supporting the view that developing countries tend to benefit in balance-of-payment terms.

The problem of controlling short-term capital movements that are destabilizing, however, is quite another story. Businessmen who recognize that a currency is under pressure may be tempted to tailor the timing of their remissions or receipts in order to reduce their risk. If a currency seems weak, they may accelerate their payments to others outside the currency area and delay the receipt of payments from outside the area.

In decades gone by, the problem of leads and lags was usually associated with the business of importers and exporters. Today, the problem is also associated with the activities of foreign-owned subsidiaries. So far, the evidence that leads and lags have actually been hurtful to currencies under pressure is inconclusive; the two serious studies of which I am aware suggest that practices vary widely.[21] Still, some foreign-owned subsidiaries clearly have a policy of trying to reduce their exposure to exchange-rate risk—hardly an unreasonable policy from their viewpoint. Thereby, however, they add to the pressures of a threatened currency. When businessmen follow such a policy, they often feel uncomfortable about its larger consequences. There is a tendency, therefore, to explain away the effects by assuming that when pressure on a currency develops, a change in its value is already overdue; hence an added push in the indicated direction may even be regarded as socially useful. But that is a self-serving assumption, whose validity in many situations is doubtful.

Still another rationalization on the part of managers of multinational enterprises is that foreign-owned subsidiaries do not engage

in these practices any more than the locally owned enterprises that
would replace them. But that assumption, too, is slightly suspect.
A foreign parent whose consolidated accounts must be reported in
another currency may be expected to see the risks of foreign exchange
fluctuations quite differently from a local firm whose income and
expenditures are principally in the weak currency itself. [22] With the
foreigner's incentive for risk reduction being stronger and his scale
of operations larger, the likelihood that multinational enterprises will
pursue a policy of risk reduction seems high when compared with
local enterprises. This is an unresolved problem that contributes to
the sense of insecurity of the local economy.

The Movement of Jobs

The concern of developing countries over the employment effects
of multinational enterprises takes a number of different forms. As
suggested earlier, some of these countries fear that multinational
enterprises may shape the national economy in ways that use more
capital and less labor. In addition, however, subsidiaries of multinational enterprises that have entered the country are thought to be
in a position to withdraw whenever the national situation becomes un-
promising. General Motors and other enterprises closed their subsidiaries in India when the government became more demanding in the
early 1960s; similar patterns could be detected at other times and
places, such as Chile and Peru in the early 1970s. The possibility
of withdrawal inhibits governments from making new demands on
foreign-owned enterprises, and limits the capacity of local labor
effectively to bargain for a larger share.

The rejoinder of multinational enterprises is that the withdrawal
of a firm established in a developing country is an exceptional event.
As the data clearly show, multinational enterprises do not often
abandon a manufacturing facility they have established in a developing
country. [23] They may at times sell out to national interests; but, in
terms of employment effects, that is quite another thing. Still, the
rejoinder is not enough. From the viewpoint of the developing countries, the latent power is palpable. Indeed, the fact that it is rarely
applied is sometimes interpreted as evidence that, in any dispute
with the host government and with local labor, the multinational
enterprises are usually strong enough to prevail.

Besides, for certain kinds of subsidiaries, the expectation is
inherently plausible that a multinational enterprise under pressure
might move to another location. Some subsidiaries are set up in
developing countries to produce for export, drawing on the advantages
of relatively cheap raw materials or cheap labor. In mining, petroleum, and agriculture, foreign subsidiaries devoted to the production

and export of raw materials always have had considerable importance. In manufacturing, foreign subsidiaries devoted mainly to export have been less common than the subsidiary that produces for the local market; but the export-oriented subsidiary appears to be growing in relative importance.[24] Developing countries assume, with obvious good reason, that if the cost advantage to the multinational enterprise is eroded, the incentive to shift locations will grow. They also assume, though the assumption is usually implicit, that national enterprises similarly situated would be less prone to withdraw from the country; this assumption, too, is easy to defend.

The developing countries' problem, one might well argue, stems from a desire to have their cake and eat it too. They would like to be able to attract foreign investors who were looking for a low-cost producing area, while retaining the power to raise the costs of production in the area. There is something to be said for this way of looking at the problem. But the ambivalence of the developing countries on this point is likely to continue, sustaining the tension that is associated with the presence of foreign-owned subsidiaries.

The Concern Generalized

If developing countries could evaluate the subsidiaries of multinational enterprises on the basis of their actual economic performance, narrowly defined, the overall evaluation would probably be more favorable than otherwise.[25] The fact that most developing countries are usually engaged in trying to attract additional foreign-owned subsidiaries suggests that this is their operating assumption as well. Of course, many cases do not fit the general pattern. Moreover, situations exist in which the developing countries feel that they should be gaining larger benefits still. The most intractable problem of all, however, stems from the foreign-owned subsidiary's potential, whether realized or latent, for rocking the national boat. Living on the lip of a volcano that is thought to be active is never very comfortable, even if the volcano rarely erupts.

The Interests of the Leaders

There is an obvious danger in ascribing to a country some given value or attitude or goal; practically every country is made up of disparate elements that cover a wide range of interests and views. The risk is especially great with regard to the developing countries. Caught up in a process of very rapid change, some of these countries include cultures that span the period from the Bronze Age to the twentieth century. In such countries, differences in outlook and

aspiration between the city and the countryside, and differences among
the various regions often are disconcertingly large. Not uncommonly,
the average income in the richest and the poorest region of a developing country differs by a ratio of ten to one, while the differences
in pay between skilled and unskilled labor can easily be five to one.
In nations with such heterogeneity, it is dangerous to regard any set
of views or values as representative.

     Despite the heterogeneous character of the developing countries,
the leaders of the various elements in these countries have tended to
have certain common reactions to their increasing interdependence
with the industrialized countries. Interdependence has often been
thought of as a continuation, even a strengthening, of the tutelary
role that the older countries had practiced for so long as colonial
powers. Nevertheless, although there has been a widespread resent-
ment among the leaders of developing countries over the pretensions
of foreigners as tutors, different segments of the national leadership
have tended to value their foreign contacts in quite different ways.[26]

     The differences could be seen in the business communities of
many developing countries. Small local businessmen, reliant on local
markets, local credit, and local supplies, have tended to be hostile
to foreign interests. Big local businessmen, however, seem to have
had a more difficult time deciding where they stood. Some have allied
themselves with foreign-owned companies, acting as suppliers or
distributors or partners; some have drawn on foreign interests to
provide capital, management, trademarks, and patents, or access
to overseas markets. In some cases, too, more complex arrangements have been developed, involving big local businessmen, government organizations, and foreign enterprises. As Securities and
Exchange Commission (SEC) disclosures indicate, the ties between
foreign business and local leaders have occasionally been more
occult, involving at times direct support for local political movements.[27]

     Other elite groups in developing countries have had less trouble
deciding where their interests lay. In politics, journalism, the arts,
and the universities, local leaders have found it both easier and
more satisfying to take a clear adversary position against the multinational enterprises. To be sure, such leaders could sometimes
benefit from partnerships with institutions in the industrial countries.
At times, such leaders could draw some support from foreign aid
programs, could secure scholarships for study abroad, and so on.
But these were ephemeral connections. Besides, they did not depend
very much on the goodwill of the foreign business community.

     The widespread hostility of many intellectual leaders in the
developing countries to foreign-owned enterprises has created fertile
ground for the development of one variant or another of the theory of

dependency.28 According to most variants of the theory, national businessmen and their political allies are linked by ties of class with foreign businessmen and their governments. As a result, the political, social, and economic control of the developing country is in jeopardy.29 Most of those who see the developing countries' problems in these terms, however, believe that the remedy requires more than the control of multinational enterprises. Their concern, as a rule, is with the basic social order of developing countries, especially with the private ownership of modern industry. By eliminating the private business class, according to this view, the developing country reduces the risk of transnational alliance with foreign capitalists and their governments.

In sum, one group of leaders in the developing countries tends to see the linkage of the national economy to foreign-owned enterprises as a betrayal of the national interests. Other groups tend to see such links as opportunities for national growth, provided the links are properly managed and carefully exploited. None of the groups in that dispute is broadly representative of the nation from which it is drawn; as ever, the peasants and the urban poor can only be heard through surrogates, and the surrogates speak mainly for themselves. Still, if the principals could speak, I assume that they would voice at least some of the values of those that are claiming to speak for them.

The Limits of Power

The interests of governments and those of foreign-owned enterprises in developing countries are usually compatible in some degree; both sides, at any rate, usually think they will gain by a continuation of the relationship. But elements of conflict are always present, in the sense that one or another would like to acquire more of the available pie. When conflict dominates the relationship, certain visible conditions usually suggest who holds the whip hand.

On the country's side lies the ineluctable attribute of sovereignty—including the power, among other things, to expel the subsidiary of the multinational enterprise. To be sure, in the specific case, that right may have been limited by contract, by law, or by treaty. But constraints of that sort provide uncertain protection for the foreign-owned subsidiary.

The expectation that a contract between a foreign-owned subsidiary and a developing country would provide some measure of protection for the foreign-owned subsidiary has never had much validity. And what validity did once exist has been greatly reduced. A government that enters into a contract with a multinational enterprise does not diminish its powers as a sovereign; and, in practice, it has proved difficult in developing countries to distinguish acts of sovereignty from acts of contract. If the contract commits the government on questions that are normally legislated, such as rates of taxation or rates of import duty, the usefulness of the contractual commitment is especially limited. The values and goals of developing countries can change with extraordinary rapidity; accordingly, a contract that seems to tie the hands of future governments on subjects that are normally legislated is vulnerable from its inception.[30]

In addition to contractual commitments, there have been commitments embodied in treaties between pairs of countries. Treaties of this sort have commonly included mutual guarantees that nationals of the other country would be entitled to the same legal protection as the country's own nationals. In countries in which the judiciary was in a position independently to interpret and enforce treaty rights, this kind of provision might be seen as providing a measure of protection. In practice, however, the executive in developing countries has not been much inhibited by treaty provisions of this sort.

One multilateral treaty has had a direct bearing on disputes between a state and a foreign-owned enterprise, the Convention on the Settlement of Investment Disputes (1965). But this agreement also has failed to impose much of a restraint on the peremptory exercist of executive power. Five years after the convention had gone into force, no dispute had yet been processed through the convention. When disputes have arisen between developing nations and foreign-owned enterprises, the parties have characteristically refrained from referring the case to outsiders for settlement.[31] In a much advertised dispute over Jamaica's decision to impose an export tax on bauxite, the Jamaican government refused to accept the convention's arbitration procedures despite the fact that it was a convention signatory.[32]

Another potential source of countervailing power against the sovereign acts of the developing countries is the home government of the multinational enterprise involved in the dispute. Pressure from home governments can take various forms, from the raw exercise of gunboat diplomacy to a slowdown on the export of military hardware to the offending country. But most managers of multinational enterprises have learned that this sort of support is an uncertain prop. History offers a succession of major incidents in which home government support was not forthcoming. In 1937, when Bolivia nationalized the holdings of the U.S. oil companies and, in 1938, when Mexico repeated the Bolivian performance, the U.S. government restrained its support of the companies because at the time it had much bigger fish to fry; it was hoping to keep the two governments from being tough on other U.S. business interests in their respective countries and from developing ties with Hitler.[33] In the 1940s, when Venezuela overturned its existing concessions with foreign oil companies, the prosecution of the war and the protection of other business interests intervened again to limit the pressures from the U.S. government.[34] In 1968, when Peru took over the International Petroleum Company, similar considerations led the U.S. government to walk softly.[35] In 1971, when the Shah of Iran undertook to rewrite his arrangements with the oil companies, the U.S. government's desire for close military ties with the Shah led it to temper sharply its support of the companies' position.[36] In 1973, when Saudi Arabia ordered Aramco to embargo shipments of oil to its partner owners in the United States and to U.S. military installations abroad, the U.S. government turned a blind eye, hoping that the problem would solve itself.[37] By that time, the naive concept that a developing country's pressure on a U.S.-owned subsidiary would lead to some sort of effective coercion on the part of the U.S. government had grown threadbare.[38]

Yet is is clear that subsidiaries of multinational enterprises can still exercise power in developing countries. The source of their power is sometimes blatantly clear. As long as these subsidiaries provide some scarce factor to the developing country, such as capital, or technology, or access to foreign markets, the host government has to weigh the losses that might be involved in driving the subsidiary out. In some situations, the government of a developing country might see the prospective gains from such a separation as outweighing the costs. The government of Guyana, for instance, saw considerable political advantage in nationalizing the bauxite holdings of Alcan in 1971. Although there was a risk that the flow of technical help from Alcan might be cut off and that access to foreign markets might be impaired, the gains were easily worth the risks. Jamaica, on the other hand, has hesitated to follow Guyana's lead with respect to nationalization. Jamaica's dependence on the aluminum companies has been heavier than that of Guyana, in terms of both access to markets and public revenues. Jamaica's tactics, therefore, have been of the salami variety; taxes have been raised, but the irrevocable step of nationalization has been put off.

The most potent source of insurance for a multinational enterprise, therefore, is its ability to threaten economic loss to a developing country if its subsidiary is expelled. That ability varies in fairly systematic ways, however, according to the function of the subsidiary and the stage at which the function is being performed.

For example, early in the life of any subsidiary, it is generally seen by the host country as bringing in at least some capital and some technology. If the subsidiary continues to produce the same product

by the same process over a period of years, however, the likelihood
is that the capital will be irrevocably sunk, and that the technology
will be available from alternative sources. Hence, the protective
mantle surrounding such a subsidiary will eventually prove a little
moth-eaten, and its vulnerability a little greater.

Nevertheless, multinational enterprises do not inevitably lose
their capacity for self-defense over the course of time. Chemical and
pharmaceutical companies roll over their products, thereby refur-
bishing their image as the indispensable enterprise. Automobile
companies widen and deepen their manufacturing activities, with the
same effect. Electronic companies ship the components they produce
in the developing country to the assembly lines of their affiliates
abroad, thus establishing their unique capabilities.

As seen through the eyes of the developing countries, therefore,
the costs and benefits associated with the presence of a given foreign-
owned subsidiary have usually shifted over time. In times of shortage
of some raw material, such as oil or copper, the foreign-owned
subsidiaries that produced these materials and marketed them abroad
have lost their bargaining strength; at such times, the developing
country has not seen the foreign-owned subsidiary's marketing connections abroad as a very important attribute. In times of surplus,
the pendulum has swung the other way; in those conditions, the marketing connections of the subsidiary have acquired a new value in the
developing countries' eyes.[39]

As the negotiating strength of developing countries toward
foreign-owned subsidiaries has waxed and waned, one pattern of
change has proved disconcerting for the developing countries. Contrary to expectations, the process of industrialization has not increased the autonomy of such countries. Instead, it has generated
a race between added autonomy and added dependence. Autonomy
has increased in industries whose technological and capital requirements were not difficult, such as standard steel products and mature
chemical products. But the dependence has simultaneously increased
in other directions. Development has generally stimulated the need
for more exotic technologies, such as those in metallurgy and electronics; it has usually increased the need for export markets to sup-
plement domestic markets, in order to accommodate plants of adequate size; and in some cases it has increased the need for added
capital, in order to underwrite more capital intensive productive
processes. Autonomy is seen as an ever receding goal and the
multinational enterprise is seen as a key villain in the process. This
adds to the propensity of many developing countries to conclude rue-
fully that such enterprises are a law unto themselves.

The indictment goes far beyond the relevant evidence. But it
can be justified in one critical sense. Nations have not yet devised

a means by which any multinational enterprise taken as a whole can be subjected to a process of social accountability and, hence, of social legitimation. The individual units that exist in some nation may be tested in terms of that nation's interests. But the controls imposed by individual nations can be hurtful to other nations or to mankind at large, and, hence, may be antisocial in their impact. The challenge is to develop a set of international arrangements to which the multinational enterprise is accountable and by which those manifold activities of the enterprise that are socially useful can be legitimated.

COMMENT

John W. Soden

Last night I spent some time reading this paper and, as I read, I traced our own experience in multinational business to see how ours and those you mention track together. We got started in the international business about 50 years ago, and when we went into these countries, it was our experience that they were pretty much interested in having employment within that country, reducing foreign exchange that went outside for the product they were consuming, and, of course, collecting their taxes. When we established there in fact, it worked out very well. We really have not experienced many of the things that we have discussed at this meeting. To some degree that makes me wonder whether many of the things we have discussed really apply on a broad front or whether they are things that maybe could happen and are in the minds more of people who analyze things and maybe in some government officials' minds than actually physically taking place.

Our own experience is that over a period of time in any country as their desires for foreign exchange and the things which this brings rise, then they become very interested in being sure that we do give that country access to what foreign markets may exist for the product manufactured there. In order to be sure that this takes place, there will be a growing demand for representation on our board and implementation of the policies of that country to ensure that entry to foreign markets is available.

We of course go along with them. We know this development will take place. We have had some interesting reactions where this

<hr/>

John W. Soden is Vice-President, Corporate Strategy, Armco Steel.

takes place. When we are there, we do try to operate as people operate within that country and live there; so that we have not experienced many of the things that we have talked about here.

One of the things that has been troublesome is trying to find within that country people who are willing to conduct the business as honestly and to pay their taxes as properly as we do. They are usually looking for some way around things in many of the developing countries.

Another thing that we have not found is this great freedom to move around, or really play a part in what happens to the currency of a country. There are adequate laws and you stay within them. Politics is a "no no" to us, and I think probably that most multinational companies stay completely away from politics.

I think maybe these things we have discussed get out of proportion. Certainly in my own opinion many of the things that we have discussed are really not true of the multinational companies.

I would just like to address one question to you, Dr. Vernon, to sort of commence this discussion. The last sentence that you used in your prepared paper says that you feel there should be development of a set of international arrangements to which the multinational enterprise is accountable and by which its socially useful activities are legitimated.

I would wonder what the real needs are in your opinion, and what you might suggest.

Dr. Vernon. My admiration for your perspicacity knows no bounds. There is only one sentence that I have revised in the draft which I have here, and it is that one sentence. The revision reads: "The challenge is to develop a set of international arrangements to which the multinational enterprise is accountable and by which those activities of the enterprise which are socially useful can be legitimated." That may have a slightly different meaning. It will in the developing countries.

I have speculated on the substance of your question a considerable amount and unhappily my present impression is that while these institutions can begin to be fashioned on a functional basis among the advanced countries, the industrialized OECD [Organization for Economic Cooperation and Development] countries, function by function, it would be premature in the year 1975 to do much vis-a-vis the developing countries.

There will be some trivial things done through the UN Centre on Transnational Corporations: more disclosure, more materials. It will gradually be discovered, however, that those materials were always available to anybody that was looking for them. There will be a tendency on the part of the developing countries to move into the field and learn a little bit more about the nature of the operation, the nature of the risks they confront, and so on; but in my opinion very little in the way of agreement.

So I must reluctantly conclude here that the challenge cannot yet be responded to in a wholehearted and forthcoming way. The direction of the response to the challenge is clear, it seems to me. Three or four areas keep coming up to the top of my list: the field of taxation; the subject of market structure (some people would call it antitrust); the problem of disclosure (including the exchange of information); and the problem of the distortion of competition through subsidies to capital. One or two other areas might lend themselves to agreement. Perhaps the most sensitive could well be an undertaking on the part of sovereigns not to avail themselves of the multinational enterprise for political ends in other countries. There is the possibility of some kind of self-denying ordinance on the part of sovereigns which could conceivably be framed in this context.

Five or six years ago, when I thought the opportunity existed, I was suggesting that the United States should do two things: it should explicitly recognize the Calvo doctrine, and it should couple its recognition with an invitation to Latin American countries to reconsider adherence to the Convention for the Settlement of Investment Disputes. That advice was greeted with a ringing silence in all quarters. In any event it is too late for that now. The psychology of the situation has changed. We will have to wait for people to mature a little bit in this field before such a step is worth suggesting again.

DISCUSSION

Question. Professor Vernon, the State, Justice, and Commerce Departments are now engaged with the OECD formulating codes of conduct for multinational enterprises. Personally I feel any such exercise, code of conduct, is demeaning to multinational enterprises, essentially negative and patently unfair to most of the international enterprises who are good corporate citizens in the countries in which they operate.

Nonetheless, we are into it. To not be in it is to not affect it.

I would like to know—you have just really skirted this issue in your last comments—if you could give us your thoughts on the utility or lack of utility of a code of conduct for multinational enterprises, both for developing countries and for industrialized countries?

Dr. Vernon. Let me separate the psychological aspects from the substantive, because the distinction is terribly important in this case.

The problems that are presented by the imperfect fit comprehend all the problems that are usually subsumed under the heading of industrial policy, national policy, market structure, taxation, labor relations, regional development—all the problems that we know of in the national setting. In addition a special set of international problems is overlaid on these, making them even more complex.

The assumption that something—a code of conduct—will, in the long run, have much bearing on these problems strikes me as a nonstarter. In the end we will have to have functional institutional approaches appropriate to this series of problems. Taxation will be handled differently from labor relations, and so on. So in a substantive sense, I regard the code approach as not operational. But it is psychologically dead wrong for the United States in the year 1975 to resist the development of a code. My guess is that we would be well to go along with this essentially useless—but also essentially harmless—exercise.

Question. I would like to follow that up by asking you whether you see any more utility in individual company codes of conduct of which the Caterpillar code is a preeminent example, in terms of dealing with some of the problems, pressures, tensions that you described.

Dr. Vernon. I am placed in a dreadfully embarrassing position by that question. With all due respect and admiration for Caterpillar's courage, I think the publication of the code itself is an unwise step. I think it puts the company's head into the lion's mouth. For example, after having heard this discussion, you will appreciate that what the code is saying at various places adds fuel to the complaints of the leaders in the developing countries.

For example, Caterpillar thinks of itself as doing the right thing when it says that it will bring to every country of the world, irrespective of the local circumstances, the finest technology and the best product. But this is interpreted by developing countries to mean that you will take your Moline techniques . . .

Mr. Morgan. Peoria, please.

Dr. Vernon. . . . and bring it to a country with different conditions, different technological needs. You will provide capital intensive lines when labor intensive lines are needed; you will provide all the exquisitely engineered add-ons of the U.S. tractor which are perfectly appropriate on an Iowa corn field and make no sense whatsoever in an Indian paddy.

Another provision in the code which is vulnerable is a perfectly reasonable and innocuous statement which says: We do not engage in any maneuvers in foreign exchange, subject of course to the legitimate concern of protecting our foreign exchange position. Interpreted into plain language this means that you do sell weak currencies short or buy strong currencies long; but you certainly do not leave a lot of money in an economy in which you expect the currency to lose value. This is a perfectly legitimate statement; but it is exactly what developing countries mean when they talk about speculation against the currency.

So that provision of the code is a hostage to fortune. I can think of codes which might not be, but so far I have not seen them.

Dr. Madden. If I could push that point a little further, I am reminded of the ancient account of the development of the commercial law, the law merchant of the thirteenth century, when businessmen, the merchants of that era, were forced to develop a legal system of their own for lack of such a system in the king's court or the ancient medieval courts. How would you suggest that the institution building you favor would go forward if it did not go forward by clumsy steps represented by these codes?

Dr. Vernon. Thirteenth century? Is that the question you are asking me?

Dr. Madden. Now, in this era, how would you expect international institution building to go forward if it did not do so under the impetus of first steps, such as codes? And in this sense, how do you defend the argument that substantively they may be useless therefore?

Dr. Vernon. Well, the codes, if I understand the analogy, and I will not hold you to the analogy . . .

Dr. Madden. Not particularly.

Dr. Vernon. . . . but those codes of course regulated the relationships among private parties in order to reduce dispute. That is not what we have here.

What we have here is one sovereign dragging at one part of an enterprise and another sovereign pulling at it from another direction, with each of them trying to get the largest possible piece. The enterprise in turn is fighting back at everybody and trying to survive.

The institution building involved here must certainly take into account an understanding of the multinational enterprise and what it does. But it must be aimed at reconciling the collective, social perceptions of the sovereigns with the efficiencies of the multinational enterprise.

Now my own guess is that you can only do this functionally. In the case of taxation, for example, you are already well started, or at least you have the underpinnings in some of the bilateral tax treaties; but they are far from being good enough.

The analogy that comes to mind is the shift in trade agreements from the bilateral trade agreements of the 1930s to the GATT [General Agreement on Tariffs and Trade] of the late 1940s, with the possibility for complaint, for review, for adjustment, and for development of new rules. Applying the approach to taxation would require a very different institution from applications in the field of, say, labor or something else.

Similarly, in the field of market structure one can picture ways of reconciling the conflicting approaches in the field of competition that exist in the various industrial countries. France from time to time wants mergers and the Americans from time to time want divestiture. Multinational enterprises scratch their heads every morning as they receive conflicting commands in the mail from different governments.

I see these institutions getting created, function by function; but they will have nothing to do with thirteenth-century codes.

Mr. Morgan. Carl, I imposed upon myself the discipline of saving my comments for the concluding remarks, but before we get too far away from the answer to Steve Crane's question on the Caterpillar code, I wonder if I might depart from that self-imposed discipline and just comment on two of your remarks about the Caterpillar code, Professor Vernon.

The first one related, as I recall it, to applying a technology in foreign countries which produce a product that is not appropriate for their use.

As I am sure you know, foreign governments have an ambivalent attitude on this question. They sometimes take the view that you expressed, but in my experience they are more likely to be critical of the company that brings them what they call obsolete or backward technology.

But be that as it may, and as a practical matter, in our particular case, your rice paddy vis-a-vis corn field-of-Iowa situation is quite inappropriate because we are really not in that business. I am not apologizing, I am not bragging about that. It is a hard fact. We are involved in earth moving and logging and mining and things of that kind.

The answer really reveals itself when you consider that if the product that we build were not built to U.S. standards, in other words according to the latest technology, they simply would not sell. The people would not want to buy less efficient, less modern technology as

it is revealed in the form of the product. So for that reason, along
with certain others, many, many years ago, we decided that the
product that is built outside the United States would in every way
possible be the equal of the U.S.-built machine.

   You commented about dealings in foreign exchange. That particular section of the code is meant to suggest that we view the availability of foreign currencies just exactly like we do availability of
any other commodities that we use in our manufacturing process.
And so in order to achieve that, we make it quite certain that we have
the foreign currencies available in the kind and in the quantity available when we need them—no more than that, hopefully no less than
that, and at no particular disadvantage in price.

   In order to achieve that, we do move currencies, we take
positions in future currencies, in order to assure that. And we want
to make absolutely certain that nobody gets carried away and tries
to engage in a business in which we do not feel compatible and which
we think it not in the best interests of the whole world monetary
situation.

Dr. Vernon. Thank you very much for that elaboration. I understand
perfectly the spirit in which it is offered.

   Let me just make one point clear. I was not addressing the
question of whether your policies were right or wrong; only the question whether your code was useful or not. That is a very different
question. I am prepared to address the appropriateness of policies
as a separate proposition.

   But the code, I suggest, is nothing more than a hostage to
fortune. That is the only point that I am making.

Question. Dr. Vernon, you did not touch upon this point, I believe.
Mr. Soden did so in his remarks about having local membership on
the board of directors, selling minority shares, entering into joint
ventures with the other government. Do you find that this really
overcomes the suspicions and attitudes in the developing countries?
Have there been any studies made on the position of those multinationals that do this as opposed to those that do not? I know that some
of the European multinationals go pretty far in having local people
on the boards of directors selling 30 percent of stock and so on. I
think Volkswagen in some of its operations does this, whereas U.S.
companies, for example, do not do this.

Dr. Vernon. You have got the world's best expert sitting in this
room. Professor Wells has written a book dealing with joint ventures. His studies up to now have dealt with U.S. companies. We
have since extended the data to cover the Europeans and Japanese.

I have two or three observations on this. One is that there is an underlying regularity in these choices which suggests that there are some pretty compelling economic forces which decide which of the choices you make. The underlying regularities look to be highly rational. For instance, a new firm that thinks of itself as not knowing a great deal about marketing, that is engaged in an import substituting operation, that cannot muster out of its own resources specialists who know how to handle each particular market, are likely to go in for joint ventures if they think they can get a distribution center that way. As the firm gets more and more experienced in markets, the tendency to use joint ventures in these circumstances declines. It does not increase.

As we look at Europeans and Japanese, what we discover is that given the strategies of their firms, the kinds of industries they are in, and the kinds of countries they are in, you would expect more joint ventures, even if they had been Americans. You see this prominently in the case of the Japanese who are rapidly getting away from joint ventures as they move into another kind of country and another kind of product requiring much more integration of firm strategies.

There may be times and places in which the joint venture system is a fairly useful device; but if you make the wrong decision, the costs are high. You do not always make the wrong decision when you choose the joint venture; but if you do, you are in real trouble.

The final point I want to make is that when the revolution comes, the local partners in joint ventures are likely to be hung first in the developing countries and then the foreigner. In terms of the internal political process, the joint venturers are characteristically seen as delivering over the economy to the foreigner, and therefore deserving to be twice slapped: once for being a businessman, and a second time for being a businessman who gave over the national economy to the foreigner. Your joint venture may prove to be a liability rather than anything else at some point.

Question. Do you think it is about time for the United States to drop OPIC [Overseas Private Investment Corporation] and not guarantee future investments in the developing countries? I raise that question in the context of your paper; namely, one of the problems is that many developing countries find it politically expedient to undervalue foreign investment or they undervalue it because it must be terribly important to the MNC if its home government will give it a guarantee for the investment.

Dr. Vernon. Well every time this question is raised, I keep thinking of the stir that was created when Esso applied for one of the first guarantees under the Marshall Plan, for an Esso refinery in Italy.

The rest of U.S. business seemed to think this was a dreadful idea, because it let the government into the foreign investment business.

Well, times have changed obviously. On the whole I am inclined to think that the period has passed in which OPIC can clearly be justified in terms of U.S. national objectives and even of global welfare. I would feel a little differently if we could move to multinational insurance, where the political aspect of administering the insurance policy did not exist or was reduced anyway. But I am troubled by the bilateral agreement and its implication in political terms. I have to confess that from time to time I have recommended to various members of the Congress that on balance I could see a very weak case for OPIC. In that case I would hope that someone would pick up its fine staff and use it in another context.

Question. I would like to know from the conclusion of your paper whether the challenge is to construct a set of international arrangements to which the multinational is accountable—if the code is not a step in the right direction, what direction specifically would these international arrangements take?

Dr. Vernon. You may not be aware that that is almost a repetition of the first question I was asked. In a long-winded answer I suggested that time was not yet, that this is a challenge which could not be very well met for the present. I would hope the United States would be as forthcoming as it possibly can on the subject of the transnational corporation and stop getting all hung up about some of the rather silly verbiage that accompanied that original report. I think there has been overreaction on the part of U.S. business. The immediate question is how to deal with the UN group, how to launch the process that UNCTAD [United Nations Conference on Trade and Development] has gone through over the last 15 years, learning about the complexity of the problem and about the need to move on a relatively evolutionary basis.

Question. Dr. Vernon, if I understood you correctly, it was your opinion that probably the codes that come out of the OECD would in effect be of little importance. What you found in the Caterpillar code are two provisions which you feared might actually be used against them.

My question is, if, as some segments in U.S. business feel, the early drafts of the OECD code contain statements which in fact would be injurious to U.S. business, is the code sufficiently trivial that U.S. business really should not get exercised, since there is no point in taking a rough stand, or could the codes be injurious even if they are no help?

<u>Dr. Vernon</u>. I would react at two levels. One is to recall some history. My first job in Washington was with the SEC in 1934 when the great battle of the corporations over disclosure was whether they should be required to disclose their gross sales.

It was argued by many serious men of affairs that the disclosure of gross sales would be such a weapon in the hands of competitors as to be disastrous to corporate life. I suggest that the first question is whether the disclosure issue is one of real substance from the viewpoint of business.

If the answer is that there is some real substance, and there may be, then the next question to ask is what alternatives are available to business. How will business fare in the absence of a code?

The virtue of a code is that for the first time a whole series of nations, all of which have multinational enterprises—Canada has about 15; Britain, 50 or 60; France, 30 or 40; and so on—confront a set of common propositions applicable to all their enterprises. I suggest that in those circumstances the problem of an egregiously injurious interpretation is sufficiently limited so that one should still worry about it very much. In a reasonably responsible society, where interests cross cut in so many different directions, you ought not anticipate an extreme interpretation, at least not very often.

NOTES

1. Assar Lindbeck, "The Changing Role of the National State," <u>Kyklos</u> 28 (1975): 2846.

2. This is an impressionistic conclusion in the process of being documented by various scholars. For data on international mail consistent with the conclusion, see United Nations, <u>Statistical Yearbook</u> (New York), various issues, reporting on letter mail; and on international trade in printed matter and records, United Nations, <u>Yearbook of International Trade Statistics</u> (New York), various issues.

3. In Mexico, for instance, manufacturing output accounted for by foreign-owned subsidiaries rose from 20 percent in 1962 to 28 percent in 1970 (from 38 percent to 45 percent if traditional branches of industry are omitted); Bernardo Sepulveda Amor and others, <u>Las Empresas Transnacionales en Mexico</u> (Mexico City: El Colegio de Mexico, 1974), pp. 4, 15.

4. See, for instance, UN Department of Economic and Social Affairs, <u>Multinational Corporations in World Development</u> (New York: United Nations, 1973), pp. 42-74; Report of the UN Group of Eminent Persons, <u>The Impact of Multinational Corporations on Development and on International Relations</u> (New York: United Nations, 1974).

5. The performance of the USSR has been fairly well studied. The emphasis on automobiles, clothing, and entertainment are about what one would expect in a capitalist country of like income. Moreover, the USSR's record in both product innovation and quality control is poor; see D.W. Bronson and B.S. Severin, "Soviet Consumer Welfare: The Brezhnev Era," in Soviet Economic Prospects for the Seventies, papers submitted to the Joint Economic Committee, 93d Cong., 1st sess. (Washington, D.C.: U.S. Government Printing Office, 1973), pp. 377-85. The case of mainland China is inadequately documented, though a book by Joan Robinson is at this writing reported forthcoming.

6. The case of pharmaceuticals in Argentina is carefully analyzed in J.M. Katz, Oligopolio, firmas nacionales y empresas multinacionales: la industria farmaceutica argentina (Buenos Aires: Siglo Veintiuno, 1974), especially Chapters 1 and 4.

7. For studies and observations bearing on the point, see David Morawetz, "Employment Implications of Industrialization in Developing Countries: A Survey," International Bank for Reconstruction and Development Staff Working Paper 170, mimeographed (Washington, D.C.: I.B.R.D., January 1974).

8. See W.A. Chudson and L.T. Wells, Jr., The Acquisition of Technology from Multinational Corporations by Developing Countries, Document no. SP/ESA/12 (New York: United Nations, 1974). One of the rare empirical analyses of this phenomenon, consistent in its general results with the few other empirical studies on the subject, is S.A. Morley and G.W. Smith, "The Choice of Technology: Multinational Firms in Brazil," Paper no. 58, mimeographed (Houston: Rice University Program of Development Studies, 1974).

9. L.T. Wells, Jr., Economic Man and Engineering Man: Choice of Technology in a Low-Wage Country, Report no. 226 (Cambridge, Mass.: Harvard University Development Research Group, 1972). For an illustration of a policy suggestive of that result, see Caterpillar Tractor Co., A Code of Worldwide Business Conduct (Peoria, Ill., 1974), p. 6: "We locate engineering facilities in accordance with need, and without reference to countries or nationalities involved. We exchange design and specification data from facility to facility, on a worldwide basis, while recognizing local restrictions that may exist."

10. For a summary of existing studies, see Chudson and Wells, op. cit.

11. For another evaluation, with accent on the positive, see Report of the Secretary-General's Ad Hoc Group on New Concepts of Science Policy, Science, Growth and Society (Paris: Organization for Economic Cooperation and Development, 1971), p. 75. For still another, leaning heavily in the opposite direction, see David Felix,

"Technological Dualism in Latin Industrializers: On Theory, History and Policy," Journal of Economic History 34, no. 1 (March 1974): 194-238.

12. G.L. Reuber, Private Foreign Investment in Development (Oxford: Clarendon Press, 1973), pp. 3-4.

13. Compilation for 1968 covering 632 U.S. parent firms with assets of $100 million or more, reported by letter from the U.S. Treasury Department to the author.

14. M.E. Kyreuz, "Effective Tax Rates and Tax Bases," mimeographed (Washington, D.C.: Office of Tax Analysis, U.S. Treasury Department, 1974), Table 1.

15. S.M. Robbins and R.B. Stobaugh, Money in the Multinational Enterprise (New York: Basic Books, 1973), pp. 91-92; M.Z. Brooke and H.L. Remmers, The Strategy of Multinational Enterprise: Organization and Finance (New York: American Elsevier Publishing, 1970), pp. 173, 177. For an unusually careful study of one kind of transfer pricing that reflected in royalties, see Daniel Chudnowsky, Aspectos Economicos de la Importacion de Technologia en la Argentina en 1972 (Buenos Aires: Instituto Nacional de Technologia Industrial, 1974). Among his striking conclusions are the heavy preponderance of royalties as fees for licenses, especially licensing of local patents and foreign trademarks; and the fact that royalty rates paid by independent Argentine national firms to foreign licensors were on average much higher than rates paid by Argentine subsidiaries to their foreign parents.

16. This reaction explains in part some extraordinary transfer prices first reported in C.V. Vaitsos, Intercountry Income Distribution and Transnational Enterprises (Oxford: Clarendon Press, 1974), pp. 158-86. See Sanjaya Lall, "Transfer Pricing by Multinational Manufacturing Firms," Oxford Bulletin of Economics and Statistics 35, no. 3 (August 1973): 173-93. The study in J.M. Katz, op. cit., p. 33, produces similar evidence for Argentina, reflecting overpricing but of a much less dramatic sort.

17. R.D. Robinson, The National Control of Multinational Corporations: A Fifteen Country Study (New York: Praeger, 1976).

18. G.D. Henderson and Peter Miller, "Proposals for Improvement of Rules of Allocation of Deductions Between Foreign and U.S. Source Income," Tax Law Review, Summer 1974, pp. 597-749; Robert Feinschreiber, "Intercompany Pricing Rules Show Need for Revision," Taxes 51, no. 3 (March 1973): 133-37; M.G. Duerr, Tax Allocations and International Business (New York: Conference Board, 1972).

19. "U.S. Director Investment Abroad in 1973," Survey of Current Business, Part II, 54, no. 8 (August 1974): 18,22.

20. Adequate empirical studies bearing on this subject are few. Most of them are listed in Sanjaya Lall, Foreign Private Manufacturing Investment and Multinational Corporations: An Annotated Bibliography (New York: Praeger, 1975), pp. 43-60; and their general purport is summarized in Raymond Vernon, "Multinational Enterprises in Development Countries: An Analysis of National Goals and National Policies," Development Discussion Paper no. 4 (Cambridge, Mass.: Harvard Institute for International Development, June 1975).

21. U.S. Senate, Committee on Foreign Relations, Subcommittee on Multinational Corporations, Multinational Corporations in the Dollar Devaluation Crisis: Report on a Questionnaire (Washington, D.C.: U.S. Government Printing Office, 1975). A second study, conducted by Rita Rodriguez, is still unpublished.

22. This is a complex subject. For an elaboration, see Robbins and Stobaugh, op. cit., pp. 117-38.

23. James W. Vaupel and Joan P. Curhan, The World's Multinational Enterprises (Boston: Harvard Graduate School of Business Administration, 1973) pp. 355-60. Of approximately 3,200 manufacturing subsidiaries established by leading multinational enterprises in developing countries after 1900, fewer than 100 had been liquidated by 1970.

24. G.K. Helleiner, "Manufactured Exports from Less Developed Countries and Multinational Firms," The Economic Journal 83 (March 1973): 21-47. See also Vaupel and Curhan, op. cit., pp. 381-82; their data show that of about 2,600 manufacturing subsidiaries of large multinational enterprises in developing countries in the early 1970s, over 90 percent sold their output mainly to the local market.

25. Careful efforts to measure such empirical effects are found in G.L. Reuber and others, Private Foreign Investment in Development (Oxford: Clarendon Press, 1973), pp. 149-84; P.P. Streeten and Sanjaya Lall, "The Flow of Financial Resources: Private Foreign Investment," mimeographed (Geneva: UN Conference on Trade and Development, May 23, 1973); Wolfgang Konig, "Towards an Evaluation of International Subcontracting Activities in Developing Countries: Interim Report," draft, UN Economic Commission for Latin America, September 1975. For summaries of the available studies, see Raymond Vernon, "Multinational Enterprises in Developing Countries: An Analysis of National Goals and National Policies," op. cit., pp. 21-35.

26. The generalizations that follow are based on bits and pieces of empirical materials drawn from various sources. See, for instance: G.R. Sherman, "Colombian Political Bases of the Andean Pact Statute on Foreign Capitals: National Influence on International Regulation of Foreign Investment," Journal of

Inter-American Studies and World Affairs 15, no. 1 (February 1973):
112-18; Jeane Kirkpatrick, Leader and Vanguard in Mass Society
(Cambridge, Mass.: MIT Press, 1971), pp. 186-88, 200, 218;
N. H. Leff, Economic Policy Making and Development in Brazil 1947-
1964 (New York: John Wiley and Sons, 1968), pp. 64-65, 132-43;
Aaron Lipman, The Colombian Entrepreneur in Bogota (Coral Gables,
Fla.: University of Miami Press, 1969), pp. 106-08; J. A. Silva
Michelena, Illusion of Democracy in Dependent Nations (Cambridge,
Mass.: MIT Press, 1971), p. 197; S. A. Kochanek, Business and
Politics in India (Berkeley: University of California Press, 1974),
Chapters 6 and 9; Arthur D. Little and Co., Mexican Attitudes Toward
Foreign Investment (Mexico City: Arthur D. Little, 1966); B. Sepul-
veda Amor and others, Las Empresas Transnacionales en Mexico
(Mexico City: El Colegio de Mexico, 1974), pp. 93-100; Warren Dena,
The Industrialization of Sao Paulo, 1880-1945 (Austin: University of
Texas Press, 1969), pp. 135-48.

27. U. S. Senate, Committee on Foreign Relations, Subcommittee on Multinational Corporations, Multinational Corporations and
United States Foreign Policy, Part 2 (Washington, D. C.: U. S. Government Printing Office, March and April 1973), pp. 599, 608-15,
618, 626-628, 640, 647, 676.

28. A classic expression of that hostility is found in P. O.
Streeten, "Costs and Benefits of Multinational Enterprises in Less-
Developed Countries," in The Multinational Enterprise, ed. J. H.
Dunning (London: George Allen and Unwin, 1971), p. 257: "Among
those who will side with [the foreign-owned firm] are bribed officials,
the small employed aristocracy of workers who enjoy high wages and
security, the satellite bourgeoisie . . . and the domestic industries
producing complementary goods . . . On the other side of the fence
are the masses of unemployed, non-employed and underemployed,
the competitors, actual and potential, and those who dislike
foreigners."

29. Susanne Bodenheimer, "Dependency and Imperialism:
The Roots of Latin American Underdevelopment," in Readings in
U. S. Imperialism, ed. K. T. Fann and D. C. Hodges (Boston: Porter
Sargent, 1971), pp. 155-78.

30. D. N. Smith and L. T. Wells, Jr., "Mineral Agreements in
Developing Countries: Structure and Substance," American Journal
of International Law 69, no. 3 (July 1975): pp. 563-65.

31. See P. K. O'Hare, "The Convention on the Settlement of
Investment Disputes," Stanford Journal of International Studies 6
(Spring 1971): 146-62; and R. C. Wesley, "The Procedural Malaise of
Foreign Investment Disputes in Latin America: From Local Tribunals
to Factfinding," Law and Policy in International Business 7, no. 3
(Summer 1975): pp. 813-61.

32. "Bauxite Tax Testing Arbitration Unit," New York Times, October 2, 1975, p. 61.

33. E.D. Cronon, Josephus Daniels in Mexico (Madison: University of Wisconsin Press, 1960), pp. 234-36, 264-67, 353; and Bryce Wood, The Making of the Good Neighbor Policy (New York: Columbia University Press, 1961), pp. 191-95, 353.

34. Wood, op. cit., pp. 272-73, 277-78.

35. J.P. Einhorn, Expropriation Politics (Lexington, Mass.: D.C. Heath, 1974); J.P. Einhorn, "Peru v. United States—Rigidity on Both Sides Perils Investors," Business Latin America, February 20, 1969, p. 57; A.J. Pinelo, The Multinational Corporation as a Force in Latin American Politics (New York: Praeger, 1973).

36. Mira Wilkins, "The Oil Companies in Perspective," in "The Oil Crisis: In Perspective," Daedalus 104, no. 4 (September 1975): 167-68.

37. R.B. Stobaugh, "The Oil Companies in Crisis," in ibid, pp. 180, 185, 188.

38. Compare the conclusion in R.F. Mikesell, Nonfuel Minerals: U.S. Investment Blues Abroad (Beverly Hills: Sage Publications, 1975), p. 88: ". . . special U.S. sanctions against governments such as those required by the Hickenlooper Amendment have not offered protection to U.S. investors and have often created embarrassment for U.S. diplomacy."

39. Raymond Vernon, Sovereignty at Bay: The Multinational Spread of U.S. Enterprises (New York: Basic Books, 1971), pp. 26-27, 47, 56.

6

ARE MULTINATIONAL CORPORATIONS FORCING US INTO NATIONAL AND INTERNATIONAL ECONOMIC PLANNING?
Richard N. Cooper

Other papers in this volume have covered many of the specific aspects of multinational corporations (MNCs). As the UN Group of Eminent Persons said in its 1974 report on the international impact of multinational corporations, they really should be called trans-national enterprises (TNEs), since a number of enterprises—the state-trading companies of the Communist countries, for example—are technically not corporations and since some of them are not yet truly multinational in their management, but only operate in several countries other than their national home base. But whether they are called MNCs or TNEs, my assignment is to assess their contribution to the drift toward increased economic planning and, more generally, to offer an overview of the impact of MNCs operating in a world of national—and often nationalistic—states.

The debate over MNCs is often couched in an adversary frame of reference, within which they are viewed either as good guys or bad guys. That seems to me to do total injustice to the complexity of the issues involved. They represent a phenomenon of today's world economy, both a response to forces not of their own making and an actor whose behavior will influence the way others must behave. It is inappropriate to cast them either into the role of messiah in a world ridden with malevolent or at best bungling governments, or into the role of a mephistopheles who first entices and then ensnares the souls of its innocent and pure-minded victims. It is satisfying to note that the debate over MNCs has cooled to some extent and has

---

Richard N. Cooper is a Fellow at the Center for Advanced Studies in Behavioral Sciences, Stanford University.

taken on a more technical, hence a more fruitful, character; but the old images flare up from time to time.

To ascertain whether MNCs will force us into national or international economic planning, we first need some common understanding about the meaning of planning. According to the dictionary, a "plan" is an arrangement of parts, usually laid out on a plane, such as a map. In a more dynamic setting, by extension, planning might be taken to refer to an arrangement of parts for the future, or, more simply, just thinking ahead and taking steps to influence future events. In this sense, every large organization and most small ones engage in planning, governments rather less than business enterprises. Unfortunately, "plan" in the economic context has been appropriated by Socialists or Communists, and then extended to developing countries. For that reason, I think, the word has taken on connotations of detailed government control or regulation of the economy, although anyone who has personal contact with planning in developing countries knows that the reality falls far short of the ambition.

In the sense of anticipating future developments and possibly taking actions to avoid unwanted consequences, planning is undertaken routinely both by government and by big business, and government does too little rather than too much of it. To anticipate the argument of this paper, I see little in the presence of MNCs to force or even to encourage governments to do more of this type of planning. In the sense of regulating or controlling the economy, I suspect that the presence of MNCs will surely alter the form and the nature of regulation, but it is unlikely to result in a major increase in planning, which, however, is on an upward trend quite independent of (but reflecting the same underlying technological and social changes that give rise to) multinational corporations.

There are many pressures in today's world calling for greater planning by governments; but their powers of resistance are remarkable. Politics, the need to arrive at compromise solutions to immediate and pressing problems, inhibits anticipatory action with regard to future events. Any group likely to be placed at a disadvantage by such actions will mobilize to resist the change, so unless the case for change is overwhelming, which it rarely is with respect to the uncertain future, little anticipatory action is likely to take place.

Despite the tendency of governments to concentrate on short- rather than long-range issues, on expediency rather than on planning, the complexities of modern society and the responsibilities placed on governments increasingly call for more planning. MNCs are involved in that process, but they are not the sole or even the principal motivation. Indeed, they are more likely to be the main objects of the planning rather than its main causes, in two quite different senses:

as the targets of government action and as the instruments for
carrying out government policies. An example of the first would be
antitrust action, where the objective of policy is to influence the
degree of economic competition. An example of the second would be
Labor Department directives on personnel policies for all firms
under government contract, where the objective of policy is to reduce racial or sex discrimination in society, and large corporations
seem to be one of the few instruments at hand for trying to accomplish
that; or controls on the prices of large firms, where the objective of
policy is to reduce the general rate of inflation.

LONG-TERM TRENDS IN THE ROLE OF GOVERNMENT

Before we turn to the main sources of friction between governments and multinational corporations, it is useful to step back and
take a broad view of trends in government policy. With each generation over the twentieth century has come a large increase in expectations concerning what government can and should do to improve the
well-being of its citizens. This increase in expectations has taken
place in part because of democratization of the political process in
all the major industrial countries; but it has occurred even more
because of the improved capacity of governments to deal with the
various afflictions to society over the ages. One of the first examples
of increased expectations—and improved performance—concerns
public health: during the nineteenth century community illness was
gradually transmuted in the public mind from being the retribution
of God to being the responsibility of government to alleviate or prevent, as our technical understanding of the basis for good health and
of the transmission of contagious diseases improved. A similar
transformation has occurred in many other areas of life: We have
set out in turn to stabilize the incomes of farmers despite the vicis-
situdes of weather, to tame the business cycle, to raise the rate of
economic growth. Denizens of the 1920s would be utterly amazed at
the things we now expect of government, indeed even take for granted.
At the same time, our expectations seem now to have run way
ahead of government's capacity for effective action, for example, in
the areas of race relations, education, and poverty. The discrepancy
between expectation and performance creates a good deal of political
tension, charges of bad faith in execution, recriminatory rhetoric,
and even threats of violent action. At the moment, in the wake of the
Vietnam war and Watergate, we are in a period of disillusionment
with government that seems to have led to a trimming back of expectations regarding what government may reasonably be expected to

accomplish by way of improving the welfare of its citizens. But my guess is that this psychological retrenchment will prove to be temporary, and that after a period of adjustment our expectations of government will resume their upward growth. The process is, moreover, a worldwide one, by no means confined to the United States or to a few Western countries. Indeed, important bodies of opinion throughout the world believe that it is within the capacity of modern government to eliminate poverty throughout the world, not merely within its wealthiest corners, within the foreseeable future; that is the sentiment which in part underlies calls for a new international economic order and their sympathetic reception by many citizens of the industrial countries.

The Consequence of Business Mobility

Multinational corporations contribute to the tension in today's world by making it more difficult in certain respects (but easier in others, as we shall see below) for national governments to achieve the objectives with which they are now charged. The key feature of the multinational corporation is its mobility, its ability to transact with ease in a number of different countries. Modern transportation and communication have increasingly taken the foreignness out of foreign transactions, so that the psychological barriers that once impeded transactions—particularly production—in several different countries are now greatly diminished.

We can speak of the domain of each enterprise—the area over which it has effective mobility. This domain will typically vary with the aspect of the enterprise in question—it is usually largest for sales, smaller for assembly, still smaller for basic production and selection of management personnel, for instance—but the various domains of the typical large firm have all increased since the 1950s, and especially since the 1960s. Multinational firms have a wider geographic domain than the national or the strictly local firm. But the geographic domains of most national and many local firms have grown as well.

Nations, on the other hand, have jurisdictions that are by and large confined geographically to a single area. Indeed, with decolonization during the 1950s the jurisdictional domains of the major European countries effectively shrank in size.

Therefore, we have in today's world (1) the expectation of publics everywhere that their governments should do more for their well-being, (2) the consequential inducement of governments to turn increasingly to major corporations both as objects and as instruments of public policies to achieve those objectives, (3) the historical fact that national jurisdictions are limited geographically, confronting

(4) the development that the domains of mobility of many large corporations have increased way beyond any particular national jurisdiction. An implication of the last two points is that corporations can in some degree escape the more onerous intrusions of national policies simply by moving some or all of their activities elsewhere. These conditions taken together create a deep structural tension in government-business relations, for mobility means the possibility of escape while attempts to regulate or to tax provide the incentives to escape.

The possibility of escape is not merely hypothetical. It can be observed in many areas of economic activity, in response both to taxation and to business and banking regulations, from disclosure of financial information to capital requirements to pollution controls. Liberia is not the most natural place for registration of the world's largest tanker fleet, and Grand Cayman island is not the most obvious location for major international banking operations. It is escape from national regulations elsewhere that has led to such quixotic features of today's international economy.

Technology has made possible a global reach by enterprises but history has provided a legacy of geographically limited national jurisdictions; the resulting tension is a characteristic of the times, not an occasion for blaming one party or the other.

It is worth pointing out that this tension is by no means confined to business firms. It applies also to individuals, especially individuals who are highly trained or who have special talents or skills. The brain drain is a major preoccupation of a number of countries, mainly but not exclusively developing countries. Britain is concerned about the emigration of doctors, and Canada has voiced concerns about the migration of some of its best talent to the United States. (Paradoxically perhaps, Canadians also have expressed concern about the immigration of Americans into teaching positions in Canadian universities, on grounds that Canada's cultural identity might thereby be threatened.) High-income actors and others maintain residence outside countries with steep progressive income tax rates, and American youths escape to Canada, Sweden, and elsewhere to evade the U.S. military draft, a regulation applicable to young males during 1966-72. Again, mobility holds open the possibility of escape, and heavy taxation or regulation provides the incentive to move. Increased mobility—made possible by the telex, by the jet aircraft, by the spreading use (at least in a number of technical disciplines and in business circles) of English, indeed by the increasing homogenization of late twentieth-century living in many areas of the world—frustrates government attempts to tax or to regulate.

To consider the normative aspects of this higher mobility would require a lengthy and technical discussion in itself, an unwarranted digression from my main theme. Suffice it to say that in terms of welfare economics a strong case can be made in favor of high mobility. But under certain circumstances high mobility for some agents combined with low mobility for others will have undesirable consequences, particularly if one is concerned about the distribution of income. And any normative judgment on mobility to escape regulations must depend in part on one's view of the importance of the regulation in question, and whether its purposes are adequately fulfilled even in the face of emigration from the region of regulation (as would be the case for certain antipollution requirements, for instance).

Possible Governmental Responses to Business Mobility

So there is the problem. What is the solution? And in particular does it reside in increased planning?

The solution can take any of three directions, or some combination of them: (1) actions to limit the mobility of enterprises and individuals, to reduce their opportunities for escape; (2) actions to extend the jurisdiction of national governments, either unilaterally by reaching out through whatever handle is available to grasp citizens operating abroad, or jointly through agreements among nations on the appropriate policies to be pursued, covering an area at least as wide as the relevant domains of enterprises or individuals; (3) abandonment of the national objectives, insofar as they require regulation or redistributive taxation of highly mobile enterprises and individuals— that is, movement to a limited regime of laissez-faire. We have seen examples of all three types of response, as shown below.

Restrictions on Movement

To help protect the autonomy of national monetary policy, a number of countries, including such basically free enterprise countries as the United States and Germany, have imposed controls on capital movements out of or (in the case of Germany) into the country. The restraints operated mainly and in the first instance on banks, but when that proved inadequate the controls were extended to business firms as well. They were not aimed especially at MNCs, but to be effective they had to encompass MNCs, and that necessarily took the authorities into the details of intracorporate (but international) financial flows.

A much older example of action to restrain mobility involves controls on immigration, introduced on a wide scale in the United

States in the 1920s and in Britain (as it affects residents of the
British Commonwealth) in the 1960s. Such measures were deemed
necessary to protect wage levels and improved working conditions
(and, in the case of Britain, to maintain some degree of racial
homogeneity) in the face of high international mobility of unskilled
individuals. A number of poor countries, on their part, place various
obstacles in the way of emigration of highly trained individuals.

Extensions of Jurisdiction

National jurisdiction has been extended unilaterally, sometimes
to the considerable irritation of other countries, in the application
of U.S. antitrust laws to firms outside the United States whose actions
might affect competition within the United States, and in the enforcement of the U.S. embargo on trade with Cuba and Communist China
with respect to U.S.-owned subsidiaries operating abroad. The list
could be lengthened to include Britain's action to close down pirate
radio stations operating outside British jurisdiction, Civil Aeronautics
Board (CAB) interference (through U.S. carriers) in International Air
Transport Association (IATA) airfare-setting activities, and so on.
While the extension of jurisdiction is frequently regarded as offensive
by other nations, it reflects more than an empire-building desire by
bureaucrats to meddle in the affairs of others; it reflects the likelihood that with high mobility the legal responsibilities of a national
agency cannot be carried out effectively without reaching across
national boundaries—without an extension of jurisdiction to match the
domain of mobility.

Extensions of jurisdiction are not always unilateral. Tax
treaties are a time-honored technique for the tax authorities of two
nations to get together on a common tax regime for firms and individuals that operate in both national tax jurisdictions. The Organization for Economic Cooperation and Development (OECD) has a number
of committees that attempt to coordinate various national regulatory
policies. And the European Community can be viewed, from this
limited perspective, as an exercise to enlarge national jurisdictions
to match the enlarged domain of business firms operating within
Europe; certainly its activities have focused heavily on creating a
harmonized regulatory and tax regime for firms operating within
its member countries, to reduce the distortions to competition that
would result from divergent national policies in the face of unimpeded
movement of goods, persons, and business enterprise within the
community.

Laissez-faire

The third possible direction of response, abandonment of national objectives insofar as they affect mobile agents, can be observed in a host of areas that have not attracted much public attention because they are not yet regarded as important, such as ease of incorporation or capital requirements for incorporation. The area that still operates under a relatively laissez-faire regime about which greatest public concern has been expressed is international banking. The Eurocurrency market represents an effective escape from rather rigorous national banking regulations, and there has been much discussion, particularly since the failure of the German bank Herstatt in mid-1974, about whether the Eurocurrency market should be brought under regulation, and if so, how. In a way, tax deferral on nonrepatriated earnings of U.S.-owned subsidiaries operating abroad also represents abandonment of national revenue objectives, on the dual grounds that accrual taxation would be technically difficult (and would intrude on the tax sovereignty of other nations) and that it would place U.S. firms operating abroad at a financial disadvantage with respect to competing local or multinational firms.

In the long run, the laissez-faire approach will not be acceptable, although mobile firms may enjoy its relative freedom for a number of years. As mobile agents, multinational corporations are able to mitigate onerous restrictions, but in so doing they may frustrate national policy. To the extent that they do, nations will try to reassert control in one way or another. The basic choice will therefore lie between restraints on mobility and extensions of jurisdiction. Moreover, since excessive unilateral extension of jurisdiction will rile other governments, the real choice is between national restraints on mobility and international joint action to extend effective jurisdiction over the domain of mobility; that is, between a strictly national or a cooperative international approach to the problem.

It is instructive to look at the early history of the United States with regard to regulation of corporate activity, for in many ways the structure of the situation parallels that in the world economy today. Under the U.S. Constitution, most regulatory authority with respect to business activity would seem to reside in the various states of the United States. And indeed in the 1880s a number of states, led by Massachusetts and Illinois, enacted legislation designed to limit the emerging abuses of incorporated business and generally to protect the welfare of investors in securities and of the general public against business fraud or malfeasance. Also under the constitution, however, contracts made in one state must be honored in others, and trade restrictions between states are prohibited. With the emergence of the railroad, the telegraph, and later the telephone, it became easier for firms to operate over a larger geographic area, and in particular it became feasible to locate corporate headquarters in a state that had little local market and that need not have had any actual production. Thus was born the era of competitively easy incorporation provisions by several states, notably New Jersey and Delaware, and one by one the states that had passed regulatory legislation were forced to repeal or greatly weaken their regulations out of fear of losing corporate citizens to other, less stringent states. There followed roughly a 40-year period of laissez-faire in many areas of corporate regulation, until in the 1930s the federal government took over responsibility from the states, under the rubric of the interstate commerce clause of the constitution. An extension of jurisdiction, to be sure with a lag, thus took place to match the enlarged domain of business enterprise in such legislation as the Securities and Exchange Act and the Banking Act. (In some areas the response was faster: the Food and Drug Act was passed in 1906, aimed at restricting the operations of fast-moving patent medicine salesmen, who could move out of the jurisdiction of any given state before fraudulence or dangerous sales could be identified.)

The parallel of the world today with the early United States is of course only a limited one, partly because constitutional limitations on the powers of states to restrict the mobility of firms is absent at the international level, and partly because of the less ready assumption earlier in the century that government action was the most effective response to all problems. As a consequence the interim period of relative laissez-faire that in certain respects we now have at the international level is unlikely to last as long as the 40 years it lasted in the United States.

National Competition for Mobile Firms

Increased mobility does not only provide firms or individuals the possibility for escape from onerous national restrictions; it also provides nations with new opportunities for attracting additional productive activity, and increasingly national governments have taken advantage of these new opportunities. The competition for location by mobile firms has occasionally been extremely keen. In Europe, most countries now have regional policies that subsidize the location of firms in regions where income is lower than the national average. Belgium, Britain, and Italy have all made heavy commitments to particular regions, and Ireland has treated the whole country as a region deserving special treatment. Foreign firms have usually been more responsive to the various incentives that have been offered than have national firms.

In 1965 Taiwan promulgated its Statute for the Encouragement of Investment and gave it much publicity in foreign circles. This act in some respects merely consolidated a number of favors that were already available to foreign investors, but it also augmented them. Within three years similar acts were promulgated in the Philippines, Malaysia, Singapore, Thailand, and Indonesia, all trying to attract export-oriented manufacturing industries, and all relying on tax holidays, rapid depreciation, exemption from import duties, and various direct assistance in getting them established. Similar competition for location of mobile firms has taken place in the Caribbean area. Again, the parallelism to developments within the United States is striking: states and municipalities have competed for years for the location of industry from out of state, mostly by offering physical facilities in the form of improved land and various other direct assistance. But the use of tax-exempt industrial development bonds to raise low-cost funds for business became so flagrant by the mid-1960s that Congress had to legislate a virtual halt to it.

In effect, all of these incentives to induce the immigration of mobile industry shift the costs of public services to the relatively immobile segments of the population. Sometimes they suffer as a result, but frequently they gain by the arrival of new business activity. Where U.S. firms are involved in international movement the principal loser is the U.S. Treasury, and hence indirectly the U.S. public, by virtue of the tax deferral and tax-crediting provisions of the U.S. tax code. The crediting provision, however, remains desirable from a cosmopolitan point of view, to encourage the most efficient use of the world's capital with minimal distortion from corporate taxes.

While the economic gains to host countries from attracting foreign firms are usually substantial, we nonetheless seem to be in a period of nationalistic and even xenophobic reaction against foreign firms, especially but by no means exclusively in the extractive industries. Restrictions on foreign firms are being tightened and the rate of nationalization seems to have risen. My guess is that these extreme reactions will be short-lived except where they continue to serve the political purposes of some important group playing on uninformed public sentiment. Serious governments will recognize the important benefits that flow from foreign investment. They may bargain harder on the terms of entry than has been the case in the past, but they will bargain. The prospective gains to the host country will surmount the xenophobic opposition to foreign-owned firms in most countries, and competition for MNCs to locate there will continue, though perhaps in more subtle ways.

CONCLUDING OBSERVATIONS

I have focused on mobility as an escape from national regulation and the consequential tension between MNCs and national governments. I do not mean to suggest by that emphasis that the international movement of business enterprise is solely motivated by a desire to escape onerous taxation or regulation in the home country. There are many reasons for locating abroad—to achieve greater proximity to new markets, to locate close to needed sources of supply, to protect markets against the intrusions of local or other foreign competitors, to reduce manufacturing costs through use of less expensive labor, and so on. But the emphasis on escape from national regulation and taxation can be defended on two grounds. First, some of the other motivating reasons turn out on close inspection to represent escape from legally enforced conditions in the home country, for example, cost-raising minimum wages or antipollution requirements that make production abroad, away from the regulations, relatively cheaper. Second and more importantly, it is a possibility of escape from national regulation rather than the other motives—and apart from the irrational xenophobia that exists in a few countries—that puts the greatest pressure on governments to take action to regulate the MNC, that is, to plan, in the control sense of the term, with greater intensity.

Furthermore, it should be understood that I refer to escape in a factual, not a normative fashion. High mobility often represents an important safety valve from politically necessary but undesirable regulations, and is sometimes even so recognized by the government imposing the regulation. Moreover, the possibility of outward movement may play a most useful role in inhibiting the adoption of undesirable regulations or taxation.

In summary, the MNC is not forcing us into greater planning in the sense of thinking ahead, and taking anticipatory action; indeed, the increasing democratization of societies will if anything impede consistent, far-sighted action. But the high mobility that the MNC enjoys does create difficulties for certain national policies, particularly those concerned with business regulation (in its broadest sense, including disclosure of information) and with redistributive taxation. The defensive response of governments when confronted with these difficulties may be the exercise of much greater control of corporations, particularly to restrain their movement. Governments increasingly recognize that it would be preferable, however, to deal with greater business mobility by extending the range of government through cooperative action among nations. The Andean Pact agreements and advanced discussions among the Associated South East Asian Nations illustrate such attempts, still admittedly in their infancy. International agreement on the policies to be pursued toward MNCs would reduce their room for maneuver relative to a laissez-faire regime, but it would not represent a fundamentally new movement toward greater control; that is taking place on the national level in any case. Indeed, the need to reach international agreement will more often than not delay the exercise of new powers by national governments, and give some respite to mobile firms.

Much public discussion of MNCs has emphasized the need for codes of good conduct by foreign-owned corporations operating in various countries. Such codes have to do with relations with the host country government, the circumstances under which appeal to the home country government is legitimate, the training of local personnel in technical and managerial jobs, the encouragement of local ownership and stimulation of local sources of supply, the undertaking of research and development expenditures in the host country, the exercise of restraint in political activities, and the like. Many of these suggestions undoubtedly have merit; and for that reason many of the suggestions are likely to be superfluous except for their public relations effect, since multinational corporations are likely to adopt these measures in any event. They are usually good and sometimes exemplary citizens of their host countries already. But these codes fail to address the fundamental issues raised by MNCs. MNCs are exploiting new opportunities opened up by improved technology, especially ease of modern communication, and they respond to the incentives and disincentives presented by different national markets. The current need is for serious discussion of which policy-induced national incentives should be allowed to operate and which should not. That, fundamentally, is a matter for governments to decide. It cannot be settled by enterprises agreeing to codes of good conduct.

COMMENT

Peter Sheppe

I agree with many of Dr. Cooper's hypotheses, but I feel his conclusions leave me—on multinational corporations as well as governments—between Scylla and Charybdis in defense of what they are not the cause of, forcing the governments to react, in terms of planning of any anticipatory nature.

Peter Sheppe is Director, International Administration, Time Incorporated.

I agree that it serves no purpose to view an MNC as a good guy or bad guy, but it is a fact that they are not all that powerful, as I think the thrust of the various discussions we have had indicates and they must operate within the structures of being good citizens of their own as well as the host country. They have a duty to shareholders and social obligation to citizens of the world

The management of the multinational corporation knows its motives for taking the actions it does. How these actions are viewed, however, depends on the frame of reference of the viewer, often much to the surprise of the multinational corporation, as Dr. Vernon implied. Thus it is the multinational corporation which is forced to plan both economically and politically to meet challenges stemming from the context or frame of reference in which it has been placed by the local public or host government.

By the same token the presence of multinational corporations today encourages planning of an anticipatory nature by governments because, as Dr. Cooper said, they are viewed as exploiters and evaders of regulations and policies. The ease of mobility, I believe, works both ways and plays today a less important role for the multinational corporation vis-a-vis the larger and growing influence it gives government with mobility aiding the exercise of its power.

I believe the increase of concentration of action will be due to governmental planning rather than despite it. Because as I see it, MNCs must meet conditions of world markets, both economic and political, given the premise that they are neither good nor bad. They must plan to cope with the national restraints on mobility and/or international joint action to extend effective jurisdiction over domains of mobility. I feel because governments may react on a short-term basis, dependent upon political reality of the moment, multinational corporations, probably more rigorously than governments, are forced or encouraged to do long-range economic planning to cope with what may turn out to be short-term politically inspired regulations both from the home and the host country.

Whether the increased authority of governments results from the exercise of national restraints or from international agreements, as Dr. Cooper suggests, will in the long run be academic, and mobility will count for little.

DISCUSSION

Question. Dr. Cooper, you presented an interesting analogy to U.S. history with respect to the extension of jurisdiction by the states and the exercise of controls, and also with respect to mobility. You cited

the fact that some corporations in the last century escaped from one
state of incorporation to another in order to avoid controls.

Now of course, as is obvious, the analogy is not complete because whereas our federal government under our constitution has
sovereign jurisdiction, that is not the case of the United Nations or
any other international body. Consequently, I wonder if you would
be able to look a little bit into the future for us. First, do you think
that history will repeat itself? Will multinational companies, for
example, desert home jurisdictions for others? We have heard this
is going to happen at various times when the United States started
imposing increased taxation on multinational companies, and some
companies were reported to have gone so far as to think of moving
to the Bahamas or something like that, but no major company has
done that. Do you think that could happen in the future?

Second, I wonder whether you could expand a bit more on what
you see as the eventual development. Because of what I just talked
about, will nations have to get together on a multilateral basis to
establish some codes of action or will we just be left to sort of per-
petual anarchy?

Dr. Cooper. Let me start out with the historical point. You say that
a major difference is that in the United States we have one federal
jurisdiction. It is worth noting that we now take that for granted.
But 75 years ago that was an open legal question. It was only over
the course of time that the legal powers which we now assume the
federal government to have—legal jurisdiction under the interstate
commerce clause of the constitution—evolved, and for a long time
there was a question about whether the federal government could
exercise jurisdiction in these areas. That was an evolutionary process.

If you ask me now what is likely to happen in the global setting,
at a high level of generalization I would see something very similar
to that taking place. We do not have world government and are not
likely to have world government in the foreseeable future, but I think
the pressures on national governments combined with their growing
perception of the advantages of having mobile corporations will together introduce greater cooperation among governments.

The developing countries will probably be the last countries to
cooperate closely because their own self-confidence is so weak at
present, and that expresses itself in nationalism. Cooperation will
take place first among industrial countries but with gradually more
and more countries coming along, and it is likely to take place piece-
meal rather than as part of some grand plan.

Taxation might illustrate the point. There will be a natural
evolution from bilateral tax treaties through a general uniform model

tax treaty to multilateral tax treaties, analogous to the General
Agreement on Tariffs and Trade. The evolution might take place
first with a limited number of countries, and then with more countries
acceding to them.

In the financial area, one can see a lot of concern today, but
not yet much action beyond the gathering of information. But that is
an important first step with the Eurocurrency market. The groping
for greater control is going to be very light at first, compared with
national regulations, but there will be a move in that direction—
essentially a standardization of approach.

A third area which is very much under discussion now in the
Law of the Sea Conference is pollution by ships. Here is an area
where we have had flags of convenience for many years. Because
of pollution of shore lines, particularly with oil, some kind of international action is going to be necessary. Whether it will take the
form of leaving it completely up to the coastal state, with the result
of a hodgepodge of different national regulations which will be onerous
to shippers and which in time gradually will be negotiated down to
some uniform regulations, or whether they will skip the hodgepodge
stage and move to something uniform at once is still under discussion
in the Law of the Sea Conference.

One can see issue by issue that these things will be resolved
by the extension of national jurisdiction, sometimes cooperatively
and sometimes not.

You raised the question of major headquarters moving, and we
have not actually seen that. I am not entirely sure what that means,
and whether it is especially meaningful to talk about the actual movement of the headquarters of the corporations. Regulated activities
are frequently moved outside the home jurisdiction. Shipping and
banking are just two examples.

There have been two major threats. One celebrated one was
Henry Ford's alleged statement back in the early 1960s that he was
going to move Ford of Britain outside Britain. Ford is a U.S.-owned
corporation, but he was dealing there with the British government.
More recently Massey Ferguson threatened to move out of Canada if
the Canadian government proceeded along a certain line. And the
threat is a credible one. As long as it is, actual movement may not
be necessary.

Question. Dr. Cooper, George Ball has suggested that an international
multilateral agreement be negotiated under which multinational corporations would be required to register, and an international organization have sanctions which it could impose upon the corporations in
the event that they violated the codes or other rules that this multinational treaty would encompass.

Would you care to comment on that as well as possibly the expansion of the jurisdiction of the world court to issue sanctions on multinational corporations' conduct?

Dr. Cooper. I do not pretend to be an expert on diverse legal forms. Perhaps what George Ball is talking about could in all of its substantive dimensions be handled in a different way, one that is legally more conventional than having an international body that can impose sanctions. That is something of a novelty.

You see it in the Coal and Steel Community in Europe. Ball has spent many years urging European unification.

But from the point of view of influencing the behavior of multinational corporations, I would have thought whether one does it through multilateral incorporation with multilateral sanctions or whether one does it through an international agreement with nations accepting an international agreement to carry out sanctions, is a matter of secondary importance. It could be achieved by either route.

My own instinct would be that the Ball route is more likely to be difficult, because novel, and hence less effective.

Question. I think one of the points that perhaps has been lost sight of in the discussion of codes of conduct guidelines, is the fact that the current OECD exercise, for example, got its start from an effort to discuss and arrive at some kind of understanding within the OECD on the conditions under which transnational investment would be received in the countries of the OECD. There was an earlier effort in the ITO (International Trade Organization) charter to deal with conditions of investment and an earlier effort in the OECD.

I think it is only fair to recognize—and this has come with respect to both our discussions this morning—it is only fair to recognize that the reason we are talking about this in the OECD is it started with discussions on conditions in which transnational investment would occur and the way it would be treated. The guidelines are sort of reciprocal on what is expected of companies, in exchange for the arrangement that would be made between governments.

It is conceivable that, referring to the last comment, this combination of efforts by governments for a framework, together with some kind of precepts for the behavior of corporations, could set a precedent in terms of a wider global situation. I wonder if Dr. Cooper would care to comment on this.

Dr. Cooper. That is a very fair point. We have come to think of codes of conduct as being something either agreed to by or imposed on corporations. Whereas the main problem, as I see it, and I gather from Dr. Vernon's paper as he sees it, is really governments.

Historically these two things have been linked. There was an implicit quid pro quo between the behavior of governments vis-a-vis corporations and what the corporations themselves would do. Is that kind of bargain possible in today's world? I am inclined to agree with Ray Vernon that as far as developing countries are concerned, the political salience of this issue is such as to prevent those countries from agreeing to any useful multinational agreement at this time.

I think that will come in time. We have this curious bifurcation. On the one hand, agencies and departments of government work vigorously to attract corporations to their shores, and on the other hand, the general antiforeign rhetoric is quite inconsistent with that. That tension will keep many developing countries from agreeing to any kind of international code that in any way seems to limit their behavior as governments.

As far as industrial countries are concerned, in Europe and North America, such an agreement is probably superfluous by now. The issues are now well enough understood and have been sufficiently refined so that governments can deal with them piece by piece, such as taxation or pollution control, without the need for that kind of overall bargain involving both governments and corporations.

Question. I was going to suggest that perhaps the analogy to the development of law in the United States is a rather interesting one. Because in the United States you have really had this movement away from state regulation of corporations to a more permissive state corporation law, like the Delaware law, and you have had response to that in development really of federal incorporation law administered basically by the SEC. One might think that this is the development which international corporations will find—the path down which they are going internationally, as well as national corporations going down that path nationally.

On the other hand, you also have at the present time a movement back by states which are beginning to regulate them much more than they did before. You have, for example, laws now with respect to take-over bids which are focused on the fact that assets of the corporation are located in a particular state. The State of Ohio has been involved—well, I think in connection with Otis Elevator, if I recall the case correctly. There are a number of state corporation statutes like those of California, for example, in which the state corporation commissioner takes a much harder look at the business wisdom of a particular corporation, tagging themselves on the fact that the corporation has assets located in the State of California. One might see a tendency I suppose in the international field to regulation of the kind that you have in connection with the development of federal incorporation law administered by the SEC, and at the same time a

kind of countervailing tendency based on immobility, the fact that
assets are located in various nations. I do not know if that is a statement or a question, but comments would be welcome.

Dr. Cooper. I am not familiar with the particular statute you mentioned. I am familiar with a related area, efforts by states to tax
corporations. Again they have gone after assets or some combination
of assets, sales, and payroll. The heavy need for revenue has pushed
states in this direction. In spite of those often urgent revenue needs,
the efforts by states to tax corporate income have been very slow in
coming and very difficult to do.

Without knowing the details of the California and Ohio statutes,
I cannot comment on them, but if they are really onerous, these
states will find that the fixity of the assets in their states is a temporary phenomenon. While fixed assets are difficult to move in one
year or even in ten, they are not difficult to move in the long run. If
the regulation is really onerous, they will be moved, through relative
expansion outside those states. Firms are always deciding where to
place new investment and where to make major renovations. If there
are cost-increasing regulatory activities in one area compared with
another, that is going to influence those decisions.

Question. My question is with regard to your last point of the paper
dealing with official incentives and disincentives to international
investment. In an ideal world the governments ought to get together
and indeed reveal what incentives and disincentives they have with
respect to foreign investment, with a view toward neutralizing those
as much as possible so that market forces can come into play in
terms of where investment goes. This is in the best interest of both
producer and consumer.

This is standard theory. However, the pragmatics are not with
it. The world is not ideal.

In the OECD, as you know, Dr. Cooper, we have been trying
very hard from our side to negotiate an agreement to consult on
official incentives and disincentives to direct investment. This has
met with a tremendous and continuing resistance by European trading
partners in the sense that they feel it is an infringement on national
policy if we discuss any measures which even have a remote domestic
motivation, rather than purely international motivation.

I do not know how to get over this hurdle, and I do not see how
one gets over it. I was wondering if you could comment on that.

Dr. Cooper. Well my first comment is that I think the theory needs
revising to some extent. That is, I am not sure that the ideal world—
of course it depends on one's ideals—is as you describe it. We have

a competitive model which often governs our thinking about the world
of private business. One can apply that competitive model to a world
of 140-odd governments as well. In the area of incentives for mobile
firms to locate, a kind of competition is also operating. One can see
it operate clearly in areas like Southeast Asia and the Caribbean,
where there is a close relationship between what one country does
and another. If you track through the theory of that, it is possible to
persuade yourself that in some circumstances this competition is a
good thing. It leads to optimization of the world's use of resources.
When Belgium or Ireland or Italy gives tax concessions for location
of a particular firm, it is shifting the tax burden from a mobile to an
immobile factor of production. Presumably they know what they are
doing and they do that only to the point at which the introduction of
mobile agents actually improves the welfare of immobile residents,
in spite of a heavier tax bill. Under certain circumstances that turns
out to be globally optimizing.

The difficulties arise when governments make mistakes and
pour good money after bad. Governments are more likely to do that
than corporations, and in an idealized competitive world business
cannot continue to operate that way.

So my reaction to the question you pose, given what I have said,
is that perhaps we should not be so concerned about the unwillingness
of European countries to agree. Maybe we ought to look at the problem
a little more critically and try to identify those areas where it really
does make sense for governments to act in concert and leave alone
those areas where it really does not make much sense.

While I do not know the details of the current negotiations, my
impression is that we have tended to lump these things together. We
have tended to talk about government policies in general, without
refining them enough.

The same thing is true in the area of pollution, for example.
The Stockholm Conference took pollution en bloc, so to speak. We
need much more refinement to that notion. There are large areas
of pollution where local option ought to be the rule. We may have
tight emission control standards. Given our stage of urbanization
and economic development, that is right for us; while in Argentina
or elsewhere lax emission control standards may be appropriate,
so long as pollution is localized. Where pollution has strong spillout
effects, if those allegations are correct, for example, on DDT, then
there is a global interest in preventing DDT runoff. That is something that should be subject to global control.

The whole area of pollution control has suffered by trying to
lump too many things together and not making distinctions where
distinctions should be made. The same is also true in business
regulations.

Question. I would just like to say I have sat here for a day and a half and listened to a lot of points of view, which I found quite diverse and very interesting. I think all of our speakers have come from one relatively common point of view. They have had the opportunity to look at these problems more on a survey basis than some of us who are in the practitioner's side of things. Some have had apparently substantial experience in various parts of the world, such as Latin America; Mexico keeps coming up all the time, Indonesia now and then, and so on.

I would just like to make some general observations taken from the point of view from which I see it. We are in the manufacturing business, which means heavy investment. We are not the fly-by-night insurance company that goes into the Bahamas. We do not go in and put a radio assembly operation in in a month and pull it out in two weeks, and things of that sort. So I start from recognition of that bias.

But we are operating in manufacturing in various degrees in 28 different countries and we sell, I guess, in almost every one of the markets except the Iron Curtain countries; we are restricted somewhat there.

I would like to suggest for consideration in this meeting some things that strike me as being reasonably fundamental. First—and most of these things have been said in one way or another here, which I find encouraging—first, multinationals are not foisted upon any country. They are there because they provide a good or a service which that country believes is best to obtain that way. There is a great ambivalence among countries, I find. For example, pollution was just mentioned by Dr. Cooper.

I recall one country where a senior member of the government said, "Do not bother us with pollution. We have not lived long enough, we have not enjoyed the benefits of the world long enough to be bothered with a little pollution." They say, "Just come and develop our country." And for the people who have never had an opportunity to do anything except walk in their life, some of these things look very good indeed.

In the United States we have had the opportunity to have the benefit of the best that the world has to offer, but not all countries have had this. So, I think we ought to start with that premise.

Second, in the pragmatic world today I think that multinationals no longer are able to dominate host countries. That may have been true in the past. That may have been true as part of colonial systems. I think that is not true in any country that I know of today.

I think the greater danger really is the other way, manipulation of multinationals for attainment of political ends. Those political ends very often are very short-range indeed. I think the problem is that in many countries where that happens, the long-range best interest of the country will not necessarily be served under those circumstances.

Basic development is something we all believe in, I think, for the good of the government, but it does not always occur.

In none of the papers that I have heard here has there been any cataloguing of the requirements that the host countries impose upon multinational corporations, or at least foreign corporations—let us speak of it that way. I have seen no paper that catalogues these requirements. They are diverse. They are very onerous indeed for those of us who have to actually live under them.

I would recommend that perhaps a survey of this type, on this subject, be developed. It seems to me it would be helpful to us all if we could see in such a survey views which we in individual companies really find very difficult indeed to collect.

The third point, it seems to me, in this day and age, and particularly in the last two or three years, is that it is essential that we distinguish between the developing country that has resources and the developing country that has no resources. We have a new phenomenon that has come out of the OPEC development of the last couple of years, and the attempts to develop cartels, which is not a new idea—it is as old as the world. I sense great arrogance that has arisen out of developing countries with resources.

One of the speakers spoke in terms of, Why do we build an automobile plant when a bicycle plant would do? I am very sympathetic with that, except the practical problem that I have seen is that the developing countries with resources do not approach it that way at all. One specific case we had, a country insisted that we come with a proposition that would start with a diesel engine plant. They wanted it from 30 horsepower to 1,600 horsepower, all in one plant, one family of design, and we suggested that was not really economical. It was not really sensible. They are a small market. They have no way possible in which they could use that. And for our trouble we got a very, very firm put-down. You see it becomes a matter of ideology. "You do not tell us—we know."

Well, I think that is a practical problem. I do think it gives us different categories that we have never had to deal with in recent times. I think we need to distinguish between legitimate issues and legitimate complaints, and what I would call the expressions of frustration which arise from these unfulfilled expectations that Dr. Cooper mentioned.

In this day and a half there is one word that I think is the root cause of so many of our problems today, and it has not been mentioned. That is inflation, and everything that that means. These frustrations that are developing simply come from shortfalls that

all of us have in any nation because none of us have really been able
to deal with that problem effectively. We have TV. We have transmission of news around the world. We have instant everything,
instant communication, and instant desire too. And that is a large
part of our problem.

I think sometimes we get these things mixed up a little bit. I
suggest we ought to separate as best we can, and it is not always easy
to do this, the problems which truly can be solved only by government-to-government contact, as distinguished from problems which
are really soluble within the range of the business community, whether
it be multinâtional or domestic.

Sometimes we get these things mixed up. I think sometimes
governments get them mixed up in what they ask us to do.

It is a very common occurrence for a government to say,
"Come and help us." One just last week said, "Would you help us
write a price control law because we do not know how to administer
price controls in our country?" Well that is a little bit off the charter,
but that is a fact. I think it is not novel. I am sure many of you
gentlemen have had the same experience.

I would like to say that I think we should not be surprised with
the fact that legitimate self-interest applies in the conduct of multinational affairs just as it applies in the affairs of domestic corporations or governments or universities or each of us in our own individual lives.

We really would not want it any other way. If it were any other
way, presumably there would be some omnipotent all-knowing someone who could solve all of our problems, and I do not know that any
of us have found that.

I think legitimate self-interest does have a place in the conduct
of affairs. This is what I would like to echo very much.

I suggest we use great caution in generalization, generalization
about unethical conduct of affairs of multinational corporations. I
think we should not lightly repeat allegations which we do not really
know to be true. I am talking about manipulation of foreign exchange.
I am talking about evasion, not avoidance of taxes. I am talking about
rigging of transfer prices, not struggling with the legitimate problems
of trying to decide what a fair price is.

We hear so much in the general community today about things
of this sort, and Dr. Cooper, I do not mean to be personal, but I do
not believe Mr. Ford ever threatened to withdraw his resources from
Britain. In the first place, Ford has a billion dollars in the ground
there.

You did make a little point which I think would be more accurate,
and that simply is that when you found that environment is hostile to
what you are trying to do, and if you find that you are not welcome

any more, you tend to wind down. Certainly a capital intensive multinational has no opportunity whatsoever to fly in the middle of the night. No way can you do that.

I think another point we would like to make is we should not overlook the importance of foreign trade to most nations of the world. Within the month the head of one of the principal industrial nations of Europe made this very point in a private conversation. He said: "You in the United States do not understand the problem of world trade because you are not very dependent upon it. We in our country are very dependent upon world trade; 50 to 60 percent of our GNP has to come from there." In the United States, of course, it is less than that. As a result, other governments make arrangements with their multinational corporations in ways in which our government does not.

I suppose the best illustration of that is the relationship of the government of Japan to its industry. Any of us who have had to deal with that knows how close and how effective that relationship is.

The words "competitive advantage" were mentioned yesterday. I thought it was passed over rather lightly. That is what it is all about.

Competitive advantage might be a month in time. It might be a piece of information. It might be knowing something about your relative cost structure. We cannot just lightly pass over those things. It seems to me that our own government might be of a little more assistance in this area.

I only have one or two other points. I wonder if we could be comewhat less myopic in defining what the real interests of the United States are. That thought came to my mind listening to the taxation discussion. What are the basic broad interests of the United States?

Sometimes we get involved in a particular specialty and we are so close to that specialty—and that happens to be the thing we are working on or we are thinking about—that we have a hard time sort of assessing the toll. We can kill the goose that laid the golden egg. I wonder if we realize how close to that we might be. As Dr. Vernon said earlier, I know there are some who will squeeze out the last egg. We may be a little closer to that than we realize. I think if you look at some of the statistics, you will understand.

Is it too much to ask that our government and others who are spokesmen outside the multinational community take a more— sympathetic is not exactly the word—perhaps a more effective role in providing assistance rather than restriction.

We have heard how to control, how to restrict, how to curtail, mostly how to police. We have heard all of these things this morning. Perhaps we can have a little bit the other way. What could we do to assist and to help and to implement in a way that would serve our national interests.

Then, I would say just one or two more things. Does anybody really have a better mechanism for the conduct of foreign trade today, given the imperfect status of the development of supranational governments? It strikes me we have more governments today than we have ever had.

Yet the trend almost necessarily has to be larger, more effective units. But the governments seem to be on only one side of that. The multinationals and governments seem to be taking opposite paths. That sort of suggests that the accomplishments of the last 25 years have been ineffectual; those great dreams of post-World War II. The EEC is going nowhere. Do we have any better mechanism for the conduct of foreign trade, is the question I would ask?

Finally I would like to say, Might it be possible to give more emphasis to the good that has resulted from multinational corporations around the world? We have heard hardly any of that. You only have to go to the country that really never had anything and to understand what it is like to have something for the first time, to understand how they feel. We in this country have had everything for so long that we have sort of forgotten what it is like to do without—until the Arabs raised the price of oil, cut off the tap, and we all stood in line at the gas station, and we began not to like it.

I doubt we would want to go back to those days. But we could talk a little bit, just a little bit, about the good as well as about the evil. I am sorry to take so much time, but I did want to express a view.

Dr. Madden. Thank you very much. As moderator, I would like to express my appreciation to the authors of the papers for the high quality of these papers and for their very disciplined and interesting and provocative presentation of the papers.

I would like to thank the group that has participated here for its attention and involvement and its probity in questions.

I feel pleased on behalf of the National Chamber Foundation that we have put together a day and a half which has seemed to justify the use of your time.

In concluding, I want first to touch very briefly on each of the
six papers in this volume, then to make some comment on the National
Chamber Foundation conference at which they were originally delivered.

J. Fred Weston addressed himself to the question, are multinational corporations (MNCs) monopolistic, are they using their
power to overprice? He examined four theories, or positions,
pointing out that MNCs do tend to be in the industries of highest concentration. The inevitable results of that are that we (MNCs) are quite
capital intensive in terms of our operations. We are responsible for,
and able to contribute, not only generally high productivity, high
efficiency, and high utilization, as I think he described it, but we
also have been in the forefront of contributing to gains and improvements in those areas.

From that I think it logically flows that we have provided lower
rates of price increases; although as I look at some of the experi-
ences of my own company and those of some of our suppliers, none
of us is in very good shape in this area—thanks to inflation, which is
one of the basic and root causes of a lot of our very real concerns.

Dr. Weston spelled out the rising, vigorous competition among
the multinationals. I found the data particularly interesting as they
relate to the non-U.S. multinationals. They are obviously energetic.
They are growing faster and are commanding a larger share of the
industry sales that they are competing for.

Louis T. Wells asked the question, are multinationals causing
more or less poverty? There are two components to that question:
poverty, first of all, at home, and then in developing countries.
Dr. Wells did not give the uniform promultinational answer that
corporate leaders from that sector necessarily like to hear. However,

208

his answer was most instructive and it seemed to me the view he presented is held by a great many within the public sector. But generally we would have to agree that some foreign investments are economically inefficient. He cited the Honduran steel mill potential as an example. I too want to echo a thought expressed at the conference that these investments are normally forced upon us for political reasons. The general notion that multinationals roam the world seeking ways to force open the doors to a particular country in order to make an investment is at the least an archaic notion. Whether or not it ever had any basis in fact, I am not too sure. In my direct experience with this process over a fair number of years now, I find we are normally being forced, coerced and at the very least, asked to come into these situations. In complying with such exhortations, we are adopting a more studied attitude toward the situations, concluding that the loss of a market in many cases may, from the corporate standpoint, be much too high a price to pay for not complying.

Incidentally, I think Professor Wells himself exemplifies a growing tendency to participate actively in and to counsel others in the negotiation process. This bodes well for the growing sophistication that I hope developing countries will eventually acquire by extending to multinationals invitations to invest.

I would like to comment on the discussion of the ten-year relationship. The assumption that technology becomes outdated or obsolete, and the fact that a licensing arrangement existed for many years may itself be an argument in favor of renegotiating for lower license fees. I speak from the framework of a manufacturing enterprise. I do want to point out in this regard that the process of technology transfer, the process of transferring managerial capabilities and skills, the process of transferring new design, is a continual one. As a matter of fact, I think none of our licensing arrangements now encompassing the building of a product covers the identical product put into production ten years earlier. In short, the licensee has the full benefit, it seems to me, of all the work that is being done by the laboratories, by the engineering and product development process. That technology is worth every bit as much today in my view as it was when the transfer was begun. I do not join in the general agreement that old license agreements are necessarily obsolete and not worth as much as they were at the time they were initially negotiated.

Robert G. Hawkins addressed the conference on the question, are multinational companies depriving the United States of economic diversity and independence? As I understand it his answer is yes— but only if you believe that interdependence detracts from independence. I found the data about our U.S. exports plus imports as a percentage of gross national product to be most interesting. In 1950,

U.S. exports plus imports as a percentage of gross national product
came to 9.7 percent. In 1974, they came to 19.9 percent. Beyond
that, however, his paper concludes that multinationals have contributed to more openness in the economy, have stimulated the process of
competition, and have created more dispersion of ownership.

Dr. Hawkins called for transparency. We may not really like
the format that has been recommended for disclosure. The line-of-
business reporting process is onerous to all of us, and the thought
that kept running through my mind during the discussion of the total
disclosure issue was that there is already a great deal of disclosure
made by business to the general public. I think probably most of our
home office accounting functions and certainly a great many of the
financial staffs of our foreign subsidiaries spend time worth millions
of dollars in the aggregate to furnish information to governments.
The practical and effective use of that information is much more of
a problem and offers much more of an opportunity for improvement
at the moment than making additional disclosure.

If you have simply tried to read and understand financial
statements that are produced in this country and to draw simple conclusions from them, or to help others understand such statements,
you recognize the great difficulty in trying to agree upon a harmonized
system that would provide useful information on an around-the-world
basis.

Thomas Horst's answer to the question, are multinational
corporations getting preferential treatment in U.S. tax policy?
found very little agreement among those attending the conference, but
his paper does sum up the arguments against the DISC legislation,
against deferral of overseas earnings, and against the practice of
calculating foreign tax credits.

One of the very useful purposes of this conference incidentally
has been the attempt to understand better the views of those who
either oppose multinational companies or misunderstand us. There
would have been a disappointment on my part if everybody had been in
total agreement. As a matter of fact, this is one of the problems of
attending meetings in this day and age. You frequently find everybody
in substantial agreement with what you have said. You may sharpen
up and add to your own biases by such a process. On the other hand,
the end result of differences of opinion is the constructive dialogue
that results from taking an introspective look at ourselves in light of
other viewpoints. I recommend Dr. Horst's paper for that very
purpose.

Raymond Vernon addressed himself to the power of multinational
enterprises in developing countries. Developing countries do indeed
associate MNCs with power. They see such power as a threat to
sovereignty. That argument, as we all know, is more political than

economic, and I think it is unfortunate we have been answering the
political viewpoint with essentially economic rationale and logic. In
effect we are creating the unfortunate situation of answering questions
that have not really been asked. I hope, therefore, that we will,
again based upon the Horst paper, tend to orient and adjust the fre-
quency of our answers to more of the political aspects than the economic aspects.

Dr. Vernon also suggested that MNCs see themselves as set
upon by powerful and sometimes arbitrary governments. I think there
is enough substance in that to justify an interesting debate. Both sides
have a deep vested interest in the outcome.

It also was suggested that if we are not able to get satisfaction,
either side could terminate the relationship. Again, it should be said
that MNCs put lots of brick and mortar and other material things into
the ground in developing countries. We are not all that mobile.

I think Dr. Vernon did suggest that at the moment we have
largely what he termed a dialogue of the deaf. For the future he
predicted that the tensions created by what he called an imperfect
fit will indeed continue. So the challenge is to find a rational means
to define and to discuss, in order to relieve those tensions.

Richard N. Cooper asked, are MNCs creating the need for
national and international economic planning? He answered that they
are not. His paper does indicate a need to alter the form or even the
nature of regulations, for reasons that he developed later. He summed
up by saying that in today's world we have (1) the expectation of
citizens that their governments should do more for their well-being,
(2) the inducement of governments to turn increasingly to major
corporations, (3) the fact that national jurisdictions are limited geographically, and (4) the development that the domains and the mobility
of many large corporations have increased beyond any particular
national jurisdiction. He suggested that these conditions taken together create a deep structural tension in government-business relationships.

He then examined three possible solutions: limiting mobility,
extending jurisdictions, and abandoning national objectives. He
emphasized mobility as the major reason for the tension between
MNCs and government.

Let me conclude with a comment about the conference overall.
I think it safe to say that the National Chamber Foundation would
probably not have undertaken such a project as recently as 1970.
Hence the question, why now?

Many MNCs, especially during the late 1950s and well into the
1960s, were going blithely down the road, secure in the belief that
they were making contributions to the balance of trade and payments
of the United States, that they were helping to feed the hungry

populations of other countries, and were contributing to the world's welfare in other ways—contributions that all of us felt very deeply about.

The advent of the Burke-Hartke proposal came as a rude shock to many of us. For me, it provided an awakening that not all employees shared the belief and understanding about the benefits of foreign investment which I believed our employees had. The effect of that shock was to cause the MNC community to mobilize its defenses—especially its data and its rhetoric.

Burke-Hartke brought us together and it brought self-examination and the need to be introspective, to be articulate and vocal about this whole matter.

From that beginning the issue has escalated and it probably will escalate still further. Your guess is as good as mine as to what was the catalytic agent that created the change in mood toward MNCs.

The world has indeed changed. It is changing very, very rapidly. The National Chamber Foundation's conference has emphasized the point very adequately that not everybody agrees that multinational corporations will indeed save the world. So again, if you disagree with some of the statements made at the conference, keep in mind that it is vital that we listen as well as speak, that we engage in dialogue. As Paul Cornelsen said in his comments on J. Fred Weston's paper, he would hope that we approach the issues with the same degree of scholarship as do some of our detractors.

It is most appropriate that we engage in dialogue and most appropriate that the National Chamber Foundation play the role that it has in providing a forum and leadership for the conference. And, finally, it is necessary that we maintain the dialogue if we are to be responsive to change and to the needs and aspirations of the people in the 143 different countries of the world.

ABOUT THE EDITOR AND CONTRIBUTORS

CARL H. MADDEN, Chief Economist for the Chamber of Commerce of the United States, 1963-76, has been Economist for the U.S. Senate Banking and Currency Committee, and was Dean, College of Business Administration, Lehigh University, 1960-63. He will assume a professorship at the School of Business, American University in the fall of 1976. Dr. Madden holds a B.A. in philosophy and M.A. and Ph.D. in economics from the University of Virginia. He is author of The Money Side of the Street, Exporting to Latin America, and Clash of Culture: Management in an Age of Changing Values, as well as co-author of The Economic Process, a high school economics text.

J. FRED WESTON, is currently Professor of Business Economics and Finance at the Graduate School of Management of the University of California at Los Angeles. He is known nationally and internationally as an authority in the field of price theory and the measurement of competition. He holds a B.A. and Ph.D. from the University of Chicago. His doctoral dissertation was on the meaning and measurement of profit, and he has done studies on pricing behavior of large firms and conglomerate performance.

LOUIS T. WELLS, Jr. is Professor of Business Administration at the Harvard Business School. He received a B.S. degree in physics and master's and doctor's degrees in business administration from Harvard. He has done research on organization structure and joint ventures in the multinational enterprise, concession agreements for hard minerals in developing countries, and foreign investment by firms from developing countries. He has recently completed a study entitled Negotiating Third World Mineral Agreements: Promises as Prologue (with David N. Smith).

ROBERT G. HAWKINS is Chairman of International Business and Professor of Economics at the Graduate School of Business Administration, New York University. He was educated at William Jewel College and at Columbia University, and received his doctor's degree in economics at New York University. His research has been in the fields of international trade policy, the economic impact of multinational corporations, international monetary relations, and sources of funds for poor nations. His publications include Gold and World Power and The United States in International Markets.

THOMAS HORST is Associate Professor of International Economics at Fletcher School of Law and Diplomacy, Tufts University. He has been Assistant Professor of Economics at Harvard University and a Research Associate at the Brookings Institution. He has published many articles in academic journals. His book At Home Abroad analyzes the domestic and international operations of the U.S. food processing industry. He is coauthor of American Multinationals and American Interests (published by Brookings in 1976).

RAYMOND VERNON, a distinguished authority in the field of international economics, is the Director of the Center for International Affairs, Harvard University. He received his doctorate from Columbia University and an honorary masters degree from Harvard. He has been with the Securities and Exchange Commission, the International Resources Division of the Department of State, and served on the Joint Presidential-Congressional Commission on Foreign Economic Policy. He was Planning and Control Director at Hawley and Hoopes, Inc., and lecturer at various colleges and universities. He has many published works, including: The Technology Factor in International Trade and Europe's Reluctant Champions.

RICHARD N. COOPER is currently a Fellow at the Center for Advanced Studies in Behavioral Sciences at Stanford. He has degrees from Oberlin College and the London School of Economics and Political Science, and received his doctorate from Harvard. He also has an honorary master's degree from Yale. He was Deputy Assistant Secretary of State for International Monetary Affairs in the mid-1960s. His published works include Economics of Interdependence, Currency Devaluation in Developing Countries, and many articles in scholarly journals.

*ECONOMIC ANALYSIS AND THE MULTINATIONAL
ENTERPRISE
edited by John H. Dunning

FOREIGN DISINVESTMENT BY U.S. MULTINATIONAL
CORPORATIONS: With Eight Case Studies
Roger L. Torneden

FOREIGN PRIVATE MANUFACTURING INVESTMENT
AND MULTINATIONAL CORPORATIONS: An
Annotated Bibliography
Sanjaya Lall

INTERNATIONAL LABOR AND THE MULTINATIONAL
ENTERPRISE
edited by Duane Kujawa

†MANAGING MULTINATIONAL CORPORATIONS
Arvind V. Phatak

MARKETING MANAGEMENT IN MULTINATIONAL
FIRMS: The Consumer Packaged Goods Industry
Ulrich E. Wiechmann

THE MULTINATIONAL BUSINESSMAN AND FOREIGN
POLICY: Entrepreneurial Politics in East-West Trade
and Investment
Jeffrey M. Brookstone

*For sale in the United States and Phillipines only
†Also available in paperback as a PSS Student Edition

MULTINATIONAL PRODUCT STRATEGY: A
Typology for Analysis of Worldwide Product
Innovation and Diffusion

> Georges Leroy

THE NATION-STATE AND TRANSNATIONAL
CORPORATIONS IN CONFLICT: With Special
Reference to Latin America

> edited by Jon P. Gunnemann

INTERNATIONAL REGULATION OF MULTINATIONAL
CORPORATIONS

> Don Wallace, Jr.